05/07

ONE WEEK LOAN

2 4 APR 2009		
2 9 APR 2010		

Telephone Renewals: 01902 321333 or 0845 408 1631
Please RETURN this item on or before the last date shown above.
Fines will be charged if items are returned late.
See tariff of fines displayed at the Counter. (L2)

Public Relations as Relationship Management

*A Relational Approach to the Study
and Practice of Public Relations*

Edited by

John A. Ledingham
Stephen D. Bruning
Capital University

Routledge
Taylor & Francis Group

NEW YORK AND LONDON

First Published by
Lawrence Erlbaum Associates, Inc., Publishers
10 Industrial Avenue
Mahwah, NJ 07430

Transferred to Digital Printing 2009 by Routledge
270 Madison Ave, New York NY 10016
2 Park Square, Milton Park, Abingdon, Oxon, OX14 4RN

Cover design by Kathryn Houghtaling Lacey

Library of Congress Cataloging-in-Publication Data

    Public relations as relationship management : a relational approach to the
    study and practice of public relations / edited by John A. Ledingham, Ste-
    phen D. Bruning
        p.   cm.
    Includes bibliographical references and index.
    ISBN 0-8058-3050-2 (alk. paper)
    1. Public Relations—Management 2. Communication in organizations.
    3. Corporations—Public Relations. I. Ledingham, John A. II. Bruning,
    Stephen D.
    HD59 2000
    659.2—dc21

                                                                            99-13642
                                                                            CIP

Publisher's Note
The publisher has gone to great lengths to ensure the quality of this reprint
but points out that some imperfections in the original may be apparent.

Contents

ဆ ✧ ભ

About the Authors

ʬ ✧ ʭ

Traci Bell earned her master's degrees in communication from the University of Tennessee, Knoxville.

Janet A. Bridges is graduate coordinator, associate professor and Board of Regents Support Fund professor of communication at the University of Southwestern Louisiana. She teaches research methods, theory and public relations. Her research interests center on understanding news and integrating the theories of publics. She holds a Ph.D. in Mass Media from Michigan State University.

Glen Broom teaches public relations, communication theory and research methods courses in the School of Communication, San Diego State University. The Public Relations Society of America named him Outstanding Educator of 1991. He was selected as Outstanding Professor in the College of Professional Studies and Fine Arts in 1993 and delivered the faculty commencement address. In addition to more than 35 scholarly papers and articles, he is co-author of *Effective Public Relations* (now in its eighth edition) and *Using Research in Public Relations*. He holds B.S. and M.S. degrees from the University of Illinois and a Ph.D. in Mass Communication from the University of Wisconsin-Madison.

Stephen D. Bruning is an associate professor of Communication at Capital University in Columbus, Ohio. His research interests focus on relationship management in public relations, developing methods to better quantify public relations, and press relations. Dr. Bruning is a member of the public relations faculty of Capital University and is coordinator of the organizational communication major. He also conducts research with a wide variety of organizations, and is the author of more than 15 scholarly articles. He holds a Ph.D. degree from Kent State University.

Samuel Burgiss is the manager of Telemedicine for the University of Tennessee Medical Center at Knoxville. He has published numerous articles on telemedicine.

W. Timothy Coombs is an associate professor of Communication at Illinois State University. His Ph.D. in Public Affairs and Issue Management is from Purdue University. His research interests include crisis management, international PR, and workplace violence. He is the author of a new book entitled *Ongoing Crisis Communication: Planning, Managing, and Responding.*

Shawna Casey was a mass communication graduate student in Professor Broom's public relations research seminar when this chapter was written.

Susan L. Dimmick is an associate professor at the University of Tennessee, Knoxville. She is the evaluation coordinator for two federal grants from the Department of Commerce and the Department of Health and Human Services. She was a Fulbright Scholar in 1996 and a USIA Academic Scholar in 1993.

Steve Esposito is a member of the Department of Communication at Capital University where he also serves as Director of University Television. A former broadcast journalist, Dr. Esposito explores television news from a critical perspective. Previous publications include TV news coverage of the O.J. Simpson criminal case, as well as network source utilization in the Timothy McVeigh Oklahoma City bombing trial.

James E. Grunig is a professor of public relations in the Department of Communication at the University of Maryland College Park. He is the co-author of *Managing Public Relations, Public Relations Techniques,* and *Manager's Guide to Excellence in Public Relations and Communication Management.* He is editor of *Excellence in Public Relations and Communication Management.* He has published more than 185 articles, books, chapters, papers, and reports. He has won three major awards in public relations: the Pathfinder Award for excellence in public relations research of the Institute for Public Relations Research and Education, the Outstanding Educator Award of the Public Relations Society of America (PRSA), and the Jackson, Jackson and Wagner Award for behavioral science research of the PRSA Foundation. He also directed a $400,000 research project for the International Association of Business Communicators Research Foundation on excellence in public relations and communication management.

Yi-Hui Huang is an associate professor at the Department of Advertising of the National Chenchi University in Taiwan. She holds a Ph.D. of public relations from the University of Maryland. Ms. Huang authored a top paper in the 2nd International, Interdisciplinary Research Conference of the Public Relations Society of America in 1999, and the top paper in the Public Relations Division of the Association for Education in Journalism and Mass Communication in 1997. Her research interests include public relations management, public relations strategies and effects, and conflict management.

Dean Kruckeberg is coordinator of the Public Relations Degree Program at the University of Northern Iowa. He was a 1995 national Public Relations Society of America "Outstanding Educator" and was awarded the 1997 "Pathfinder Award" of the Institute for Public Relations Research & Education. He is co-author of *Public Relations and Community: A Reconstructed Theory* and *This Is PR: The Realities of Public Relations.* He is academic co-chair of the Commission on Public Relations.

John Ledingham is a member of the Department of Communication at Capital University in Columbus, Ohio. Dr. Ledingham is the author of more than 60 scholarly articles, chapters, or papers and is the faculty advisor to Capital University's student chapter of the Public Relations Society of America. Dr. Ledingham has served as principal or co-principal investigator on numerous grants from a variety of sources. He received his Ph.D. degree (1980) from the Ohio State University.

Richard Alan Nelson is Associate Dean at Louisiana State University's Manship School of Mass Communication. Accredited by Public Relations Society of America, he also is president of the International Academy of Business Disciplines. Nelson's books include *A Chronology and Glossary of Propaganda in the United States* and co-authorship of *Issues Management: Corporate Public Policymaking in an Information Society.*

Caroline Ragsdale is press secretary for the director of the Tennessee Department of Economic and Community Development.

James Ritchey was a mass communication graduate student in Professor Broom's public relations research seminar at San Diego State University.

T. Dean Thomlison is a communication educator, consultant, trainer, and a nationally recognized expert in interpersonal communication. Dr. Thomlison is also the author of *Toward Interpersonal Dialogue*, co-author of *Let's Talk* (in press), and a contributing author to *Listening in Everyday Life*. Dr. Thomlison has participated in numerous research projects on the application of interpersonal communication theory to relationship management. He is Professor of Communication at the University of Evansville.

Elizabeth L. Toth, Ph.D. is Associate Dean for Academic Affairs. at the S. I. Newhouse School of Public Communications, Syracuse University. Dr. Toth has co-authored or co-edited several books and has served the editor of *The Journal of Public Relations Research*. For her research, Toth won the 1998 Institute for Public Relations Pathfinder Award.

Laurie J. Wilson, APR, is Chair of the Brigham Young University Department of Communications. An award winning teacher, author, lecturer, and researcher, her qualifications include 10 years directing the preparation of public relations and marketing efforts for government contractors, 6 years as a freelance writer and communications consultant, and she was also a participant in political campaigns. She serves on the educational affairs committee of the Public Relations Society of America (PRSA) and is an ongoing member of the Joint Commission on Public Relations Education. She also serves on United Way of Utah County's Board of Directors as a public relations advisor, and is Emeritus President of the Association of Latter-day Saints Public Relations Professionals.

Introduction: Background and Current Trends in the Study of Relationship Management

80 ✧ 03

John A. Ledingham
Capital University

Stephen D. Bruning
Capital University

Public relations is a field more often characterized by what it does than what it is. Ask a practitioner to define the field and the likely response is a listing of the activities that are included under the rubric of public relations: publicity, press agentry, advertising, events management, media relations and so on. Moreover, many public relations professionals seem to perceive that the production and dissemination of communication messages is the answer to every public relations problem (Ledingham & Bruning, 1998a). As others have noted, the end result of that view is "communication [that] is simply functionary, the generation of messages as an end in themselves, a perpetual motion machine, squirting ink" (Broom, 1986). Moreover, a misplaced emphasis on communication production and dissemination can lead to a basic confusion as to the purpose of public relations, and a tendency to measure programmatic initiatives in terms of communication output rather than in relational or behavioral outcomes.

A BRIEF HISTORICAL PERSPECTIVE

Public relations traces its beginnings to the late 1800s. However, the field began to emerge as a powerful corporate tool in the early 20th century as industrial and business leaders, under attack by a new breed of investigative journalists termed *muck-*

rakers, sought to shape public opinion and stave off governmental interference by hiring experts in "public relations." The battlefield for these campaigns and counter-campaigns was the mass media. Most early public relations practitioners traced their careers to first-hand work in the media, a practice that continues today. Moreover, many of these early public relations practitioners viewed their corporate role as a "journalist in residence." To their credit, some also considered themselves the "conscience" of their organization—making certain the interest of the public was top-of-mind—a view reflected today in the social consciousness perspective of public relations (Wilson, 1994). However, it also may be said that the dominance of the field of public relations by former journalists reinforced the notion of manipulation of the mass media as the central focus of public relations practice, and generating favorable publicity was the number one goal of most public relations practitioners. Indeed, it is fair to say that public relations initially was publicity (Wilcox, 1992, p. 41). As an early practitioner noted: "I was in the publicity business. I was a press agent. Very simply, my job was to get the client's name in the paper" (Cutlip, 1994, p.11). As the field grew it attracted visionaries such as Edward Bernays, Arthur Page, and Harwood Childs who saw public relations a way of balancing the interests of organizations and their publics (Cutlip, 1994). However, that perspective was often ignored in the rush to garner "free" favorable publicity through the semiotic relationship of public relations practitioners and the mass media (Broom & Dozier, 1990; Seitel, 1995).

Recently, the role of "journalist in residence"—offering advice on ways to get an organization's name in the press—has been supplanted to some degree by that of the "expert prescriber"—a public relations counselor who advises client companies on matters of public policy and beyond (Broom & Dozier, 1986, pp. 611–614). Nonetheless, many organizations still view public relations primarily as a means of generating favorable publicity. Their rationale for public relations is found not in the management of reciprocal relationships between an organization and its publics, but rather in "the credibility attached to information that has been examined by reporters (through) third party endorsement by the media" (Nakra, 1991, p. 42), a concept that recently has been challenged by public relations scholars (Hallahan, 1998).

Despite the fact that public relations is a field undergoing continuing change in terms of perspective, role and evaluation, numerous scholars contend that the contribution of public relations to corporate goals is still a mystery to much of senior management (Hon, 1998) and many practitioners (Broom & Dozier, 1990; Dozier, 1995) and that the field suffers from the lack of an agreed-on approach for evaluating public relations initiatives (Broom & Dozier, 1990; Hon, 1998).

Thus, public relations is a field that continues to seek a theoretical framework to guide its practical application. Botan (1993) observed that "public relations is in an ongoing state of change … branching out from a single applied focus driven by the knowledge needs of practitioners into two major branches … [the] applied branch [and] a new theory based research and scholarship branch" (p. 107). According to Botan, these include "symmetrical/systems, [the] rhetorical/critical, [the] feminist, and [the] social scientific" and "a dominant applied model, based … on a journalistic heritage and business orientation"(p. 108).

THE EMERGENCE OF THE
RELATIONAL PERSPECTIVE

Of the various perspectives that can be brought to bear on issues of public relations form and function, one of the most intriguing is that of *relationship management*. The relational perspective that relationship management encompasses holds that public relations is "the management function that establishes and maintains mutually beneficial relationships between an organization and the publics on whom its success or failure depends" (Cutlip, Center, & Broom, 1994, p. 2). The emergence of relationship management as a paradigm for public relations scholarship and practice calls into question the essence of public relations—what it is and what it does or should do, its function and value within the organizational structure and the greater society, and the benefits generated not only for sponsoring organizations but also for the publics those organizations serve and the communities and societies in which they exist. The relationship paradigm also provides a framework in which to explore the linkage between public relations objectives and organizational goals, for constructing platforms for strategic planning and tactical implementation, and approaching programmatic evaluation in ways understood and appreciated by the ruling management group, that which Dozier (1995) termed the organization's "dominant coalition" (p. 15).

The notion that relationships ought to be at the core of public relations scholarship and practice appears first to have been advocated by Ferguson (1984). The perspective then advanced through the rapid adoption of a relational definition of public relations in leading texts, such as that of Cutlip, Center and Broom (1987). The relational perspective then emerged as an area for exploration for public relations scholars. For example, Broom and Dozier (1990) suggested a co-orientational approach to measure organization–public relationships, rather than communication efficiencies, as a function of public relations evaluation. J. E. Grunig underscored the importance of "building relationships with publics that constrain or enhance the ability of the organization to meet its mission" (1992, p. 20). Ehling termed the shift away from the manipulation of public opinion and toward a relationship-centered approach "an important change in the primary mission of public relations" (1992, p. 622).

Today, the notion of organization–public relationships as central to public relations is the focus of scholarship operating from varying approaches. Noting that "the purpose and direction of an organization (its mission) is affected by relationships with key constituents [publics] in the organization's environment," Dozier (1995) called for the use of communication as "a strategic management function (that helps) manage relationships with key publics that affect organizational mission, goals and objectives" (p. 85). Based on a wide-sweeping review of relationship literature from interpersonal and organizational communication, social psychology, and other fields, Broom, Casey, and Ritchey (1997) constructed a model for developing theory around the notion of relationship management. Central to that model is recognition of the need to identify the antecedents, states, and consequences of organization–public relationships. For our part, we approached the study of organization–public relationships by identifying dimensions of organization–public relationships (Ledingham & Bruning, 1998a) and by applying the relational perspective to issues such as consumer satisfaction, competitive choice, and media relations (Ledingham & Bruning, 1998b, 1998c, 1998d). Eschewing the management approach as inherently manipulative, Wilson (1994) instead focused on the relationship between corporations and community within the social responsibility perspective. The cumulative effect of this scholarship has been to establish the concept of relationship management as a useful and fruitful perspective for public relations study and education.

There is much that the reports in the literature of organization–public relationships have in common. First, they tend to draw on a variety of disciplines, including interpersonal communication and relationship building, organizational behavior, marketing, social psychology, and others. Additionally, they generally reflect a concern with the purpose, direction, planning, execution and evaluation of public relations initiatives, primarily within the organizational setting but with the notion of mutual benefit foremost in mind. Moreover, most of the scholarship in this area exhibits an appreciation for systems theory approach as an overarching construct.

IMPETUS FOR THE BOOK

This book grows out of our interest in cross-disciplinary exploration, the need for a framework for understanding public relations, and the implications of organization–public relationships for the study, practice, and teaching of public relations. Moreover, we are enthusiastic about the potential of relationship management as a framework for demonstrating the value of public relations to sponsoring organizations, the immediate community, and the larger societal and global environment. In putting this collection together, we purposely invited contributions from established and emerging public relations scholars, as well as those from other areas of scholarship. It was hoped that, in that way, the book would serve as a guide to the current state of scholarship in this area, but also would offer new directions in organization–public relationship scholarship. It also was hoped that this diverse collection would encourage the exchange of ideas and enthusiasm for this line of scholarship that we have found in our collaboration with each other and with others. All the chapters are original and have not appeared in other collections or academic journals.

STRUCTURE OF THE BOOK

Part I

The book is divided into three distinct parts. Part I is entitled "The State of Organization–Public Relationship Research." In this section, we attempt to offer state-of-the-art research in terms of two theoretical models and a longitudinal study of relationship management. The lead chapter is by Glen Broom, Shawna

Casey, and James Ritchey. In this chapter, the authors report the results of a case study of their pioneering organization–public relationship model and delineate the four conditions under which relationships occur. In the second chapter, James E. Grunig and Yi-Hui Huang build on Broom, Casey, and Ritchey's original model, articulating the permutations of organization–public situations within the framework of environmental scanning, and adding "relationship maintenance" strategies as well as relational outcomes. The third chapter contains a report of our research concerning the influence of a managed communication program on perceptions of previously identified organization–public relationship dimensions, and the implications of the findings for the role of communication within the relationship management perspective.

Part II

Part II is entitled "Applications of the Relational Perspective." It consists of a series of chapters dedicated to applications of the relational perspective to various components of public relations. The lead chapter in this section is by Timothy Coombs, in which he approaches crisis management from the perspective of attribution theory, contending that building and nurturing key relationships can lessen the impact of crises when they occur. This is followed by a chapter by Janet Bridges and Richard Nelson, in which the authors explore the necessity of making difficult decisions regarding relationships as part of the issues management process. The subsequent chapter is by Susan Lucarelli Dimmick, with Traci E. Bell, Samuel G. Burgiss, and Caroline Ragsdale. In it, the authors examine the importance of the relationship dimension of trust and offer a promising model of health care relationships, with antecedents and consequences. In the next chapter, Wilson uses the case study method to examine previously identified relationship dimensions and their role in developing employee and community relationships through volunteerism. In the concluding chapter in this section, Dean Kruckeberg contends that public relations practitioners cannot realize global professionalism—and its dependence on appropriate relationship building—without a greater understanding of themselves as a professional body and an ability to articulate their worldview.

Part III

Part III is entitled "Implications of the Relational Perspective." The first chapter in this section, by T. Dean Thomlison, should be particularly useful for those with an interest in organization–public relationships, but who lack familiarity with the literature of interpersonal communication and relationship building. Elizabeth Toth's chapter demonstrates how the interpersonal perspective can serve as the basis for a "personal model" of public relations, based on her contention that public relations is an interpersonal function occurring between an organization and its significant publics. In the following chapter, we report on our exploration of organization–public relationship dimensions in a business-to-business context. We included this chapter in the hope it would be useful for public relations professionals practicing in environments in which key constituencies are other companies, not public members. Media relations promises to continue to be a crucial component of the practice of public relations and the changing nature of the media represent challenges to those seeking to utilize media to influence organization–public relationships. In the final chapter of the book, Steven Esposito and Stephen Koch trace the evolution of "relationship news" over the past decade, with implications for the practice of public relations. They demonstrate that the quest for ratings that characterizes network news today involves a re-examination of what "news" means, both to network producers and viewing audiences.

A FINAL NOTE

We are excited about the continuing potential of the relational paradigm as a framework for public relations study and practice. The notion of relationship management brings with it an opportunity for theory-building and cross-discipline integration. Moreover, the perspective serves as a platform for developing public relations initiatives that generate benefit for organizations and for the publics they serve. Relationship management also provides a structure for relating public relations strategies and organizational goals in ways understood and appreciated by an organization's dominant coalition. Finally, relationship management can serve as the conceptual overview for demonstrating the value of public relations within the larger organizational environment and, in that way, help public relations finally achieve the level of recognition it deserves an a valuable and integral component of sponsoring organizations.

In the process of putting together this book, we are reminded of Broom, Casey, and Ritchey's invitation for other scholars to join in the process of explicating the organization–public relationship concept. It is our similar hope that this book will stimulate colleagues from diverse disciplines—with the richness their different backgrounds and training affords—to join in the process of building theory and practice around the notion of relationship management. It is that hope that motivated us throughout the process of serving as editors of this book. We thank all the contributing authors for their patience as well as their intellectual efforts, and especially our spouses, Pegge Ledingham and Kathy Bruning for their continuing support.

REFERENCES

Botan, C. (1993). Introduction to the paradigm struggle in public relations. *Public Relations Review* (summer edition).Broom, G. M. (1986, August). *Public relations roles and systems theory: Functional and historicist causal models.* Paper presented at the annual meeting of the International Communication Association, Chicago, IL.

Broom, G. M. & Dozier, D. M. (1990), *Using research in public relations: Applications to program management.* Englewood Cliffs, NJ: Prentice-Hall, Inc.

Broom, G., Casey, S. and Ritchey, J. (1997). *Toward a concept and theory of organization–public relationships.* Journal of Public Relations Research, 9(2), 83–98.

Bruning, S. D. and Ledingham, J. A., (1998b, August). *Public relations and consumer decisions: Effectively managing the relationships that impact consumer behavior.* Paper presented at the Annual Convention of the Association for Education in Journalism and Mass Communication, Baltimore, MD.

Bruning, S. D. and Ledingham, J. A. (1998a). *Organization–public relationships and consumer satisfaction: Role of relationships in the satisfaction mix.* Communication Research Report.

Bruning, S. D. & Ledingham, J. A., (1998b, August). *PR, price, and product features.* Paper presented at the Annual Convention of the Association for Education in Journalism and Mass Communication, Baltimore, MD.

Cutlip, S. M., Center, A. H. & Broom, G. M., (1994). *Effective public relations.* Englewood Cliffs, NJ: Prentice-Hall, Inc.

Dozier, D. M., with Grunig, L. A., & Grunig, J. E., (1995). *Manager's guide to excellence in public relations and communication management.* Mahwah, NJ: Lawrence Erlbaum Associate.

Hallahan, K. (1998, August). *No Virginia, it's not true what they say about publicity's "implied third-party endorsement" effect.* Paper presented in the Advertising & Public Relations Division of the annual conference of the Association for Education in Journalism and Mass Communication, Baltimore, MD.

Ehling, W. P. (1992). Estimating the value of public relations and communication to an organization. In J. E. Grunig, D. M. Dozier, W. P. Ehling, L. A. Grunig, F. C. Repper, & J. White (Eds.), *Excellence in public relations and communication management* (pp. 617–638). Hillsdale, NJ: Lawrence Erlbaum Associates.

Ferguson, M. A. (1984, August). *Building theory in public relations: Interorganizational relationships.* Paper presented to the Association for Education in Journalism and Mass Communication, Gainesville, FL.

Grunig, L. A., Grunig, J. E., & Ehling, W. P. (1992). What is an effective organization? In J. E. Grunig, D. M. Dozier, W. P. Ehling, L. A. Grunig, F. C. Repper, & J. White (Eds.), *Excellence in public relations and communication management* (pp. 65–90). Hillsdale, NJ: Lawrence Erlbaum Associates.

Hon, L. C. (1998). Demonstrating effectiveness in public relations: Goals, objectives, and evaluation. *Journal of Public Relations Research, 10*(2), 103–135.

Ledingham, J. A., & Bruning, S. D. (1997). Building loyalty through community relations. *The Public Relations Strategist, 3*(2), 27–29.

Ledingham, J. A., & Bruning, S. D. (1998a, Spring). Relationship management and public relations: Dimensions of an organization–public relationship. *Public Relations Review, 24.*

Ledingham, J. A. and Bruning, S. D. (1998b). A management approach to media relations. *Business Research Yearbook,* 752–756.

Nakra, P. (Spring, 1991). The changing role of public relations in marketing communication. *Public Relations Quarterly.*

Wilcox, D. L., Ault, P. H., & Agree, W. K. (1992). *Public relations strategies and tactics.* NY: HarperCollins.

Wilson, L. J. (1994). The return to Gemeinschaft: A theory of public relations and corporate community relations as relationship-building. In A. F. Alkhafaji (Ed.), *Business research yearbook: Global business perspectives* (Vol. 1, pp. 135–141). Lanham, MD: International Academy of Business Disciplines and University Press of America, Inc.

I

The State of Organization–Public Relationship Research

1

Concept and Theory of Organization–Public Relationships[1]

ಔ ✧ ಚ

Glen M. Broom, Shawna Casey, and James Ritchey
School of Communication, San Diego State University

This chapter explores the concept of *relationships* in public relations theory and practice. Even though the public relations function builds and maintains organizations' relationships with publics, we found few definitions of such relationships in public relations literature. We also found the same paucity of useful definitions in the literature of other fields in which the concept of relationships is central.

We conclude that the absence of a fully explicated definition precludes the development of valid operational measures of organization–public relationships and limits theory building in public relations. Without such definition, both scholars and practitioners will continue using indirect measures to draw inferences about relationships without measuring the relationships themselves.

We suggest a concept of relationships with measurable properties distinct from their antecedents and their consequences, and independent of the perceptions held by individuals in the relationships. We also posit a theoretical model for constructing theory about public-organization relationships.

---

[1]An earlier version of this chapter was published in the *Journal of Public Relations Research*, 9(2) (1997), pp. 83–98.

Many scholars and practitioners say that public relations is all about building and maintaining an organization's relationships with its publics. However, anyone reading the literature of the field would have difficulty finding a useful definition of such relationships in public relations. Instead, we assume that readers know and agree on the meaning and the measurement of the important concept of relationships. Unfortunately, the assumption is not supported by evidence. What follows is a framework for explicating the concept of relationships in a public relations context and for building theory around this concept.

NEED FOR DEFINITION

Public relations literature is replete with references to relationships that neither define the concept nor indicate how to measure them. For example, Center and Jackson (1995) emphasized the central role of relationships in public relations management: "The proper term for the desired outcomes of public relations practice is public relationships. An organization with effective public relations will attain positive public relationships" (p. 2). However, the authors neither defined the concept nor indicated how practitioners are to measure and monitor the relative "positiveness" of public relationships.

The authors of *Effective public relations* (Cutlip, Center, & Broom, 1994) defined *public relations* as "the management function that establishes and maintains mutually beneficial relationships between an organization and the publics on whom its success or failure depends" (p. 6). Ehling (1992) said that the shift from influencing opinion to establishing and maintaining relationships "indicates an important change in the conceptualization of the primary mission of public relations." He cautioned, however, that the notion of relationships "may be far too open-ended to be helpful in giving needed specificity to this kind of end state" (p. 622).

Broom and Dozier (1990) also acknowledged that few researchers actually measure organization–public relationships:

> Conceptually, public relations programs affect the *relationships* between organizations and their publics, but rarely is program impact on the relationships themselves measured. In practice, impact measures are made on one or both sides of relationships and then inferences made—sometimes explicitly, usually implicitly—about how the relationships changed. (pp. 82–83)

Broom and Dozier did not, however, explicate the nature of or the attributes of relationships. L. A. Grunig, Grunig, and Ehling (1992, p. 81) argued that the concept of relationships between organizations and stakeholders is central to their theory of public relations and organizational effectiveness. After reviewing the literature, however, the authors found few public relations scholars who have studied relationships. They also found little agreement on the essential nature of relationships in other fields of study.

Again, however, these same authors devoted little attention to defining relationships in ways that would help either practitioners or scholars measure the phenomenon in the empirical world. Instead, Grunig, Grunig, and Ehling (1992) proposed a mix of attributes, perceptions, and constructs to measure relationships:

> Researchers and practitioners could use any of these concepts to measure the quality of the strategic relationships of organizations, but we suggest that the following are most important: reciprocity, trust, credibility, mutual legitimacy, openness, mutual satisfaction, and mutual understanding. (p. 83)

Pavlik (1987, p. 122) observed that even though public relations focuses mainly on publics and relationships, there has been little research on relationships. He pointed out that essentially no public relations research has used the relationship as the unit of analysis. Rather, research on relationships typically employs survey research using individuals as the unit of analysis. Ferguson (1984) pointed to the need for the definition and measurement of relationships between organizations and their publics. Her suggested approaches, however, mix characteristics of relationships with perceptions of the parties in relationships, as well as constructs based on the reports of those in relationships.

Broom (1977) found that although definitions of public relations include terms such as *relationships* and *mutual relations*, the practice more typically deals with "measuring, analyzing and influencing public opinion" (p. 111).

> They say the function of public relations is to establish and maintain communication linkages between an organization and its various publics in order to maintain mutually beneficial *relationships*.

> This view of public relations calls for measuring the relationships in the social system composed of an organization and its publics. Public opinion surveys designed to find out how similar the public's definition of an issue is to corporate views, however, do not provide all the information needed to adequately describe corporate–public relationships on issues of mutual concern. (p. 111)

Broom went on to suggest intrapersonal measures of "perceptions of agreement," in addition to actual agreement, for calculating coorientational indices of relationships. However, these indices are based on participants' views, they do not represent phenomena independent of those views.

Although those who practice and study public relations talk about relationships as a focal concept, few have defined the concept or have carefully measured attributes of relationships. More commonly, measures of relationships rely on participants' perceptions, as if those reports were valid indicators of the relationships under study.

DEFINING CONCEPTS: EXPLICATION

Chaffee (1991) defined *explication* as the process of linking the conceptual world with the real world—an intellectual process that links theoretical propositions to observable phenomena (operational definitions). According to Chaffee, *primitive terms*—words accepted as having generally understood meanings and treated as givens—are basic to the explication process. Primitive terms are used to define other terms, with the goal of specifying observable phenomena to represent the concept. The usefulness of a conceptual definition, therefore, is a function of how effectively the definition suggests attributes or properties that distinguish the concept from other objects. According to Chaffee, "An explication of a concept specifies the operations a scientist must perform to produce an instance of the concept; validity is the general criterion by which we assess the adequacy of that operationalization once we have established our explication" (p. 12).

Without clearly explicated concepts, researchers cannot make empirical observations and construct meaningful theories. A survey of public relations textbooks and of scholarly journals found no definition of relationships in public relations that is generally understood and accepted. Instead, it appears that public relations scholars and authors in other fields use the term relationships as a primitive term when defining public relations and when posing theoretical propositions. Yet the term relationship stands for a complex phenomenon for which few practitioners and scholars share a common definition and a set of measures. Without that definition, researchers cannot derive valid and reliable measures useful for positing and testing public relations theory. Also without that definition, practitioners cannot describe and compare organization–public relationships with any validity or reliability.

Theoretical Framework

A number of fields other than public relations also use relationships as a central concept. Interpersonal relations, family relations, group dynamics, labor–management relations, counselor–client psychotherapy relations, organizational studies, and international relations are but a few of the many domains of theory and practice based on understanding and observation of relationships. A review of literature in some of these fields indicates that they also share with public relations similar explication problems. These explication problems include the absence of a precise and widely used definition of relationships, as well as a paucity of systematic theory construction based on a commonly accepted definition of relationships. The reviews that follow illustrate these problems in just a few of the many fields that use the concept in both theory and practice.

Perspectives From Interpersonal Communication. Throughout the interpersonal communication and interaction literature reviewed, the definition of relationships included both behavioral and cognitive elements. For example, Surra & Ridley (1991) defined *degree of relationship* as comprising observable "moment-to-moment interaction events" and "intersubjectivity" or "cognitive interdependence" (p. 37). Millar and Rogers (1976) cast relationships in a symbolic interaction perspective: "People become aware of themselves only within the context of their social relationships. These relationships, whether primarily interpersonal or role specific, are bestowed, sustained, and transformed through communicative behaviors" (p. 87).

Surra and Ridley (1991) suggested that relationships are both objective realities and subjective realities. These realities provide the context within which each partner in the relationship "know how to behave toward the other and to understand, predict, and interpret the other's behavior ... " (p. 38). Likewise, the social relations model central to the study of social interaction and "relational science" includes both observable behavior and subjective elements ("reciprocal liking") in the concept of relationships (Kenny & Kashy, 1991).

In an early installment of his many reports using the concept of relationships, Duck (1973) argued that relationships do not exist outside of the cognition and the values of the interactors. According to Duck, "Social relationships must be defined in terms of the individual's viewpoint" (p. 147). In a subsequent article, Duck (1986) added behavior and the imagery of process, and suggested that the term relationship may not be definable in ways amenable to empirical observation:

> A relationship takes its existence from the partners thinking that they have one and represent that belief in their behavior toward one another. Such behavior change; our views of a partner or friend can alter; attitudes about the relationship can be affected by mood, circumstances, and the state of the rest of our lives. Accordingly, relationships should be regarded not as permanent "things" that we investigate clinically, but as potentially changing mental and behavioral creations of participants and outsiders. (p. 92)

Similarly, Andersen (1993) wrote, "Relationships are the combined product and producers of both the interpersonal interactions and the cognitive activity of the interactants" (p. 2). However, Andersen did not define the concept as an observable phenomenon independent from the perceptions of the "interactants." Cappella (1991) suggested that understanding relationships requires studying "the association between *patterns* of message interchange between partners and the partners' experienced state of the relationship" (p. 103).

Those studying close relationships typically treat relationships as combinations of subjective and objective attributes associated with the participants and with their interaction (Huston & Robins, 1982):

> *Relationship properties* are recurrent patterns of interpersonal or subjective events. These patterns can be discerned only by reference to samples of interactions or of subjective experiences at the event level ...

> When we speak of data about relationships, we include not only overt interpersonal activity but also cognitions and emotions that result from or contribute to such activity. In other words, we include those subjective features that are relevant to the behavioral interdependence of the particular relationship. Thus, interpersonal and subjective *events*, interpersonal and subjective relationship *properties*, and *subjective conditions* are all data about relationships. (pp. 904, 905)

Berscheid and Peplau (1983) offered a list of properties useful for classifying a relationship as "close":

> (1) the individuals have *frequent* impact on each other, (2) the degree of impact per each occurrence is *strong*, (3) the impact involves *diverse* kinds of activities

for each person, and (4) all of these properties characterize the interconnected activity series for a relatively long *duration* of time. (p. 13)

Millar and Rogers (1987) argued that "dyadic structure cannot be additively reconstructed from monadic measures" (p. 127). They proposed nine indices for measuring relationships, all but one of which are based on measures taken from one of the relationship members. Most of the attributes attributed to relationships are actually ratios in which one member's score is divided by the other's score.

Ballinger (1991) adapted Millar and Rogers' (1987) relational communication perspective to propose a nine-cell "relational model of public–organizational relationships" (see Table 1.1): "The relational dimensions of Millar and Rogers (1987), intimacy, trust and control, were thus integrated into a preliminary relational model of public–organizational relationships which also includes the dimensions of perceptions, communication behavior and relational outcomes" (p. 75).

Recent theorizing, however, has expanded the concept of relationships to explicitly include qualities and properties of the "links" between parties in relationships. For example, Kerns (1994) said that relationships represent "summaries" or "traits" that "refer to the consistencies in the affect, cognition and behavior of a particular dyad" (p. 130). Likewise, I. G. Sarason, Sarason, and Pierce (1995) raised the now obvious question: "Where do individuals end and relationships begin?" (p. 617). They concluded that "relationships are basic units of analysis whose distinctive properties and processes need to be specified" (p. 618).

In summary, however, interpersonal communication scholars operationally define relationships as a measure of participants' perceptions or as a function of those perceptions. Much of the interpersonal communication literature does not suggest measures of relationships

TABLE 1.1

Ballinger's Relational Model of Public–Organizational Relationships

	Intimacy	*Trust*	*Control*
Perceptions	Dependence	Confidence	Power
Communication Behaviors	Frequency	Openness	Dominance
Relational Outcomes	Knowledge	Reciprocity	Functionality

Note. From *Relational dimensions of public-organizational relationships* (p. 54), by J. D. Ballinger, 1991, Unpublished master's thesis, San Diego State University, San Diego, CA, p. 54. Copyright 1991 by San Diego State University. Reprinted with permission.

that are independent of the participants' perceptions (Burnett, McGhee, & Clarke, 1987; Duck, 1988; Duck, 1991; Gilmour & Duck, 1980, 1986; Harvey, Arbuch, & Weber, 1992). As Berscheid (1995) concluded, these "individualistic causal conditions" suggest that the "psychological perspective ... is becoming dominant in theory and research on interpersonal relationships" (p. 529). At the same time, however, there is a growing recognition that the "mentalistic" approach is not the only approach and that "the relationship itself has distinctive emergent properties" (I. G. Sarason, Sarason, & Pierce, 1995, p. 613).

Perspectives From Psychotherapy.   Psychotherapy also employs the concept of relationships as central to both study and practice, particularly the relationship between counselor and client. This field also mixes subjective and objective indicators to represent the existence and the nature of relationships. For example, Gelso and Carter (1985) defined the *counselor–client relationship* as "the feelings and attitudes that counseling participants have toward one another, and the manner in which these are expressed" (p. 159).

Gelso and Carter (1985) included three elements of relationships: First, they described the "working alliance ...an emotional alignment that is both fostered and fed by the emotional bond, agreement on goals, and agreement on tasks" (p. 163). Second, they defined the *transference relationship*, or *unreal relationship*, as representing the displacement of feelings from previous relationships onto the therapist, and vice versa. Clearly, displacement feelings are intrapersonal projections, not observable attributes of something independent of the participants' perceptions of each other. And third, they referred to the *real relationship* as "something that exists and develops between counselor and client as a result of the feelings, perceptions, attitudes, and actions of each toward the other" (p. 185).

Sexton and Whiston (1994) undertook a review of the literature on therapeutic relationships covering publications dated 1985 through 1992. They used Gelso and Carter's (1985) three-element definition as the organizing structure for their analysis. It was not surprising, then, that the review reflected a similar reliance on individual introspection. Sexton and Whiston referred to "perceptions and interpretations of another's behavior that are appropriate and realistic, in which feelings are genuine and the behaviors are congruent" (p. 8). Their definition of the counseling relationship, however, mixes these perceptions with interaction and even the environment: "Those aspects of the client and counselor and their interaction that contribute to a therapeutic environment, which in turn may influence client change" (p. 8).

In 1994, Gelso and Carter revisited their 1985 definition of client–counselor relationships. They concluded that humanistic therapists define the counselor–client relationships in terms of the counselor's perceptions of empathetic understanding, unconditional positive regard, and congruence. Instead of measuring the actual client–counselor relationships, these indicators represent only therapists' perceptions of the relationships. However, Gelso and Carter's (1994) revised definition mixes perceptions of relationships with participants' expressions of those perceptions. They defined the counselor–client relationship as "the feelings and attitudes that counseling participants have toward one another, and the manner in which these are expressed" (p. 297).

Perspectives From Interorganizational Relationships (IORs). The study of IORs, by necessity, does not employ subjective, introspective attributes to describe relationships. Rather, organizational theorists focus on organizational behavior. Theoretically, organizations enter relationships because of their dependence on other organizations for resources (Hougland & Sutton, 1978; Van de Ven, 1976). The emphasis is on the exchange of resources: "An interorganizational relationship occurs when two or more organizations transact resources (money, physical facilities and materials, customer and client referrals, technical staff services) among each other" (Van de Ven, p. 25).

Van de Ven and Walker (1984) specified three conditions, one of which must be present for the formation of IORs: First, a scarcity of resources may cause an organization to become dependent on another. Second, a requirement for specialized skills or services needed to fulfill obligations may cause IORs. Third, relationships may result when organizations operate in similar domains in which they have similar clients, similar services, similar skills, or similar needs. Under the third condition, the resulting relationships may take the form of competition.

The term *linkages* appears frequently in discussions of IORs. For example, Oliver (1990) summarized the literature on IORs as "the relatively enduring transactions, flows, and linkages that occur among or between an organization and one or more organizations in its environment" (p. 241). Oliver's "contingencies of relationship" formation can be recast as characteristics of linkages or exchanges. These include the following:

1. *Necessity* refers to the quality of the relationship derived from legal or regulatory requirements. In other words, a governing body mandates the relationship, as opposed to a relationship entered voluntarily. Research suggests that greater frequency of interaction occurs in mandated relationships than in voluntary relationships.
2. *Asymmetry* refers to the potential exercise of power or control over another organization or its resources. Research suggests that scarcity of resources prompts organizations to form asymmetric relationships, even if the formation of relationships necessitates the loss of autonomy.
3. *Reciprocity* refers to cooperation, collaboration, and coordination among organizations, rather than domination, power, and control. Research on reciprocity in interorganizational relationships draws from exchange theory. Exchange theorists posit that a linkage produces benefits that outweigh any disadvantages, particularly the loss of autonomy and the cost of managing the linkage.
4. *Efficiency* refers to arrangements that are consequences of the need to improve internal input/output ratios. The theory suggests that organizations enter formal "efficiency" relationships to reduce the cost of transactions that would otherwise occur in the marketplace.
5. *Stability* refers to the relative predictability of interorganizational relationships in the face of environmental uncertainty. Researchers have reported that uncertainty prompts organizations to establish and manage linkages with other organizations in order to achieve orderly, reliable patterns of resource flows and exchanges.
6. *Legitimacy* refers to aspects of interorganizational relationships that lend justification and the appearance of agreement with prevailing norms, rules, beliefs, or expectations of external constituents. In other words, the nature or quality of the linkage adds or detracts value. (Oliver, 1990, pp. 243–246)

The dominant paradigm for studying interorganizational relationships draws from *resource dependency theory* (Aldrich, 1976; Lincoln & McBride, 1985) and *exchange theory* (Cook, 1977; Levine & White, 1961; Stearns, Hoffman, & Heide, 1987). According to resource dependency theory, relationships form in response to an organization's need for resources. Satisfying the need for resources allows an organization to survive, to grow, and to achieve other goals. Relationships consist of the transactions involving the exchange of resources between organizations.

Similarly, exchange theory suggests that voluntary transactions result from knowledge of domain similarity and lead to mutual benefit, as well as to mutual goal achievement. It should be noted that exchange theorists define relationships in terms of the voluntary transactions and of the mutuality of interests and rewards.

Other theorists working in the area of interorganizational relationships also have hypothesized about the contingencies or causes of such relationships, as well as their consequences. They defined interorganizational relationships as something distinct from the participant organizations. For example, Laumann, Galaskiewicz, and Marsden (1978) conceived of interorganizational relationships as concrete and observable transactions in which resources are transferred across organizational boundaries.

Perspectives From Systems Theory. Katz and Kahn (1967) described systems theory as "basically concerned with problems of relationships, of structure, and of interdependence rather than with the constant attributes of objects" (p. 18). The authors suggested that defining social systems and determining their functions requires "tracing the pattern of energy exchange or activity of people as it results in some output and ascertaining how the output is translated into energy which reactivates the pattern" (p. 18).

Miller (1978) defined a system as "a set of interacting units with relationships among them" (p. 16). Miller also stated that relationships can be empirically observed using spatial, temporal, spatiotemporal, and causal qualities (p. 17). Relationships also take on symbiotic or parasitic forms to perform processes which one element in the relationship lacks (p. 18). The structure of a system is defined by the relationships among the units. To the extent that communication is the primary exchange in social systems, it serves as a major determinant of both relationships and of the overall functioning of most systems. However, when communication flows through specialized systems—presumably technology designed to facilitate information transfer and interactions—spatial propinquity is less important to system structure and relationships (p. 19).

Klir (1991) pointed out that there are two basic types of systems—those concerned with the *things* in the system, and those concerned with the *relations* among the things. Klir went on to make the point that the relations of phenomena are independent of the things that comprise the system:

The *relation-oriented classification* of systems is of primary concern to systems science, which focuses on those phenomena of systems which are independent of the kind of things involved in the systems. Since systems characterized by different types of relations require different theoretical treatment, this classification is predominantly *theoretically based.* (p. 219)

In summary, the various perspectives on relationships lead to several observations and conclusions. First, many who write about relationships assume the term has a common meaning that does not need explication. Second, many attempts to define the concept mix attributes of those involved in the relationship with attributes of the relationship itself. Third, some who portend to describe relationships instead measure antecedent states and consequences of relationships. Fourth, some definitions combine the processes by which relationships are formed with the states achieved by the processes. And last, some systems theorists say that relationships among interacting units can be described using attributes of the relationships themselves independent of the units involved.

Table 1.2 illustrates the diversity of definitions found in the literature of areas in which the concept of relationships is central to a theoretical framework. Some scholars conceive of relationships as processes observed over time, whereas others define relationships as states that can be measured at a single point in time. Still others use combinations of processes and states to represent what they refer to as relationships. Likewise, some scholars define relationships as subjective reality; others define them as objective reality. The majority of works reviewed for this

TABLE 1.2

Summary of Perspectives on Relationships

Relationships as:	Process	Process and State	State
Subjective Reality			Duck (1973, 1986)
Combinations of Subjective and Objective Realities	Hinde (1988)	Andersen (1993) Ballinger (1991) Capelle (1991) Huston & Robins (1982) Millar & Roger (1987) Surra & Ridley (1991)	Gelso & Carter (1985, 1994) Kerns (1994) Sexton & Whiston (1994)
Objective Reality	Laumann, Galaskiewicz, & Marsen (1978)	Katz & Kahn (1967) Oliver (1990) Van de Ven (1976) Van de Ven & Walker (1984)	Klir (1991) Miller (1978)

study, however, employed notions of relationships that combine subjective perceptions of the participants with qualities of relationships independent of the participants.

Defining Organization–Public Relationships

Since Cutlip and Center (1952) first wrote about the "ecology" of public relations in the first edition of their classic textbook, systems theory has served as a useful framework for theory building in public relations. Recent editions include an entire chapter devoted to system theory and the development of an open systems model of public relations (Cutlip et al., 1994).

A Theoretical Framework. Systems theorists posit that interacting units develop patterns of interaction that form the structure of the system, but the structure and the process of creating it are not the same:

> Structure is the arrangement of a concrete system's parts at a moment in three-dimensional space. Process is change in the matter-energy or information of that system over time. The two are entirely different and need not be confused. (Miller, 1978, p. 24)

Systems theorists base their definitions of systems on the central notion of *interdependence,* or relatedness, of elements.

Similar to propositions of systems theory, relational communication scholars suggest that mutual adaptation forms the essence of all interpersonal interaction. Researchers find that over time, social interactions lead to mutual changes in accents, speech rates, vocal intensity, gestures, gaze, and so forth (Cappella, 1991, p. 104). Functional causal imagery in interpersonal relationships research "focuses on communication as a central means through which people both pursue and service relevant relationship functions" (Burleson, 1995, p. 576). Relationships, then, reflect the conjoint, purposive behaviors of the actors in the relationships.

The imagery of systems theory also suggests a concept of relationships similar to those in the literature on interorganizational relationships: Relationships represent the exchange or transfer of information, energy, or resources. Therefore, attributes of those exchanges or transfers represent and define the relationship. At the level of organization–public systems, the attributes of linkages among the participants describe the relationships within the system as well as the structure of the system.

Antecedents to relationships include the perceptions, motives, needs, behaviors, and so forth, posited as contingencies or as causes in the formation of relationships. In the open systems model of public relations, antecedents are the sources of change, pressure, or tension on the system derived from the environment. The *consequences* of relationships are the outputs that have the effects of changing the environment and of achieving, maintaining, or changing goal states both inside and outside the organization (Cutlip et al., 1994, p. 213).

Figure 1.1 incorporates these elements to explicate the concept of relationships and to develop theoretical propositions about the formation and the impact of relationships. This model shows relationships as both the consequences of and the causes of other changes. In other words, relationships act as both dependent and independent variables, as well as intervening variables in the construction of theory about public–organizational relationships.

The Communication Linkage.   It would be difficult to overstate the importance of the communication linkage in organization–public relationships. Walton (1969) suggested that communication is "the most significant factor accounting for the total behavior of the organization" and that "the dynamics of the organization can best be understood by understanding its systems of communication" (p. 109). Ehling (1992) said that the "primary end state" of public relations is "the maximization through communication of the difference between cooperation and conflict such that cooperation becomes the prime benefit" (p. 633).

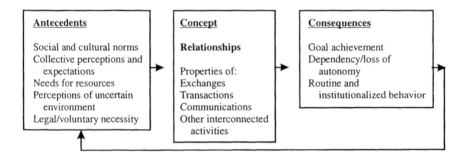

FIG. 1.1. Antecendents and consequences of organization–public relationships.

Similar to the imagery of Van de Ven (1976) in his discussion of interorganizational relationships, the communication linkage represents interactions aimed at attaining mutual goals, patterns that develop through the division of tasks and functions among the communicators, and qualities separate from the those of communicators. Qualities of the communication linkage independent of the communicators include the symmetry of the exchange, the intensity of the exchange, the content of the exchange, the frequency of the exchange, the valence of the exchange, and the duration of the exchange. Surely, communication offers the richest domain of literature and theory from which to build a theory of organization–public relationships.

TENTATIVE CONCLUSIONS AND SUGGESTIONS

Even though the explication of the concept of organization–public relationships is not complete, the study reported here provides the basis for some tentative conclusions:

1. Public relations researchers and practitioners can study relationships as phenomena distinct from the perceptions held by parties in the relationships.
2. The formation of relationships occurs when parties have perceptions and expectations of each other, when one or both parties need resources from the other, when one or both parties perceive mutual threats from an uncertain environment, or when there is either a legal or voluntary necessity to associate.
3. Relationships consist of patterns of linkages through which the parties in them pursue and service their interdependent needs.
4. Relationships are the dynamic results of the exchanges and reciprocity that manifest themselves as the relationships develop and evolve, yet they can be described at a given point in time.
5. Relationships may lead to increased dependency, loss of autonomy, goal achievement, and structured interdependence in the form of routine and institutionalized behavior.
6. Relationships have unique and measurable properties that are not shared with the participants in the relationships and that define relationships as being something separate from the participants.

7. The antecedents and consequences of relationships also have unique properties that distinguish them from the relationship.
8. Relationship formation and maintenance represents a process of mutual adaptation and contingent responses.
9. The absence of a useful definition precludes measurement of organization–public relationships and forces both scholars and practitioners alike to measure one part of them or another and make potentially invalid inferences about the relationships.
10. The absence of a fully explicated conceptual definition of organization–public relationships limits theory building in public relations.

Whatever definition results from the continued exploration, the primary concern must be with defining the concept in ways that lead to valid operational definitions for use in both theory and in practice. In the meantime, those in both the scholarly and the professional communities will continue to speak of the central role of relationships in public relations. Without explication, however, researchers and practitioners alike will continue to use measures that may not measure the relationships themselves, hence the need for attending to the concept itself, as well as for developing empirical descriptions and measurements of the phenomenon.

POSTSCRIPT

Since the publication of the earlier edition of this chapter in the *Journal of Public Relations Research*, we have pilot tested some of the ideas in a thesis research case study (Casey, 1997). We also have written a summative statement defining organization–public relationships:

> Organization–public relationships are represented by the patterns of interaction, transaction, exchange, and linkage between an organization and its publics. These relationships have properties that are distinct from the identities, attributes, and perceptions of the individuals and social collectivities in the relationships. Though dynamic in nature, organization–public relationships can be described at a single point in time and tracked over time.

Based on the imagery of this concept of organization–public relationships, we studied the relationships between an adult continuing education center (CEC) and its significant publics. For two weeks, the second author observed the CEC's dealings with its various publics, logging interaction, transaction, exchange, and other linkages. In addition to observing, the researcher also assisted with some of the work, reducing the distance between the observer and those being observed. Logs documented the CEC's dealings with its members, business community contacts, instructors, program alumni, and staff at the affiliated university.

The observer's logs described three dimensions of the state of relationships between the CEC and its publics: *formalization, standardization,* and *complexity.* Formalization included recorded indicators of the extent to which rules, policies, procedures, instructions, and communication between the CEC and its publics were contractual, prescribed, and in written form. Standardization logs recorded the degree to which interaction, transaction, exchange, and transfer between the CEC and its publics were planned and routine. Complexity represented the number of different types of linkages between the CEC and each of its publics.

Logs also documented the *intensity* and *reciprocity* of two major relationship processes—*information flow* and *resource flow.* Observation of the intensity dimension produced logs of how frequently the CEC and each of its publics exchanged information and resources. For example, the information intensity log recorded contacts that included face-to-face contact, written communications, and phone calls. Resource intensity recorded exchanges of money, materials, services, and physical facilities.

Reciprocity logs recorded the relative balance (symmetry) in the exchanges of information and of resources. This dimension was operationalized for each organization–public relationship as a ratio of CEC-initiated contact or resource distribution divided by the number of public-initiated contacts or resource transfers. A ratio of 1.0 means that the relationship is perfectly reciprocal. Ratios greater than or less than 1.0 indicates degrees of asymmetry in the relationships with respect to information and resource exchange processes.

Following the 2-week participant observation, CEC staff members completed questionnaires about their perceptions of the state and process dimensions of the CEC's various relationships. Mean staff ratings paralleled the empirical data from participant observation on most dimensions, thus providing some validation of the relationship measures. Staff perceptions of the CEC's relationship with its university affiliate, however, portrayed a relationship unlike the one documented by the observer.

CEC staff rated the organization's relationship with the university on each of the dimensions much higher than was suggested by the observer's logged data. This finding suggests that the staff perceived the CEC–university relationship to be much more complex, intense, and reciprocal with respect to information and resource exchanges than was in reality. Finally, the staff typically perceived a greater level of reciprocity in relationships with other publics than what was recorded in the observer's logs.

In summary, this pilot test demonstrated that state and process measures can provide useful profiles of organization–public relationships. Differences found between staff perceptions of relationships and the observer's logs also suggest that independent observation may help identify otherwise undetected problems in organization–public relationships.

Although clearly beyond the scope of this case study application of the relationship measures, we conclude that conceptualizing organization–public relationships as observable phenomena distinct from their antecedents and consequences, and independent of the parties in the relationship, provides a useful paradigm for research and for theory building. To that end, we close by inviting you to join us in continuing the explication and theory-building processes.

ACKNOWLEDGMENTS

The authors acknowledge the contributions of fellow seminarians Margo Dwoskin, Jeff D. Sojka, Kimberly J. White, and Maureen M. Wisener. We also acknowledge the work done on this topic by Jane R. Ballinger, Jeannie Brittingham, Leona Patterson, Eugenia Roberts, Susan Ruckman, and Christine Zimmerman during an earlier seminar. The authors also thank San Diego State University communication professor, Dr. Brian Spitzberg, for his suggestions, support, and encouragement.

REFERENCES

Aldrich, H. (1976). Resource dependence and interorganizational relations: Local employment service sector organizations. *Administration and Society, 7*, 419–453.
Andersen, P. A. (1993). Cognitive schemata in personal relationships. In S. W. Duck (Ed.), *Individuals in relationships* (pp. 1–29). Newbury Park, CA: Sage.

Ballinger, J. D. (1991). *Relational dimensions of public–organizational relationships.* Unpublished master's thesis, San Diego State University, San Diego, CA.

Berscheid, E. (1995). Help wanted: A grand theorist of interpersonal relationships, sociologist or anthropologist preferred. *Journal of Social and Personal Relationships, 12,* 529–533.

Berscheid, E., & Peplau, L. A. (1983). The emerging science of relationships. In H. H. Kelley, E. Berscheid, A. Christensen, J. H. Harvey, T. L. Huston, G. Levinger, E. McClintock, L. A. Peplau, and D. R. Peterson (Eds.), *Close relationships* (pp. 1–19). New York: Freeman.

Broom, G. M. (1977). Coorientational measurement of public issues. *Public Relations Review, 3,* 110–119.

Broom, G. M., & Dozier, D. M. (1990). *Using research in public relations: Applications to program management.* Englewood Cliffs, NJ: Prentice-Hall.

Burleson, B. R. (1995). Personal relationships as a skilled accomplishment. *Journal of Social and Personal Relationships, 12,* 575–581.

Burnett, R., McGhee, P., & Clarke, D. (Eds., 1987). *Accounting for relationships: Explanation, representation and knowledge.* London: Methuen.

Cappella, J. N. (1991). Mutual adaptation and relativity of measurement. In B. M. Montgomery & S. W. Duck (Eds.), *Studying interpersonal interaction* (pp. 103–117). New York: Guilford.

Casey, S. (1997). *A framework for studying organization–public relationships: Measuring relationship state and process.* Unpublished master's thesis, San Diego State University, San Diego, CA.

Center, A. H., & Jackson, P. (1995). *Public relations practices: Management case studies and problems* (5th ed.). Englewood Cliffs, NJ: Prentice Hall.

Chaffee, S. H. (1991). *Explication* (Communication Concepts 1). Newbury Park, CA: Sage.

Cook, K. S. (1977). Exchange and power in networks of interorganizational relations. *The Sociological Quarterly, 18,* 62–82.

Cutlip, S. M., and Center, A. H. (1952). *Effective public relations.* Englewood Cliffs, NJ: Prentice-Hall.

Cutlip, S. M., Center, A. H., & Broom, G. M. (1994). *Effective public relations* (7th ed.). Englewood Cliffs, NJ: Prentice-Hall.

Duck, S. W. (1973). *Personal relationships and personal constructs.* London: Wiley.

Duck, S. W. (1986). *Human relationships: An introduction of social psychology.* Beverly Hills, CA: Sage.

Duck, S. W. (1988). *Relating to others.* Stony Stratford, UK: Open University Press and Belmont, CA: Dorsey/Brooks/Cole/Wadsworth.

Duck, S. W. (1991). *Understanding relationships.* New York: Guilford.

Ehling, W. P. (1992). Estimating the value of public relations and communication to an organization. In J. E. Grunig, D. M. Dozier, W. P. Ehling, L. A. Grunig, F. C. Repper, & J. White (Eds.), *Excellence in public relations and communication management* (pp. 617–638). Hillsdale, NJ: Lawrence Erlbaum Associates.

Ferguson, M. A. (1984, August). *Building theory in public relations: Interorganizational relationships.* Paper presented at the annual convention of the Association for Education in Journalism and Mass Communication, Gainesville, FL.

Gelso, C. J., & Carter, J. A. (1985). The relationship in counseling and psychotherapy: Components, consequences, and theoretical antecedents. *The Counseling Psychologist, 13,* 155–243.

Gelso, C. J., & Carter, J. A. (1994). Components of the psychotherapy relationship: Their interaction and unfolding during treatment. *Journal of Counseling Psychology, 41,* 296–306.

Grunig, L. A., Grunig, J. E., & Ehling, W. P. (1992). What is an effective organization? In J. E. Grunig, D. M. Dozier, W. P. Ehling, L. A. Grunig, F. C. Repper, & J. White (Eds.), *Excellence in public relations and communication management* (pp. 65–90). Hillsdale, NJ: Lawrence Erlbaum Associates.

Gilmour, R., & Duck, S. W. (Eds., 1980). *The development of social psychology.* New York: Academic Press.

Gilmour, R., & Duck, S. W. (Eds., 1986). *The emerging field of personal relationships.* Hillsdale, NJ: Lawrence Erlbaum Associates.

Harvey, J. H., Orbuch, T. L., & Weber, A. L. (Eds., 1992). *Attributions, accounts, and close relationships.* New York: Springer-Verlag.

Hinde, R. A. (1988). Introduction. In R. A. Hinde and J. Stevenson-Hinde (Eds.), *Relationships within families: Mutual influences* (pp. 1–4). Oxford: Clarendon.

Hougland, J. G., & Sutton, W. A. (1978). Factors influencing the degree of involvement in interorganizational relationships in a rural county. *Rural Sociology, 43,* 649–670.

Huston, T. L., & Robins, E. (1982). Conceptual and methodological issues in studying close relationships. *Journal of Marriage and the Family, 44,* 901–925.

Katz, D., & Kahn, R. L. (1967). *The social psychology of organizations.* New York: Wiley.

Kenny, D. A., & Kashy, D. A. (1991). Analyzing interdependence in dyads. In B. M. Montgomery & S. Duck (Eds.), *Studying interpersonal interaction* (pp. 275–285). New York: Guilford.

Kerns, K. A. (1994). A developmental model of the relations between mother-child attachment and friendship. In R. Erber and R. Gilmour (Eds.), *Theoretical Frameworks for Personal Relationships* (pp. 129–156). Hillsdale, NJ: Lawrence Erlbaum Associates.

Klir, G. J. (1991). *Facets of systems science.* New York: Plenum.

Laumann, E. O., Galaskiewicz, J., & Marsden, P. V. (1978). Community structures as interorganizational linkages. *Annual Review of Sociology, 4,* 455–484.

Lincoln, J. R., & McBride, K. (1985). Resources, homophily, and dependence: Organizational attributes and asymmetric ties in human service networks. *Social Science Research, 14,* 1–30.

Levine, S., & White, P. E. (1961). Exchange as a conceptual framework for the study of interorganizational relationships. *Administrative Science Quarterly, 5,* 583–601.

Millar, F. E., & Rogers, L. E. (1976). A relational approach to interpersonal communication. In G. R. Miller (Ed.), *Explorations in interpersonal communication* (pp. 87–103). Newbury Park, CA: Sage.

Millar, F. E., & Rogers, L. E. (1987). Relational dimensions of interpersonal dynamics. In M. E. Roloff & G. R. Miller (Eds.), *Interpersonal processes: New directions in communication research* (pp. 117–139). Newbury Park, CA: Sage.

Miller, J. G. (1978). *Living systems.* New York: McGraw-Hill.

Oliver, C. (1990). Determinants of interorganizational relationships: Integration and future directions. *Academy of Management Review, 15,* 241–265.

Pavlik, J. V. (1987). *Public relations: What research tells us.* Newbury Park, CA: Sage.

Sarason, I. G., Sarason, B. R., & Pierce, G. R. (1995). Social and personal relationships: Current issues, future directions. *Journal of Social and Personal Relationships, 12,* 613–619.

Sexton, T. L., & Whiston, S. C. (1994). The status of the counseling relationship: An empirical review, theoretical implications, and research directions. *The Counseling Psychologist, 22,* 6–78.

Stearns, T. M., Hoffman, A. N., & Heide, J. B. (1987). Performance of commercial television stations as an outcome of interorganizational linkages and environmental conditions. *Academy of Management Journal, 30,* 71–90.

Surra, C. A., & Ridley, C. A. (1991). Multiple perspectives on interaction: Participants, peers, and observers. In B. M. Montgomery & S. Duck (Eds.), *Studying interpersonal interaction* (pp. 35–55). New York: Guilford.

Van de Ven, A. H. (1976). On the nature, formation and maintenance of relations among organizations. *Academy of Management Review, 1*(4), 24–36.

Van de Ven, A. H., & Walker, G. (1984). The dynamics of interorganizational coordination. *Administrative Science, 29,* 598–621.

Walton, R. (1969). *Interpersonal peacemaking.* Reading, MA: Addison-Wesley.

2

From Organizational Effectiveness to Relationship Indicators: Antecedents of Relationships, Public Relations Strategies, and Relationship Outcomes

ಐ ✧ ಚ

James E. Grunig
University of Maryland

Yi-Hui Huang
National Cheng-chi University, Taiwan

In an invited paper to the Public Relations Division of the Association for Education in Journalism in the mid-1980s, Ferguson (1984) reviewed 9 years of research published in *Public Relations Review* and concluded that a paradigm focus for the field "would greatly enhance the probability of productive theory development" (p. ii.). That paradigm focus, she added, should be on relationships: "By this, the author means that the unit of study should not be the organization, nor the public, nor the communication process. Rather the unit of study should be the *relationships* between organizations and their publics" (p. ii).

L. A. Grunig, Grunig, and Ehling (1992), in the focal chapter of the literature review for the IABC study of Excellence in Public Relations and Communication Management, developed a general premise of how public relations contributes to organizational effectiveness, which they then used to integrate several subtheories of public relations. They concluded that public relations contributes to organizational effectiveness " ...when it helps reconcile the organization's goals with the expectations of its strategic constituencies. This contribution has monetary value to the organization. Public relations contributes to effectiveness by building quality, long-term relationships with strategic constituencies" (p. 86).

Quantitative research based on a sample of over 300 organizations in the United States, in Canada, and in the United Kingdom confirmed that excellent public relations programs were much more likely to have "change of relationship effects" and "conflict avoidance effects" than were less excellent programs (Dozier, L. A. Grunig, & Grunig, 1995, pp. 226–229). In subsequent qualitative interviews, heads of public relations and CEOs of organizations with the most excellent public relations programs were asked to estimate the value of public relations to their organizations. Although some assigned extremely high monetary values to public relations, most CEOs were reluctant to assign such values. Instead they generally explained that public relations has value when it develops good relationships with strategic publics—relationships that, in particular, helped the organizations withstand crises (pp. 230–235).

Public relations practitioners, like scholars, also increasingly are pointing to relationships as the key indicator of successful public relations. For example, Williams (1996) titled her Vernon C. Schranz Distinguished Lecture at Ball State University, "Putting Relationships Back Into Public Relations." She explained:

> I believe that the public relations business on the whole is moving away from being a relationship-based business and towards becoming a more impersonal, technologically based business. We think about placements, sound bytes, canned stories. We forget about people. But the basis of the very words "public relations" is connections between people. (p. 2)

> ... Remember, people don't call on us because of our technology. They communicate with us because of relationships. Think about it. The only reason we talk to half of the people in our families is because of relationships. (p. 10)

Kathleen Larey Lewton, senior vice-president of the public relations firm Porter Novelli, and the 1997 recipient of the Frank Weaver Lifetime Achievement Award of the Public Relations Society of America's Heath Academy, attributed declining confidence in the U.S. health-care system to a failure to build relationships:

Hospitals responded to the lure of marketing gimmicks (this year it's "branding"—too often superficial logo and slogan efforts) rather than focusing on dialogue with the communities they serve, nurturing relationships with key stakeholders and making substantive changes to adapt to a new environment. (Lewton, 1998, p. 6)

In October 1996, the Institute for Public Relations Research & Education, *Inside PR*, and the Ketchum Public Relations Research and Measurement Department invited 21 leading public relations practitioners, counselors, researchers, and academicians to an evaluation summit meeting to discuss and then define minimum standards for measuring the effectiveness of public relations. The group developed and agreed upon a report describing the state-of-the-art in public relations evaluation (Lindenmann, 1997). Nevertheless, many participants expressed the need to move beyond the state-of-the art to the measurement of relationships, as described in a summary of the meeting:

Several participants in the summit meeting were convinced that there is a need for practitioners to focus more attention on the notion of "relationships" in public relations, and to determine what it is about these relationships that can be measured. (*Seeking minimum standards*, p. 16)

The summary of the meeting also reported that "the following conversation took place":

My perspective is that most, if not all, of marketing and public relations has to do with changing or building relationships. I wonder if we shouldn't go at this from the point of view of evaluating these relationships. Can we come up with a definitive, industry-accepted methodology for demonstrating that reputation is in fact important to corporate success? I would say that we could agree that we could measure that by saying how do we measure the strengths of relationships, and how do we then demonstrate the stronger the relationships are with whichever groups we are looking at—employees, communities, shareholders, and customers seem to be the four that come up most often—that good relationships with those contribute to corporate success. (*Seeking minimum standards*, p. 17)

Although the concept of relationships is implicit in the term public relations and both scholars and practitioners regularly use the term in explaining the value of public relations, neither scholars nor practitioners have defined the concept carefully or have developed reliable measures of relationship outcomes. A psychologist serving on a doctoral dissertation committee at the University of Maryland a few years ago expressed the shortcoming well when she said, "Just what do you people mean by relationships?"

Broom, Casey, and Ritchey (1997) said the same thing in more academic language:

> A survey of public relations textbooks and scholarly journals turned up no generally understood and accepted definition of relationships in public relations. Instead, it appears that public relations scholars and authors in other fields use the term *relationships* as a primitive term when defining public relations and when posing theoretical propositions. Yet the term *relationship* stands for a complex phenomenon for which few practitioners and scholars share a common definition and set of measures. Absent that definition, researchers cannot derive valid and reliable measures useful for positing and testing public relations theory. Also absent that definition, practitioners cannot describe and compare organization–public relationships with any validity or reliability. (p. 86)

Public relations scholars and practitioners conducting evaluation research began to move from measuring one-way effects of communication programs toward definitions and measures of two-way relationships in the 1970s. However, their efforts were restricted to short-term effects that public relations messages, campaigns, and programs have on relationships between organizations and publics. In this chapter, we attempt to move from defining and measuring one-way, short-term effects to effects of public relations on long-term relationships. In doing so, we hope to move public relations theory and methods of evaluation toward a point where relationships are more than primitive concepts used in public relations jargon.

FROM SHORT- TO LONG-TERM
COMMUNICATION EFFECTS

In the 1970s, client organizations began to demand that both in-house public relations practitioners and consultancies demonstrate the effectiveness of communication programs (J. E. Grunig, 1977). Although many practitioners still claim that it is difficult to measure and evaluate the effects of public relations, public relations scholars and applied research firms have known for years how to conceptualize and measure the short-term effects of communication programs. The report that resulted from the 1997 summit conference on evaluation of public relations, for example, described the current best practices for measuring both the outputs of public relations processes and their outcomes (Lindenmann, 1997).

Evaluation, in other words, can be done by measuring both process and outcome indicators (Broom & Dozier, 1990, J. E. Grunig & Hunt, 1984, chap. 9; Lindenmann, 1997). A process indicator might include, for example, a count of the number of press releases issued, media monitoring and content analysis, or a count of attendance at a special event. Process indicators alone have little value, but when they can be linked both theoretically and empirically to outcome indicators, process indicators can be useful in monitoring the processes that eventually result in desirable outcomes.

Public relations researchers learned early that evaluation can be managed most easily if it is limited to specific communication programs such as media relations, community relations, or employee relations or to specific campaigns (Tirone, 1977). When they measured outcomes of public relations, however, researchers generally considered only one-way effects on exposure to messages by publics and changes in their cognitions, attitudes, and behavior. The 1997 summit report, for example, described measures of public relations outcomes in this way:

> As important as it might be to measure PR *outputs*, it is far more important to measure PR *outcomes*. These measure whether target audience groups actually *received* the messages directed at them ... paid *attention* to them ... *understood* the messages ... and *retained* these messages in any shape and form. Outcomes also measure whether the communication materials and messages which were disseminated have resulted in any *opinion, attitude,* and/or *behavior* changes on the part of those targeted audiences to whom the messages were directed. (Lindenmann, 1997, p. 5)

These outcomes of communication processes, as suggested in this quote, almost always were one-way (only effects on publics were measured) and asymmetrical (the purpose of public relations was seen as affecting publics for the benefit of client organizations). If the purpose of public relations is to build relationships between organizations and publics, however, then we must conceptualize and measure both communication processes and outcomes as two-way—by looking for effects on management as well as on publics. As we maintain in the following paragraphs, we can build relationships more effectively if we build symmetrical ones, which benefit both organizations and publics, than if we build asymmetrical ones that benefit only the organization.

The coorientation model developed by McLeod and Chaffee (1973) and adapted for public relations by Broom (1977) and J. E. Grunig and Hunt (1984) made it possible to reconceptualize the traditional out- comes of public relations as two-way relationship variables: communica- tion (extent of dialogue or mutual exposure), understanding (shared cognitions), agreement (shared attitudes), and complementary behavior (J. E. Grunig & Hunt, p. 134). In addition, a variable called *accuracy* in the coorientation model made it possible to identify gaps between organizations and publics. To measure accuracy, members of organiza- tions and members of publics are asked to predict the cognitions, attitudes, and behaviors of each other. The discrepancies between what one party thinks, feels, and how they behave and what the other thinks it thinks and feels and how it thinks it behaves can identify significant gaps in, at least, short-term relationships.[1]

Nevertheless, these coorientational measures are more useful in evaluating short-term effects of specific messages or of communication programs than they are in evaluating the long-term characteristics of the relationship between an organization and a public. Logically, there is a link between short-term coorientational effects and long-term rela- tionships—that is, relationships are likely to be better in the long term when organizations and publics understand one another, agree with one another, and behave in complementary ways. However, senior manage- ment and clients generally demand more than logic when they fund communication programs. They want evidence that they make organi- zations more effective. To provide that evidence, it is necessary to conceptualize and measure indicators of long-term relationships.

In her paper calling for a focus on relationships in public relations, Ferguson (1984) moved toward such long-term indicators of the quality of organization-public relationships. She identified five attributes of relationships: dynamic versus static; open versus closed; the degree to which both the organization and the public are satisfied with the relationship; distribution of power in the relationship; and the mutuality of understanding, agreement, and consensus.

In developing the theory for the Excellence study, L. A. Grunig, Grunig, and Ehling (1992) reviewed Ferguson's (1984) paper as well as literature on interorganizational and interpersonal relationships and

---

[1]Gap analyses, for example, make up a large part of the research that Kathleen Ladd Ward provides to her research clients (Ward, 1997).

concluded that the following attributes of relationships are the most important: "reciprocity, trust, credibility, mutual legitimacy, openness, mutual satisfaction, and mutual understanding" (p. 83). Vercic and J. E. Grunig (1995) went one step further when they related the concept of trust to theories of economics and of strategic management and pointed out that trust is the characteristic that allows organizations to exist—trust by stockholders, employees, consumers, governments, and communities, for example. Without trust, stockholders will not buy stock, employees will not work, consumers will not buy products, and governments will interfere with the organization's mission.

More recently, Broom et al. (1997) reported the results of a graduate research seminar that was dedicated to reviewing the literature of relationships from the fields of interpersonal communication, psychotherapy, interorganizational relationships, and systems theory. They developed a three-stage model that consisted of relationship concepts, antecedents to relationships, and consequences of relationships. The *relationship concepts* defined the nature of a relationship, which they specified as "properties of exchanges, transactions, communications, and other interconnected activities" (p. 94). They did not specify specific properties, however, that defined relationships or, especially, good relationships.

Broom et al.'s (1997) *antecedents of relationships* explained reasons why organizations enter into relationships with specific publics. They defined antecedents as "social and cultural norms, collective perceptions and expectations, needs for resources, perceptions of uncertain environment, and legal/voluntary necessity" (p. 94). Finally, they specified four *consequences of relationships*: "goal achievement, dependency/loss of autonomy, and routine and institutionalized behavior" (p. 94).

We have found Broom et al.'s (1997) model to be an excellent framework into which we can fit elements of the Excellence theory, but we believe we can offer more concrete variables under the categories of antecedents, relationship concepts, and consequences than Broom et al. offered. In doing so, we first followed Stafford and Canary (1991) and described Broom et al.'s middle category as "maintenance strategies" rather than relationship concepts. In this chapter, therefore, we conceptualize the antecedents that describe the publics with which organizations need relationships, the *strategies* used to maintain those relationships, and the consequences or *outcomes* of those strategies.

The antecedents can be derived from the general excellence theory of public relations and its subtheory of the role of public relations in strategic management (J. E. Grunig, 1996; J. E. Grunig, 1997a; J. E. Grunig & Repper, 1992). The maintenance strategies can be derived from models of public relations (J. E. Grunig & Grunig, 1992) and theories of conflict resolution (Huang, 1997; Plowman, 1996). The relational outcomes can be derived in part from the excellence study, but primarily they have been developed by Huang (1997).

We begin the conceptualization of this three-part model by reviewing some of the basic premises and theories from the excellence study.

ANTECEDENTS AND CONSEQUENCES OF RELATIONSHIPS IN THE EXCELLENCE THEORY

In the excellence project, we began by reviewing the literature on organizational effectiveness (L. A. Grunig et al., 1992) to determine what an effective organization is so we then could conceptualize how different public relations variables can be linked to organizational effectiveness. The literature on organizational effectiveness is large and contradictory. In fact, some theorists question the value even of trying to define effectiveness (for overviews of the literature, see, e.g., Goodman and Pennings, 1977; Hall, 1991; Price, 1968; Robbins, 1990). Robbins (1990) and Hall (1991), however, integrated this literature into a coherent framework that leads to the basic premise of the excellence theory: Public relations makes organizations more effective by building relationships with strategic publics. Strategic publics are publics with which organizations need relationships—that is, they possess the antecedent characteristics in the model we are developing.

These organizational theorists identified four approaches, each of which contributes to a comprehensive theory of organizational effectiveness:

The *goal attainment* approach states that organizations are effective when they meet their goals. The goal-attainment approach is limited, however, because it cannot explain effectiveness when an organization has multiple goals and different stakeholders of an organization have conflicting goals. It also cannot explain the role of the environment in organizational effectiveness.

The *systems* approach states that organizations are effective when they survive in their environment and successfully bring in resources necessary for their survival. The systems approach, therefore, adds the environment to the equation of organizational effectiveness, but it is limited because survival is an extremely weak goal. The systems approach also defines the environment in vague terms. It does not answer the question of how an organization determines what elements of the environment are important for its success.

The *strategic constituencies* approach puts meaning into the term "environment" by specifying the parts of the environment that are crucial for organizational survival and success. Strategic constituencies are the elements of the environment whose opposition or support can threaten the organization's goals or help to attain them. Taken broadly, the environment is both external and internal so employee groups and management functions can be strategic constituencies as much as can external groups.

The fourth piece of the effectiveness puzzle comes from the *competing values* approach. That approach provides a bridge between strategic constituencies and goals. It states that an organization must incorporate the values of strategic constituencies into its goals so the organization attains the goals of most value to its strategic constituencies. Thus different organizations with different strategic constituencies in their environments will have different goals, and their effectiveness will be defined in different ways—what Hall (1991) called the contradiction model of effectiveness:

> Put very simply, a contradiction model of effectiveness will consider organizations to be more or less effective in regard to the variety of goals which they pursue, the variety of resources which they attempt to acquire, the variety of constituents inside and outside of the organization, and the variety of time frames by which effectiveness is judged. (p. 247)

A theory of organizational effectiveness that incorporates the competing values of strategic constituencies into the goals chosen to define success fits logically with theories of strategic management that provide a model for organizations to develop missions (sets of goals) that fit with the threats and opportunities provided by strategic constituencies in the environment (J. E. Grunig & Repper, 1992). Such a theory also makes the role of public relations in organizational effectiveness clear. Robbins (1990) described that role well when he discussed the limitations of the strategic constituencies model. The role of public relations is to provide the information about the environment that Robbins said is difficult for other managers to attain:

The task of separating the strategic constituencies from the larger environment is easy to say but difficult to do in practice. Because the environment
changes rapidly, what was critical to the organization yesterday may not be so
today. Even if the constituencies in the environment can be identified and are
assumed to be relatively stable, what separates the strategic constituencies
from the "almost" strategic constituencies? Where do you cut the set? And
won't the interests of each member in the dominant coalition strongly affect
what he or she perceives as strategic? An executive in the accounting function
is unlikely to see the world—or the organization's strategic constituencies—in
the same way as an executive in the purchasing function. Finally, identifying
the expectations that the strategic constituencies hold for the organization
presents a problem. How do you tap that information accurately? (p. 67)

The theory of strategic management and public relations developed
by J. E. Grunig and Repper (1992) provides the mechanism that Robbins
(1990) called for in this quote. It states that public relations managers
can begin to identify strategic constituencies by identifying stakeholder
categories and then by segmenting members of those categories into
active and passive publics. Active publics—or potentially active publics—are most strategic for an organization. Thus, it is their values that
must be incorporated into organizational goals. To do so means that an
organization must build both short- and long-term relationships with
strategic publics to be effective.

If there are more strategic constituencies than the organization has
the resources to build relationships with, it must separate the strategic
constituencies from the "almost" strategic constituencies, to use Robbins' words. To help make that decision, the excellence research team
used theories of cost–benefit analysis to help set such priorities (Ehling,
1992). Likewise, the research team also found that excellent public
relations managers help to bring the values and goals of different
functional managers together by working with them to build relationships with relevant publics and to bring the perspectives of those publics
into strategic management (L. A. Grunig, Dozier, and Grunig, 1994)—another of Robbins' questions about strategic constituencies.

This integrated theory of organizational effectiveness, therefore,
provided the basic integrating premise for a general theory of public
relations developed by the excellence team (J. E. Grunig, 1992a). When
public relations helps the organization build relationships with strategic
constituencies, it saves the organization money by reducing the costs of
litigation, regulation, legislation, pressure campaigns, boycotts, or lost
revenue that result from bad relationships with publics—publics that

become activist groups when relationships are bad. It also helps the organization make money by cultivating relationships with donors, consumers, shareholders, and legislators who are needed to support organizational goals. Good relationships with employees also increase the likelihood that they will be satisfied with the organization and with their jobs, which makes them more likely to support and less likely to interfere with the mission of the organization (see J. E. Grunig, 1992b, for a review on the relationship between employee communication and job satisfaction).

Antecedents and a Consequence in a Model of Relationships

Table 2.1 contains a three-stage model of organization–public relationships that we have developed to parallel Broom et al.'s (1997) model. The excellence theory can be used to conceptualize the antecedents and one of the consequences in the model. The one consequence discussed so far is that of goal achievement. Goal achievement is the first outcome listed in the Broom et al. model, and it is one of the indicators of organizational effectiveness in the excellence theory. It is an outcome of good relationships because organizations and publics that have good relationships with one another are both more likely to choose appropriate goals and to attain them. Table 2.1 also describes mutual goal achievement as complementary behavior, which logically connects this concept to the coorientational concept of complementary overlapping behaviors (J. E. Grunig & Hunt, 1984, p. 134).

Table 2.1 includes four additional outcomes of relationships that we will describe in a later section. At this point, however, we can use the excellence theory and earlier theorizing by J. E. Grunig and Hunt (1984) to describe the antecedents of relationships. J. E. Grunig and Hunt theorized that organizations have a public relations problem (a reason to develop a public relations program) when management decisions have consequences on nonmanagement people inside or outside of the organization (publics) or when the behavior of these publics has consequences on the success with which the decision can be implemented. The concept of consequences explains why people become members of publics (Dewey, 1927) and why they organize into the activist groups (J. E. Grunig & Grunig, 1997) that make issues out of the consequences of decisions—the way in which J. E. Grunig and Repper (1992) explained

TABLE 2.1

Stages and Forms of Relationships

Situational Antecedents (Behavioral Consequences on Each Other [Interpenetration])	Maintenance Strategies	Relationship Outcomes

Organization affects public $(O_1 — P_1)$
Public affects organization $(P_1 —> O_1)$
Organization-public coalition affects another organization $(O_1P_1 —> O_2)$
Organization-public coalition affects another public $(O_1P_1 —> P_2)$
Organization affects an organization–public coalition $(O_1 —> O_2P_2)$
Multiple organizations affect multiple publics $(O_i —> P_i)$
	Symmetrical
	  Disclosure (openness)
	  Assurances of legitimacy
	  Participation in mutual
	    networks
	  Shared tasks (helping to
	    solve problems of interest
	    to the other party)
	  Integrative negotiation
	  Cooperation/collaboration
	  Be unconditionally
	    constructive
	  Win-win or no deal
	Asymmetrical
	  Distributive negotiation
	  Avoiding
	  Contending
	  Compromising
	  Accommodating
		Control mutuality
		  (Joint acceptance of
		  degrees of symmetry)
		Commitment
		  (Interdependence, loss of
		  some autonomy)
		Satisfaction/liking
		Trust
		Goal attainment
		  (Complementary behavior)

Measures of Concepts		
Environmental scanning	Ongoing observations of management and publics (such as monitoring of disclosure by management and publics, expressions of legitimacy, building networks with activist groups	Coorientational measures of management and publics: Perceived by either or both parties. Observed by third party (overlap in coorientation model) Predicted for other party (Accuracy and congruence in coorientation model)

the relationship of issues management to strategic management and public relations.

It should be noted that our conceptualization of the antecedents to relationships both builds on and also departs from the literature on such antecedents. Broom et al. (1997) concluded by defining antecedents to relationships as "sources of change, pressure, or tension on the system derived from the environment" (p. 94)—a general definition that describes the publics, organizations, and coalitions we have included in Table 2.1. Earlier, however, after reviewing the literature on interorganizational relationships, they pointed out that the dominant theories for studying the antecedents to relationships come from *resource dependency theory* and *exchange theory*:

> According to resource dependency theory, relationships form in response to an organization's need for resources. Satisfying the need for resources allows an organization to survive, to grow, and to achieve other goals. Relationships consist of the transactions that involve the exchange of resources between organizations. Similarly, exchange theory suggests that voluntary transactions result from knowledge of domain similarity and lead to mutual benefit, as well as mutual goal achievement. Importantly, exchange theorists define relationships in terms of the voluntary transactions and the mutuality of interests and rewards. (p. 91)

Resource dependency theory and exchange theory may be adequate for explaining relationships between organizations and the relationships between organizations and consumers. However, these theories do not describe all of the "change pressures" from the environment. These pressures may have little or nothing to do with resources or with exchanges. Instead, they may come from publics, activist groups, government, or media who simply want to change the behavior of the organization in specific situations, thus interfering with the behavior the organization wants to implement.

Because specific decisions, such as closing a factory or marketing a new product, have specific consequences in specific situations, the antecedents of relationships are situational, just as publics are situational (J. E. Grunig, 1997b). That is, publics come and go and change as situations change. In addition, consequences stem from the behaviors of both organizations and publics. Therefore, Table 2.1 emphasizes behavioral relationships rather than purely symbolic relationships that are embodied in such concepts as identity and image (J. E. Grunig, 1993). Behavioral relationships also are implicit in concepts such as interpenetrating publics (Preston & Post, 1975) and in the loss of autonomy that organizations face when they enter into relationships (L. A. Grunig, Grunig, & Ehling, 1992; Kelly, 1991)—one of Broom et al.'s (1997) relationship outcomes. Likewise, corporate reputation is highly connected with behavioral relationships because reputation essentially consists of the corporate behaviors that publics remember (J. E. Grunig, 1993).

The first column of Table 2.1 also extends the idea of organization–public relationships beyond the simple relationship between one organization and one public. As Vercic (1997) pointed out, organizations today typically face multiple publics with different interests and conflicting goals. These publics often organize into coalitions, and organizations enter into similar coalitions (Pien, 1994; Tucker & McNerney, 1992). Therefore, Table 2.1 extends the concept of situational antecedents from single publics and single organizations to multiple publics and multiple organizations that have consequences on each other.

In addition to describing theoretical concepts of relationships, Table 2.1 also suggests potential measures of these concepts at each of the three stages of the model. The first-stage situational concepts, therefore, are measured through formal and informal techniques of environmental scanning (see, e.g., Dozier et al., 1995; Stoffels, 1994)—techniques that public relations practitioners can use to identify strategic publics with which an organization needs to build relationships.

MAINTENANCE STRATEGIES

We, like the authors of other chapters in this book, have looked to the literature on interpersonal communication for concepts that can be adapted or modified for a theory of organizational–public relationships. Typically, scholars of interpersonal communication have studied how different communication strategies affect the development, maintenance, and dissolution of relationships—that is, the effect of communication strategies on relationship outcomes (Stafford & Canary, 1991). Stafford and Canary studied the strategies that couples use to maintain relationships, although they also pointed out that extensive research has been done on conflict and on problem solving in relationships.

Analogues of Interpersonal Strategies

Stafford and Canary (1991) developed questionnaire items from the interpersonal literature to use in a study of how romantic couples maintain their relationships. Factor analysis yielded five dimensions of strategies: positivity (such as attempts to make the relationship enjoyable for both), openness (such as disclosure of thoughts and feelings), assurances (of love and commitment), networking (having common friends), and shared tasks (taking joint responsibility for household tasks). These five dimensions seem to be analogous to public relations strategies, especially those characterized by J. E. Grunig's two-way symmetrical model (e.g., J. E. Grunig, 1989; J. E. Grunig & Grunig, 1992; J. E. Grunig & White, 1992).

These five dimensions suggest ways for developing the symmetrical model theoretically and for developing practical public relations strategies that fit within the broad framework of the model. For example, *positivity* brings to mind Fisher and Brown's (1988) principle of "Be Unconditionally Constructive" in building relationships, which J. E. Grunig and Grunig (1992) and Plowman (1995) appropriated into the symmetrical model.

Openness, or *disclosure*, has a long tradition of research in interpersonal communication (see, e.g., Chellune, 1979). Disclosure also has a critical role in a theory of public relations ethics (Bivins, 1987; J. E. Grunig & Grunig, 1996). In her book *Secrets*, Bok (1989) pointed out that having secrets and restricting access to information is the essence of power and that disclosure can produce more symmetry in the distribution of power in a relationship. Although Bok maintained that it is necessary to keep some secrets, she added that those in a position of power have the burden of proof that withholding information is in the interest of those with less power.

Assurances of love and commitment in interpersonal relationships can be extended to *assurances of legitimacy* in the relationships between organizations and publics. For example, L. A. Grunig et al. (1992) included legitimacy as one of their dimensions of good organization–public relationships, and Jensen (1997) developed a theory of public relations that used legitimacy as the central concept. Jensen said, for example, that "Building up a successful strategic concept could be considered a process of building up a legitimate field of activities" (p. 229). L. A. Grunig (1992), likewise, concluded that organizations must acknowledge the legitimacy of all constituencies as a necessary step in developing relationships with activist groups.

In interpersonal relationships, *networking* consists of having common friends and enjoying spending of time with the same friends. In organization–public relationships, this same concept could be seen as organizations building networks with the same groups as their publics, such as environmentalists, unions, or community groups. Likewise, in interpersonal communication, *sharing of tasks* typically means that couples share in household duties. In organization–public relationships, organizations and publics would share in such tasks as reducing pollution, providing employment, making a profit, and staying in business, which are in the interest of either the organization, the public, or both.

Conflict Resolution Strategies

In addition to these symmetrical maintenance strategies derived from
Stafford and Canary (1991), Table 2.1 contains several strategies of
conflict resolution that Huang (1997) and Plowman (1995) derived
from the literature in that field to apply to public relations. J. E. Grunig
and Grunig (1992) first suggested that theories of negotiation and
conflict resolution would provide a basis for developing the symmetrical model of public relations from a vague, general idea into a useful,
practical model. These negotiation strategies can be defined broadly
as integrative strategies, which are symmetrical in nature, and distributive strategies, which are asymmetrical. In general, we propose that
integrative, symmetrical strategies will be more effective in developing
organization-public relationships than will distributive, asymmetrical
strategies.

Integrative Strategy.   Walton and McKersie (1965) created the
term *integrative negotiation* in labor negotiation. Integrative bargaining
functions by searching out common or complementary interests and
solving problems confronting both parties. An integrative strategy,
according to Putnam (1990), "aims to reconcile the interests of both
parties, reach joint benefits, or attain 'win-win' goals through open
information exchange and joint decision making" (p. 3). As Canary
and Cupach (1988) suggested, an integrative management style emphasizes mutual interests rather than an individual orientation. Sillars (1980a) held that an integrative strategy emphasizes cooperative
and disclosive actions that promote a neutral or positive climate.
Putnam and Wilson's (1982) solution–orientation strategy is similar
to the integrative style, which entails open discussion of alternatives
and compromise.

Integrative bargaining has special relevance to public relations, first,
because it is bounded by a symmetrical worldview, which values the
integrity of a long-term relationship between an organization and its
publics. Second, integrative bargaining aims to cultivate trust and sup-
portiveness (Putnam, 1990); and trust is a central concept in organization–public relationships.

Distributive Strategy.   In contrast to integrative bargaining, distributive bargaining refers to efforts to maximize gains and minimize

losses within a "win–lose" or self-gain orientation (Putnam, 1990, p. 3). Putnam and Wilson (1982) equated a distributive strategy with a control strategy. Tactics such as domination, argument, insistence on a position, and showing anger might appear in distributive strategies (Putnam & Wilson). In the same vein, Sillars (1980a, 1980b) said that distributive strategy includes tactics such as faulting the other party, hostile questioning, presumptive attribution, demands, and threats. Likewise, Morrill and Thomas (1992) labeled a similar strategy as a "forcing" strategy. They suggested that this strategy is to impose one's position on to that of an adversary without concern for his or her position.

Dual Concern Strategies. Although an integrative strategy seems most consistent with the symmetrical model of public relations, Plowman (1995) reviewed several dual-concern theories of conflict resolution that seem to fit well with Dozier and associates' (1995) most recent version of the symmetrical model. That model, which Murphy (1991) has called a mixed-motive model and Spicer (1997) has called collaborative advocacy, emphasizes that symmetry involves balancing the interests of publics with the interests of the organization. Several writers, such as Cancel, Cameron, Sallot, and Mitrook (1997) have mistakenly equated the symmetrical model with accommodation of the public's interest at the expense of the organization's interest. In contrast, the Dozier and associates model emphasizes that accommodation of the public's interest at the expense of the organization's interest is just as asymmetrical as accommodation of the organization's interest at the expense of the public's interest.

Plowman (1995) searched the literature on conflict resolution looking for strategies that could be applied in public relations. Then he conducted case studies of 10 organizations, 6 of which also were participants in the qualitative portion of the excellence study. Plowman began with five dual-concern strategies identified by Thomas (1976) and found that all of the organizations used one or more of these strategies of resolving conflict as well as two others that were mentioned in the interviews but that also had been discussed in the literature.

Plowman (1995) identified two asymmetrical strategies in use that emphasize the interest of the organization over the interest of the public. We hypothesize that these strategies will not be effective in developing or maintaining organization–public relationships:

Contending.   The organization tries to convince the public to accept its position.

Avoiding.   The organization leaves the conflict, either physically or psychologically.

Two other strategies accommodate the public's interest at the expense of the organization. We hypothesize that they will be equally ineffective as maintenance strategies:

Accommodating.   The organization yields, at least in part, on its position and lowers its aspirations.

Compromising.   The organization meets the public part way between their preferred positions, but neither party is completely satisfied with the outcome.

In contrast, Plowman found three truly symmetrical strategies that would be most effective in building and maintaining a relationship:

Cooperating.   Both the organization and the public work together to reconcile their interests and to reach a mutually beneficial relationship.

Being unconditionally constructive.   This strategy, put forward by Fisher and Brown (1988), means that the organization should do whatever it thinks is best for the relationship, even if it means giving up some up of its position and even if the public does not reciprocate. Organizations often used this strategy for intransigent activist groups that refused to negotiate or compromise.

Saying Win–Win or No Deal.   Covey (1989) defined this strategy. If the organization and the public cannot find a solution that benefits both, they agree to disagree—no deal. Covey explained: "It would be better not to deal than to live with a decision that wasn't right for us both. Then maybe another time we might be able to get together" (p. 214).

The second column of Table 2.1, therefore, lists the maintenance strategies we have described as symmetrical and as asymmetrical strategies. The theory of symmetrical public relations, which is a critical part of the excellence theory, states that symmetrical strategies build relationships more effectively than asymmetrical strategies.

Measures of Maintenance Strategies

A true evaluation of the effectiveness of public relations must come from measuring the relational outcomes described in Table 2.1, which we discuss in the next section. As we said previously, however, evaluation can be done by measuring both process and outcome indicators. Process indicators are valuable when they can be linked both theoretically and empirically to outcome indicators. Process indicators then can be used to monitor the processes that eventually result in desirable relationship outcomes.

For example, Table 2.1 lists monitoring of disclosure as a particularly useful measure of a maintenance strategy, logically connected with the symmetrical model, that indicates when a positive relationship outcome is likely to occur. For example, in an evaluation of AT&T community relations teams in the 1970s, J. E. Grunig and Hunt (1984) found that community leaders were more likely to disclose their concerns to effective teams than to less effective teams. They reported that community leaders " ... directed most of their behaviors toward the company, expressing approval or disapproval to company representatives, rather than by expressing dissatisfaction to political leaders, opposing the company in policy or regulatory conflicts, or refusing to use company services" (p. 277).

In other words, public relations managers can measure disclosure by publics to the organization by counting suggestions, complaints, inquiries, and other contacts that members of publics, the media, government, or leaders of activist groups make with the organization, rather than to regulatory bodies, regulators, or the media. Likewise, public relations practitioners can measure their effectiveness in counseling management by keeping a count of the occasions when management seeks them for advice or is willing to disclose its intentions, decisions, and behaviors to outside publics or to the media through the public relations function.

Table 2.1 suggests other process indicators of effective maintenance strategies, such as counts of what management has done to show publics that their interests are legitimate, of contacts with networks of activist groups, or in social responsibility reports showing the extent to which management has worked on problems of interest to publics.

RELATIONSHIP OUTCOMES

Although these antecedents of relationships and maintenance strategies previously have not been organized into a process model of relationships as we have done in this chapter, none of them are really new to the public relations literature. In contrast, the relationship outcomes listed in Table 2.1 were identified by Huang (1997) and are new to the public relations literature.

Citing Burgoon and Hale (1984), Canary and Spitzberg (1989) emphasized the importance of conceptualizing relational characteristics in terms of universal features. Among the numerous relational features that have been proposed, Huang (1997) suggested that trust, control mutuality, relational commitment, and relational satisfaction are the most essential and pertinent indicators representing the quality of organization–public relationships. These key relational features appear consistently in the literature of interpersonal and organizational relationships, that is, trust (L. A. Grunig et al., 1992; Stafford & Canary, 1991), control mutuality (Burgoon & Hale, 1984, 1987; Canary & Spitzberg, 1989; Canary & Stafford, 1992; Ferguson, 1984; Stafford & Canary, 1991), commitment (Aldrich, 1975, 1979; Burgoon & Hale, 1984, 1987; Canary & Spitzberg, 1989; Canary & Stafford, 1992), and satisfaction (Ferguson, 1984; L. A. Grunig et al., 1992).

These four features also seem to represent the essence of organization–public relationships. For example, control mutuality reflects the unavoidable asymmetry of power in organization–public relationships. Likewise, both trust and satisfaction reflect the cognitive and affective aspects of relationships. Finally, level of commitment reflects the degree of resource interchange, which includes emotional and psychological aspects of interpersonal relationships and behavioral aspects of interorganizational relationships.

To sum up, using Canary and Spitzberg's (1984) way of describing relationships in general to describe organization–public relationships in particular, we believe that organization–public relationships are likely to be considered successful to "the degree that the organization and publics trust one another, agree on who has rightful power to influence, experience satisfaction with each other, and commit oneself to one another" (pp. 633–634). The characteristics of these four relational outcomes can be described as follows.

Control Mutuality

Stafford and Canary (1991) defined control mutuality as "the degree to which partners agree about which of them should decide relational goals and behavioral routines" (p. 224). They conceptualized this notion as whether the contending parties in a relationship agree that one or both may rightfully influence the other (Stafford & Canary), or whether partners agree on the power balance in the relationship (Canary & Stafford, 1992). Stafford and Canary (1991) also quoted Kelley (1979) to distinguish bilateral, or mutual, control from unilateral attempts to control the partner (p. 224).

The notion of control mutuality is similar to other concepts suggested as being critical in relationships, such as Aldrich's (1975, 1979) concept of reciprocity, Ferguson's (1984) idea of "distribution of power in the relationship," Millar and Rogers' (1976) construct of "power," and Moore's (1986) notion of "empowerment." Along the same lines, L. A. Grunig et al. (1992) argued that equality of power may not be necessary but that a norm of reciprocity may produce a quality relationship even if power is unequal.

Power asymmetry is natural in reality. The critical issues in power asymmetry can be addressed in the following four circumstances. First, one party is completely powerless. Ross (1970) suggested that this situation "could not meaningfully be called negotiation," inasmuch as power balance generally favors the powerful one. However, there also is evidence that a high level of absolute power makes the parties fear escalation and hence exercise care not to antagonize each other (Pruitt & Carnevale, 1993, p. 150). Second, if the power difference is only slight, the result is likely to be a power struggle in which neither party does well. Third, when the power asymmetry is reasonably large, it would be appropriate to involve a trustful third party to balance power, inasmuch as the third party would subjectively favor the weaker one in order to provide a balance and come to an equitable resolution. Fourth, it should be noted that the sources of power asymmetry also might include experience, information, costs of delay, or going to court (Ross, 1970).

Although power asymmetry is inevitable in interpersonal, interorganizational, and organization–public relationships, the sense of control mutuality between and among the opposing parties in a relationship is critical to interdependence and relational stability (Stafford & Canary, 1991). Intensive research has been conducted regarding the relationship between control mutuality and relational outcomes (Canary & Cupach, 1988; Canary & Stafford, 1992; Millar & Rogers, 1976; Rogers & Farace, 1975; Stafford & Canary, 1991). For example, research has revealed that unilateral attempts to achieve control are associated with decreases in perceptions of communicator competence and relational satisfaction (Bochner, Kaminski, & Fitzpatrick, 1977; Canary & Cupach, 1988) and increases in the level of activism (L. A. Grunig, 1992). In summary, all of the relevant conceptualizations and research suggest that for a stable, positive relationship, control mutuality among the parties should exist to some degree.

Trust

Trust is a widely accepted and critical construct both in interpersonal relationships (Canary & Cupach, 1988) and in organizational conflicts in which risk is involved (Carlson & Millard, 1987; Fitchen, Hearth, & Ressenden-Raden, 1987; Huang, 1994; Krimsky & Plough, 1988; National Research Council, 1989). Likewise, in the public relations literature discussed previously, L. A. Grunig et al. (1992) emphasized trust and credibility as components of relationships, and Vercic and J. E. Grunig (1995) maintained that trust from publics enables an organization to exist.

Parks, Henager, and Scamahorn (1996) defined trust as the belief that others will not exploit one's goodwill (Yamagishi, 1986; see also Komorita & Carnevale, 1992). According to Canary and Cupach (1988), trust suggests "a willingness to risk oneself because the relational partner is perceived as benevolent and honest" (p. 308). From the perspective of relationship marketing, Morgan and Hunt (1994) conceptualized trust "as existing when one party has confidence in an exchange partner's reliability and integrity" (p. 23). They also quoted Moorman, Deshpande, and Zaltman (1993), who defined trust as "a willingness to rely on an exchange partner in whom one has confidence" (p. 23). In summary, trust highlights one's confidence in and willingness to open oneself to the other party.

Several researchers have examined trust and the lack of trust in relationships. For example, Canary and Cupach (1988) cited Larzelere and Huston (1980) to emphasize that trust is essential to promoting and maintaining a relationship, whereas suspicion undermines favorable growth in a relationship. Likewise, Lahno (1995) maintained that the value of a trustworthy reputation is so great that it becomes rational not to try to seize any short-term advantage.

Relational Satisfaction

Relational satisfaction also has been widely acknowledged as a crucial attribute of the quality of a relationship (Ferguson, 1984; Millar & Rogers, 1976; Stafford & Canary, 1991). As suggested in Hendrick (1988), relationship satisfaction is one of the established areas of relationship assessment; and there are numerous measures available to assess feelings, thoughts, or behaviors in intimate relations. Likewise, Ferguson (1984) held that the degree to which both organization and public are satisfied with their relationship is one of the significant indicators for gauging the quality of an organization's relationship with its strategic publics.

Unlike control mutuality and trust, which involve cognitive dimensions, satisfaction encompasses affection and emotion. Hecht (1978), for example, conceptualized satisfaction as a favorable affective response to the reinforcement of positive expectations in a certain kind of situation. From a social exchange perspective, Stafford and Canary (1991) held that a satisfying relationship is one in which "the distribution of rewards is equitable and the relational rewards outweigh costs" (p. 225). They also indicated that a partner who perceives the other partner's maintenance behaviors to be positive increases his or her satisfaction with the relationship. They thus concluded that relational satisfaction is probably the most important outcome of effective maintenance of a relationship.

Relational Commitment

Morgan and Hunt (1994), from the perspective of relationship marketing, defined commitment to a relationship as

> an exchange partner believing that an ongoing relationship with another is so important as to warrant maximum efforts at maintaining it; that is, the committed party believes the relationship is worth promoting and savoring to ensure that it endures indefinitely. (p. 23)

Again, they quoted Moorman, Zaltman, and Deshpande (1992), who emphasized that commitment is "an enduring desire to maintain a valued relationship" (p. 23) and concluded that commitment is central to the relationship of the firm and its partners.

The literature reveals that commitment has long been a central notion in the social exchange approach (Stafford & Canary, 1991). Cook and Emerson (1978) used the concept of commitment to distinguish social from economic exchanges. Likewise, commitment has been found to be an effective indicator of internal relationships in an organizational setting. For example, commitment has been associated closely with increased organizational citizenship, recruiting and training practices, and support for the organization (Morgan & Hunt, 1994). In service relationships, Berry and Parasuraman (1991) held that relationships are built on the foundation of mutual commitment. Likewise, in relationship marketing literature, Morgan and Hunt conceived of brand loyalty as a form of commitment. Following the logic of these conceptualizations, we interpret the four components of a relationship between organizations identified by Aldrich (1975, 1979; formalization, intensity, reciprocity, and standardization) to be forms of commitment in organization–public relationships.

Two aspects of commitment seem relevant for an organization–public relationship: affective commitment and continuance commitment. According to Meyer and Allen (1984), *continuance commitment* means commitment to continue a certain line of action. On the contrary, *affective commitment* is an affective or emotional orientation to an entity. The traditional instrument used to measure organizational commitment focuses on affective commitment (Meyer & Allen). For example, Mowday, Steers, and Porter (1979) conceptualized organizational commitment (characterized by Meyer and Allen as affective commitment) as having the following characteristics: "(1) a strong belief in and acceptance of the organization's goals and values, (2) a willingness to exert considerable effort on behalf of the organization, and (3) a strong desire to maintain membership in the organization" (p. 226).

On the other hand, Meyer and Allen (1984) emphasized continuance commitment. They defined *continuance commitment*, in an organizational setting, as "the extent to which employees feel committed to their organizations by virtue of the costs that they feel are associated with leaving" (p. 375). Therefore, we believe that both affective commitment and Meyer and Allen's "continuance commitment" should be incorporated into the conceptualization of relational commitment as an outcome of public relations programs.

In summary, trust, control mutuality, commitment to a relationship, and satisfaction with a relationships are four focal characteristics representing the quality of organization–public relationships. Research has revealed that attempts to control a relationship unilaterally lead to relational dissatisfaction and misunderstanding (e.g., Bochner et al., 1977). Moreover, published studies have demonstrated high intercorrelations among these four features of relationships. Confirmatory factor analyses have revealed that trust, commitment, satisfaction, and control mutuality often are perceived by respondents to be interrelated (Stafford & Canary, 1991). Therefore, we can conclude that these four distinguishable, yet intercorrelated, factors can be used to conceptualize and measure the quality of relationships between organizations and publics.

Measures of Relationship Outcomes

Broom et al. (1997) pointed out an obvious dilemma in the measurement of relationship outcomes: Most measures are of one party's perception of a two-party relationship. To truly measure the properties of relationships, researchers must develop measures of "relationships as phenomena distinct from the perceptions held by parties in the relationships" (p. 95). Nevertheless, we believe that the best starting point for developing measures of the relationship outcomes we have described is to ask one or both parties to describe the relationship features we have identified in the literature.

Once we have perfected these one-party indicators, we recommend moving toward coorientational measures as suggested in Table 2.1. With coorientational measures, each partner in a relationship can indicate their perception of the relationship as well as what they believe the perception of the other party to be. In addition, a third-party observer can measure the perceptions of both parties and compare the two. As a starting point in measuring relationship outcomes, however, we suggest items that Huang (1997) developed from the literature on interpersonal relationships to measure control mutuality, trust, commitment, and satisfaction.

The instrument for *control mutuality* contained three items described by Stafford and Canary (1991), which also have been found to be reliable and valid in research by Canary and Cupach (1988) and Canary and Spitzberg (1989):

1. Generally speaking, the organization and we are both satisfied with the decision-making process.
2. In most cases, during decision making both the organization and we have equal influence.
3. Both the organization and we agreed on what we can expect from one another.

For *trust*, Huang (1997) adapted Morgan and Hunt's (1994) instrument:

1. Generally speaking, I don't trust the organization.
2. Members of the organization are truthful with us.
3. The organization treats me fairly and justly, compared to other organizations.

For *satisfaction with the relationship*, Huang (1997) adapted items from Hendrick's (1988) Relationship Assessment Scale:

1. Generally speaking, organization members meet our needs.
2. Generally speaking, our relationship with the organization has problems.
3. In general, we are satisfied with the relationship with the organization.
4. Our relationship with the organization is good.

To measure *commitment to the relationship*, Huang (1997) reviewed Stafford and Canary's (1991) measurement of commitment, Morgan and Hunt's (1994) construct of relationship commitment, and Mowday and associates' (1979) notion of continuance commitment to create these items:

1. I do not wish to continue a relationship with the organization.
2. I believe that it is worthwhile to try to maintain the relationship with the organization.
3. I wish to keep a long-lasting relationship with the organization.
4. I wish I had never entered into the relationship with the organization.

Huang (1997) found these measures to have acceptable to high levels of reliability in a study of the relationship between members of the public relations department of the executive branch of the Taiwanese government and representatives and staff members in the legislative branch. Therefore, we believe they can serve as a starting point for operationalizing and measuring the relational outcomes we have conceptualized and for developing additional coorientational measures of the outcomes.

CONCLUSIONS

In this chapter, we have followed the lead of Broom et al. (1997) and have developed a theoretical model of the antecedents of relationships, the strategies public relations practitioners can use to develop and maintain relationships, and the outcomes of relationships. For each stage in the model, we also have suggested indicators that can be used to identify antecedents, to monitor ongoing public relations processes used to maintain relationships, and to measure and evaluate the long-term effects of public relations programs. In doing so, we believe we have moved the excellence theory to the next level of theoretical and empirical development—to new theory and to practical measures of long-term relationships among organizations and publics.

REFERENCES

Aldrich, H. E. (1975). An organization–environment perspective on cooperation and conflict between organizations in the manpower training system. In A. R. Negandhi (Ed.), *Interorganizational theory* (pp. 49–70). Kent, OH: Kent State University Press.

Aldrich, H. E. (1979). *Organizations and environments*. Englewood Cliffs, NJ: Prentice-Hall.

Berry, L., & Parasuraman, A. (1991). *Marketing service*. New York: The Free Press.

Bivins, T. H. (1987). Applying ethical theory to public relations. *Journal of Business Ethics, 6,* 195–200.

Bochner, A. P., Kaminski, E. P., & Fitzpatrick, M. A. (1977). The conceptual domain of interpersonal communication behavior. *Human Communication Research, 3,* 291–302.

Bok, S. (1989). *Secrets—On the ethics of concealment and revelation*. New York: Vintage Books.

Broom, G. M. (1977). Coorientational measurement of public relations. *Public Relations Review, 3*(4), 110–119.

Broom, G. M., Casey, S., & Ritchey, J. (1997). Toward a concept and theory of organization–public relationships. *Journal of Public Relations Research, 9,* 83–98.

Broom, G. M., & Dozier, D. M. (1990). *Using research in public relations: Application to program management*. Englewood Cliffs, NJ: Prentice-Hall.

Burgoon, J., & Hale, J. (1984). The fundamental topoi of relational communication. *Communication Monographs, 51,* 193–214.

Burgoon, J., & Hale, J. (1987). Validation and measurement of the fundamental themes of relational communication. *Communication Monographs, 54,* 19–41.

Canary, D. J., & Cupach, W. R. (1988). Relational and episodic characteristics associated with conflict tactics. *Journal of Social and Personal Relationships, 5,* 305–325.

Canary, D. J., & Spitzberg, B. H. (1989). A model of the perceived competence of conflict strategies. *Human Communication Research, 15,* 630–649.

Canary, D. J., & Stafford, L. (1992). Relational maintenance strategies and equity in marriage. *Communication Monographs, 59,* 243–267.

Cancel, A. E., Cameron, G. T., Sallot, L. M., & Mitrook, M. A. (1997). It depends: A contingency theory of accommodation in public relations. *Journal of Public Relations Research, 9,* 31–64.

Carlson, W. B., & Millard, A. J. (1987). Defining risk within a business context: Thomas A. Edison, Eliihu Thomson, and the a.c.–d.c. controversy, 1885–1900. In B. B. Johnson and V. T. Covello (Eds.), *The social and cultural construction of risk* (pp. 275–293). Dordrecht, Holland: D. Reidel.

Chellune, G. J. (ed.). (1979). *Self-disclosure: Origins, patterns, and implications of openness in interpersonal relationships.* San Francisco: Jossey-Bass.

Cook, K. S., & Emerson, R. M. (1978). Power, equity, and commitment in exchange networks. *American Sociological Review, 43,* 721–739.

Covey, S. R. (1989). *The seven habits of highly effective people.* New York: Fireside.

Dewey, J. (1927). *The public and its problems.* Chicago: Swallow.

Dozier, D. M., Grunig, L. A., & Grunig, J. E. (1995). *Manager's guide to excellence in public relations and communication management.* Hillsdale, NJ: Lawrence Erlbaum Associates.

Ehling, W. P. (1992). Estimating the value of public relations and communication to an organization. In J. E. Grunig (Ed.), *Excellence in public relations and communication management* (pp. 617–638). Hillsdale, NJ: Lawrence Erlbaum Associates.

Ferguson, M. A. (1984, August). *Building theory in public relations: Interorganizational relationships as a public relations paradigm.* Paper presented to the Association for Education in Journalism and Mass Communication, Gainesville, FL.

Fisher, R., & Brown, S. (1988). *Getting together: Building a relationship that gets to yes.* Boston: Houghton Mifflin.

Fitchen, J. M., Hearth, J. S., & Ressenden-Raden, J. (1987). Risk perception in community context: A case study. In B. B. Johnson and V. T. Covello (Eds.), *The social and cultural construction of risk* (pp. 31–54). Dordrecht, Holland: D. Reidel.

Goodman, P. S., and Pennings, J. M. (eds.; 1977). *New perspectives on organizational effectiveness.* San Francisco: Jossey Bass.

Grunig, J. E. (1977). Measurement in Public Relations—An overview. *Public Relations Review, 3*(4), 5–10.

Grunig, J. E. (1989). Symmetrical presuppositions as a framework for public relations theory. In C. Botan & V. T. Hazelton (Eds.), *Public relations theory* (pp. 17–44). Hillsdale, NJ: Lawrence Erlbaum Associates.

Grunig, J. E. (1992a). Communication, public relations, and effective organizations: An overview of the book. In J. E. Grunig (Ed.), *Excellence in public relations and communication management* (pp. 1–30). Hillsdale, NJ: Lawrence Erlbaum Associates.

Grunig, J. E. (1992b). Symmetrical systems of internal communication. In J. E. Grunig (Ed.), *Excellence in public relations and communication management* (pp. 531–576). Hillsdale, NJ: Lawrence Erlbaum Associates.

Grunig, J. E. (1993). Image and substance: From symbolic to behavioral relationships. *Public Relations Review, 91*(2), 121–139.

Grunig, J. E. (1996, December). *Public relations in strategic management and strategic management of public relations: Theory and evidence from the IABC excellence project.* Paper presented to the conference on Strategic Planning in Public Relations, Department of Mass Communication, Faculty of Humanities and Social Sciences, United Arab Emirates University, Al Ain, United Arab Emirates.

Grunig, J. E. (1997a). Public relations management in government and business. In J. L. Garnett and A. Kouzmin (Eds.), *Handbook of administrative communication* (pp. 241–283). New York: Marcel Dekker.

Grunig, J. E. (1997b). A situational theory of publics: Conceptual history, recent challenges, and new research. In D. Moss, T. MacManus, & D. Vercic (Eds.), *Public relations research: An international perspective* (pp. 3–48). London: International Thomson Business Press.

Grunig, J. E., & Grunig, L. A. (1992). Models of public relations and communication. In J. E. Grunig (Ed.), *Excellence in public relations and communication management* (pp. 285–326). Hillsdale, NJ: Lawrence Erlbaum Associates.

Grunig, J. E., & Grunig, L. A. (1996, May). *Implications of symmetry for a theory of ethics and social responsibility in public relations*. Paper presented to the International Communication Association, Chicago, May 23–27.

Grunig, J. E., & Grunig, L. A. (1997, July). *Review of a program of research on activism: Incidence in four countries, activist publics, strategies of activist groups, and organizational responses to activism*. Paper presented to the Fourth Public Relations Research Symposium, Managing Environmental Issues, Bled, Slovenia.

Grunig, J. E., & Hunt, T. (1984). *Managing public relations*. New York: Holt, Rinehart & Winston.

Grunig, J. E., & Repper, F. C. (1992). Strategic management, publics, and issues. In J. E. Grunig (Ed.), *Excellence in public relations and communication management* (pp. 117–158). Hillsdale, NJ: Lawrence Erlbaum Associates.

Grunig, J. E., & White, J. (1992). The effect of worldviews on public relations theory and practice. In J. E. Grunig (Ed.), *Excellence in public relations and communication management* (pp. 31–64). Hillsdale, NJ: Lawrence Erlbaum Associates.

Grunig, L. A. (1992). Activism: How it limits the effectiveness of organizations and how excellent public relations departments respond. In J. E. Grunig (Ed.), *Excellence in public relations and communication management: Contributions to effective organizations* (pp. 483–501). Hillsdale, NJ: Lawrence Erlbaum Associates.

Grunig, L. A., Dozier, D. M., & Grunig, J. E. (1994). *IABC excellence in public relations and communication management, phase 2: qualitative study, initial analysis: cases of excellence*. San Francisco: IABC Research Foundation.

Grunig, L. A., Grunig, J. E., & Ehling, W. P. (1992). What is an effective organization? In J. E. Grunig (Ed.), *Excellence in public relations and communication management: Contributions to effective organizations* (pp. 65–89). Hillsdale, NJ: Lawrence Erlbaum Associates.

Hall, R. H. (1991). *Organizations: Structures, processes, and outcomes* (5th ed.). Englewood Cliffs, NJ: Prentice-Hall.

Hecht, M. L. (1978). The conceptualization and measurement of interpersonal communication satisfaction. *Human Communication Research, 4*, 253–264.

Hendrick, S. S. (1988). A generic measure of relational satisfaction. *Journal of Marriage and the Family, 50*, 93–98.

Huang, Y. H. (1994). *Technological risk and environmental activism: Case studies of public risk perception in Taiwan*. Taipei: Wu-Nan Publishers.

Huang, Y. H. (1997). *Public relations strategies, relational outcomes, and conflict management strategies*. Unpublished doctoral dissertation, University of Maryland, College Park, MD.

Jensen, I. (1997). Legitimacy and strategy of different companies: A perspective of external and internal public relations. In D. Moss, T. MacManus, & D. Vercic (Eds.), *Public relations research: An international perspective* (pp. 225–246). London: International Thomson Business Press.

Kelley, H. (1979). *Personal relationships: Their structure and processes*. Hillsdale, NJ: Lawrence Erlbaum Associates.

Kelly, K. S. (1991). *Fund raising and public relations: A critical analysis*. Hillsdale, NJ: Lawrence Erlbaum Associates.

Komorita, S. S., & Carnevale, P. J. (1992). Motivational arousal vs. decision framing in social dilemmas. In W. B. G. Liebrand, D. M. Messick, and H. A. M. Wike (Eds.), *Social dilemmas* (pp. 209–24). Tarrytown, NY: Pergamon.

Krimsky, S., & Plough, A. (1988). *Environmental hazards: Communicating risks as a social process*. Dover, MA: Auburn House Publishing Company.

Lahno, B. (1995). Trust, reputation, and exit in exchange relationships. *Journal of Conflict Resolution, 39*, 495–510.

Larzelere, R. E., & Huston, T. L. (1980). The dyadic trust scale: Toward understanding interpersonal trust in close relationships. *Journal of Marriage and the Family, 42*, 595–604.

Lewton, K. L. (1998). From costs to confidence: Resuscitating health care. *Public Relations Tactics, 5*(3), 1, 6.

Lindenmann, W. K. (1997). *Guidelines and standards for measuring and evaluating PR effectiveness.* Gainesville, FL: The Institute for Public Relations.

McLeod, J. M., & Chaffee, S. H. (1973). Interpersonal approaches to communication research. *American Behavioral Scientist, 16,* 469–500.

Meyer, J. P., & Allen, N. (1984). Testing the side-best theory of organizational commitment: Some methodological considerations. *Journal of Applied Psychology, 69,* 372–378.

Millar, F. E., & Rogers, L. E. (1976). A relational approach to interpersonal communication. In G. R. Miller (Ed.), *Explorations in interpersonal communication* (pp. 87–104). Beverly Hills, CA: Sage.

Moore, C. W. (1986). *The mediation process.* San Francisco: Jossey-Bass.

Moorman, C., Deshpande, R., & Zaltman, G. (1993). Factors affecting trust in market research relationships. *Journal of Marketing, 57*(1), 81–101.

Moorman, C., Zaltman, G., & Deshpande, R. (1992). Relationships between providers and users of marketing research: The dynamics of trust within and between organizations. *Journal of Marketing Research, 29,* 314–329.

Morgan, R. M., & Hunt, S. D. (1994). The commitment–trust theory of relationship marketing. *Journal of Marketing, 58*(3), 20–38.

Morrill, C., & Thomas, C. K. (1992). Organizational conflict management as disputing process: The problem of social escalation. *Human Communication Research, 18,* 400–428.

Mowday, R. T., Steers, R. M., & Porter, L. W. (1979). The measurement of organizational commitment. *Journal of Vocational Behavior, 14,* 224–247.

Murphy, P. (1991). The limits of symmetry: A game theory approach to symmetric and asymmetric public relations. *Public Relations Research Annual, 3,* 115–131.

National Research Council. (1989). *Improving risk communication.* Washington, DC: National Academy Press.

Parks, C. D., Henager, R. F., & Scamahorn, S. D. (1996). Trust and reactions to messages of intent in social dilemmas. *Journal of Conflict Resolution, 40,* 134–151.

Pruitt, D. G., & Carnevale, P. J. (1993). Relationship among negotiating parties. *Negotiation in social conflict.* Pacific Grove, CA: Brooks/Cole.

Pien, M. J. (1994). *The use of coalitions in the practice of strategic public relations.* Unpublished master's thesis, University of Maryland, College Park, MD.

Putnam, L. L. (1990). Reframing integrative and distributive bargaining: A process perspective. In B. H. Sheppard, M. H. Bazeramn, and R. J. Lewicki (Eds.), *Research on negotiation in organizations* (Vol. 2, pp. 3–30). Greenwich, CT: JAI Press.

Putnam, L., & Wilson, C. E. (1982). Communication strategies in organizational conflict: Reliability and validity of a measurement scale. In M. Burgoon (Ed.), *Communication yearbook 6* (pp. 629–652). Beverly Hills: Sage.

Plowman, K. D. (1995). *Congruence between public relations and conflict resolution: Negotiating in the organization.* Unpublished doctoral dissertation, University of Maryland, College Park, MD.

Price, J. L. (1968). *Organizational effectiveness: An inventory of propositions.* Homewood, IL: Irwin.

Preston, L. E., & Post, J. E. (1975). *Private management and public policy: The principle of public responsibility.* Englewood Cliffs, NJ: Prentice-Hall.

Robbins, S. P. (1990). *Organization theory: The structure and design of organizations.* Englewood Cliffs, NJ: Prentice-Hall.

Rogers, L. E., & Farace, R. V. (1975). Analysis of relational communication in dyads: New measurement procedures. *Human Communication Research, 1,* 222–239.

Ross, H. L. (1970). *Settled out of court: The social process of insurance claims adjustment.* Chicago: Aldine.

Seeking minimum standards for measuring public relations effectiveness (1996, November). Summary of an extended discussion held in New York City, October 10, 1996. New York: The Institute for Public Relations Research & Education, *Inside PR,* and the Ketchum Public Relations Research and Measurement Department.

Sillars, A. L. (1980a). Attributions and communication in roommate conflicts. *Communication Monographs, 47,* 180–200.

Sillars, A. L. (1980b). The sequential and distributional structure of conflict interactions as a function of attributions concerning the locus of responsibility and stability of conflicts., In

D. Nimmo (Ed.), *Communication Yearbook 4* (pp. 217–235). New Brunswick, NJ: Transaction Books.

Spicer, C. (1997). *Organizational public relations: A political perspective.* Mahwah, NJ: Lawrence Erlbaum Associates.

Stafford, L., & Canary, D. J. (1991). Maintenance strategies and romantic relationship type, gender, and relational characteristics. *Journal of Social and Personal Relationships, 8,* 217–242.

Stoffels, J. D. (1994). *Strategic issues management: A comprehensive guide to environmental scanning.* Tarrytown, NY: Pergamon.

Thomas, K. (1976). Conflict and conflict management. In M. Dunnette (Ed.), *Handbook of industrial and organizational psychology* (pp. 889–936). Chicago: Rand-McNally.

Tirone, J. F. (1977). Measuring the Bell System's public relations. *Public Relations Review, 3*(4), 21–38.

Tucker, K., & McNerney, S. L. (1992). Building coalitions to initiate change. *Public Relations Journal, 48*(1), 28–30.

Vercic, D. (1997). Towards fourth wave public relations: A case study. In D. Moss, T. MacManus, & D. Vercic (Eds.), *Public relations research: An international perspective* (pp. 264–279). London: International Thomson Business Press.

Vercic, D., & Grunig, J. E. (1995, July), *The origins of public relations theory in economics and strategic management.* Paper presented to the Second International Public Relations Research Symposium, Bled, Slovenia.

Walton, R. A., & McKersie, R. B. (1965). *A behavioral theory of labor negotiations.* New York: McGraw-Hill.

Ward, K. L. (1997, November). *Research to evaluate and cultivate relationships.* Presentation to the Public Relations Society of America, Nashville, TN.

Williams, T. M. (1996). *Putting relationships back into public relations.* Vernon C. Schranz Distinguished Lectureship in Public Relations. Muncie, IN: Department of Journalism, Ball State University.

Yamagishi, T. (1986). The provision of sanctioning system as a public good. *Journal of Personality and Social Psychology, 51,* 110–116.

3

A Longitudinal Study of Organization–Public Relationship Dimensions: Defining the Role of Communication in the Practice of Relationship Management

ဆ ✧ ၛ

John A. Ledingham
Capital University

Stephen D. Bruning
Capital University

Since its inception, public relations scholars and practitioners have struggled with defining what public relations is, what it does, and what it should be doing. As the field evolved, the practice of public relations expanded from mere press agentry to also include publicity, advertising, public affairs, issues management, lobbying, investor relations, and development (Cutlip, Center, & Broom, 1994). At the theoretical level, simplistic dissemination models gave way to the normative two-way symmetrical model that envisions public relations functioning in such a way as to generate mutual benefit for organizations and for their key publics. Today, public relations increasingly is seen as a management function, practiced within the four-step process of analysis, strategic planning, implementation, and evaluation. Moreover, Botan (1993) has observed that "public relations is in an ongoing state of change ... branching out from a single applied focus driven by the knowledge needs of practitioners into two major branches ...(the) applied branch (and) a new theory-based research and scholarship branch" (p. 107). According to Botan, these include "symmetrical/systems, (the) rhetorical/critical, (the) feminist, and (the) social scientific" and "a dominant applied model, based ...on a journalistic heritage and business orientation" (p. 108).

One perspective that has been the focus of a good deal of recent scholarly interest is that of *relationship management*; the notion of public relations as the management of relationships between an organization and its key publics. The emergence of relationship management as a paradigm for public relations scholarship and practice calls into question the essence of public relations—what it is and what it does or should do, its function and value within the organizational structure and the greater society, and the benefits generated not only for sponsoring organizations but also for the publics those organizations serve and the environments in which they exist.

The genesis of the relationship management perspective may be found in Ferguson's (1984) call for increased attention to relationships within the study and practice of public relations. The concept was given impetus by the inclusion of a relational definition of public relations in Cutlip, Center, and Broom's (1987) public relations text, and through J. E. Grunig's (1992) definition of the purpose of public relations as "building relationships with publics that constrain or enhance the ability of the organization to meet its mission" (p. 20). Ehling (1992) contended that the relationship perspective represents a shift away from *manipulation* of public opinion and toward a focus on building, nurturing and maintaining *relationships* as the core function of public relations, and he describes the shift as "an important change in the primary mission of public relations" (p. 622).

The scholarly literature concerning public relations as relationship management is integrative, drawing on concepts from the disciplines of mass media, interpersonal communication, interorganizational behavior, social psychology concepts, and marketing and management. The research reported herein also is integrative, centered around relationship dimensions gleaned from related fields and tested in an organization–public setting. Specifically, the research focuses on the linkage between public perceptions of an organization–public relationship and the behavior of public members, and the role of communication within this process. Additionally, the research provides a basis for exploring the notion of mutual benefit for organizations and their key publics as an outcome of two-way symmetrical public relations, for examination of the interaction of symbolic and behavioral relationships, and for discussion of the implications of relationship management for the study and practice of public relations. Finally, the research provides an opportunity for reflection concerning the connectiveness of a relational approach to public relations and the corporate social responsibility perspective.

Review of Organization–Public Relationship Literature

The literature of organization–public relationships consists of a good deal of scholarly review and discourse, accompanied by a limited amount of empirical research. Early scholarship includes Toth and Trujillo's (1987) call for scholars to integrate concepts from organizational communication, management research, and public relations to develop an overbridging theory. The integrative approach was further advanced by Toth's (1995) suggestion that public relations be thought of as a form of interpersonal communication with public relations practitioners functioning between an organization and its publics. Broom and Dozier's (1990) contribution to this area of inquiry focused on evaluation of organization–public relationships. They suggested a coorientational approach to relationship audits centered around issues of agreement, accuracy, and perceptual alignment between an organization and its publics. Additionally, L. A. Grunig, Grunig, and Ehling (1992) suggested that the quality of organization–public relationships might be measured through the dimensions of reciprocity, trust, mutual legitimacy, openness, mutual satisfaction, and mutual understanding. J. E. Grunig has emphasized the importance of linking organization–public relationships to organizational goals, arguing that "for public relations to be valued by the organizations it serves, practitioners must be able to demonstrate that their efforts contribute to the goals of these organizations by building long-term behavioral relationships with strategic publics" (p. 136). Such long-term relationships are the result of both symbolic and behavioral relationships, "intertwined like the strands of a rope" (p. 123).

Increased attention on relationship management has brought into sharp focus the paucity of theoretical concepts concerning these relationships as well as the lack of an agreed-upon definition of the term *organization–public relationship*. Those needs were addressed in a pivotal study by Broom, Casey, and Ritchey (1997). They observed:

> Many scholars and practitioners say that public relations is all about building and maintaining an organization's relationships with its publics. However, anyone reading the literature of the field would have difficulty finding a useful definition of such relationships in public relations. Instead, it appears that authors assume that readers know and agree on the meaning and measurement of the important concept of *relationships*. Unfortunately, the assumption is not supported by evidence. (p. 83)

They further contended that

> the absence of a fully explicated definition (of organization–public relationships) precludes the development of valid operational measures of organization–public relationships and limits theory building in public relations. Without such definition, both scholars and practitioners will continue to use indirect measures to draw inferences about relationships without measuring the relationships themselves. (p. 83)

Based on a review of the literature of interpersonal and organizational communication, social and other related fields, Broom and associates (1997) advanced a model for constructing theory concerning organization–public relationships centered around the properties, antecedents, and consequences of organization–public relations. However, they concluded: "We are not yet ready to propose either (the) conceptual or operational definitions of organization–public relationships. Our goals ... were to initiate the process of explication and to invite others to join us in the task" (p.96).

We also looked to the literature of related disciplines for concepts that could be brought to focus on the organization–public setting. As a result of such a review, coupled with qualitative research with public members, we suggested that the concepts of *openness, trust, involvement, investment* and *commitment* may act as dimensions of the organization–public relationship (Ledingham, Bruning, Thomlison, & Lesko, 1997). Subsequent quantitative research revealed that the organization–public relationship dimensions of openness, trust, involvement, investment, and commitment differentiated those who would stay with an organization from those who were undecided or would leave when presented with an alternative choice in the form of competition (Ledingham & Bruning, 1998c). We also concluded that the research

> suggests a role for communication initiatives within the framework of rela-
> tionship management; in that role, goals are developed around relationships,
> and communication is used as a strategic tool in helping to achieve those goals.
> Moreover, while measurement of communication efficiencies should certainly
> be part of the evaluation process, their importance eventually may rest upon
> their ability to impact the achievement of relationship objectives. (p. 63)

Moreover, our research indicates that the organization–public relationship dimensions of openness, trust, involvement, investment, and commitment influence perceptions of *satisfaction* with the organization by
public members (Bruning & Ledingham), influence perceptions of satisfaction with the organization for business owners, managers, or both
(Bruning & Ledingham, 1998a), and may be more influential than price
or product features in predicting consumer behavior (Bruning & Ledingham, 1998c). We also found that the amount of time in a relationship
influences perceptions of the relationship dimensions (Ledingham,
Bruning, & Wilson, 1998), and our research regarding media and community relations suggests the importance of building and maintaining
relationships in that context (Ledingham & Bruning, 1997, 1998a,
1998b). Finally, we turned again to the literature of interpersonal relationships for insight into the development of diagnostic tools to catego-
rize the state of an organization–public relationship as a part of the
process of relationship management (Bruning & Ledingham, 1998b).

Wilson (1994b) states that the role of public relations "is to facilitate
positive communication between an organization and its publics (and)
that requires building relationships" (p. 136). However, she adds that "at
the foundation of those relationships must be a public perception of
what has come to be called corporate social responsibility" (p. 136). The
agent of corporate social responsibility, in Wilson's (1994b) view, is the
public relations practitioner who "functions in the role of corporate
conscience ... a 'community' role in a 'societal' organization ... perhaps
the last bastion of community within a corporate structure built on the
assumption and principles of society" (p. 136). According to Wilson
(1994a), American corporations are realizing a need to move away from
a rational approach and toward a "more people-oriented, relational
approach based on a few core corporate values like quality and service"
(p. 334). Wilson (1994b) contends this movement impacts public relations in two ways:

> First, now, more than ever, the emphasis in public relations is on relationship
> building. The era of press agentry, and publicity is past and attempts to

integrate public relations part and parcel with marketing are falling on hostile ears. It (public relations) is focused on developing relationships with all the publics in a corporation's community: government, industry, suppliers, employees, special interests, and local and national communities. The second change is that corporate credibility in those relationships is based less on successful business performance and more on demonstrated commitment to and support of community ...Relationships are based on employee and public perceptions of honest, corporate commitment, trust, and mutual respect. (p. 138)

The notion of public relations as relationship management has sparked the interest of practitioners as well as scholars. In 1996, Ketchum Public Relations and the Institute for Public Relations Research and Education created a task force to explore evaluation of relationships in public relations. Task force member and practitioner Kitty Ward observed: "My perspective is that most, if not all, of marketing and public relations has to do with changing or building relationships" (in Hon, 1998, p.112). Fellow task force member J. E. Grunig also argued that "public relations needs to evaluate maintenance strategies that are predictors of relationship outcomes such as commitment and trust" (p.112).

Purpose of the Study

As the review of the literature indicates, a good deal of progress has been accomplished in terms of exploration of issues concerning organization–public relations. Nonetheless, those contributing to the literature have offered several suggestions as to future research that is needed. As a result of her broad review of planning and evaluation practices used by practitioners of public relations, Hon (1998) found that "no one described experimental research designs whereby a strong case could be made for causal inferences between public relations activities and specific outcomes. Most often, the link was assumed" (p.130). Wilson's (1994b) admonition concerning the need to focus on "employee and public perceptions of corporate commitment, trust and mutual respect" (p. 138) underscores the need for research concerning the influence of those perceptions on both organizational and on public behavior. We have suggested that there is a need

to expand current models of public relations to include identified relationship dimensions, as well as the antecedents and consequences of those dimensions (and) the need to explore the dimensions of an organization–public relationship within a longitudinal design that includes benchmark measurement, intervention, and subsequent follow-up. (Ledingham & Bruning, 1998c, p. 63)

Moreover, we have posited that the role of communication within the relational perspective is "as a strategic tool" used to "help ... achieve (relationship) goals" (Ledingham & Bruning, 1998c, p. 63), a notion that needs further exploration.

Research Questions

Communication is a form of public relations activity. Indeed, communication has always been central to the study and practice of public relations. The emergence of the relationship management perspective raises the question of the role of communication within that framework. We employed a longitudinal research design to address our concerns and those of Hon as to the need for linking public relations activities and outcomes by exploring the role of communication within the relational perspective. We did so through an investigation of the influence of a managed communication program on perceptions of the organization–public relationship. The two research questions this investigation seeks to answer, then, are:

RQ1: Can a managed communication program influence the perceptions of public members of the organization–public relationship dimensions of openness, trust, involvement, investment, and commitment?

RQ2: What influence would a managed communication program have on public behavior?

METHOD

A research design employing qualitative and quantitative research methods was conducted. The design consisted of three focus groups, followed by a benchmark survey, an intervention, and a subsequent, follow-up survey (see Ledingham, Bruning, Thomlison & Lesko [1997] for a review of the qualitative research).

The Setting for the Study

"Relationville" is a midwestern community of some 80,000 residents. The community was selected, in part, because of its relatively isolated geographic location. Relationville is located about 100 miles from the nearest metropolitan area. Moreover, the community has been served exclusively by the local telephone company, under one corporate banner or another, since the inception of telephone service. The authors felt that if they were going to see relationships operating, the best opportunity would be afforded in a situation where longevity was prevalent.

Developing the Survey Instrument

The organization–public relationship questions reported in this investigation were created by conducting a review of interpersonal communication, social psychology, and marketing literature. From this review, the authors developed a list of 17 potential relationship dimensions (investment, commitment, trust, comfort with relational dialectics, cooperation, mutual goals, interdependence/power imbalance, performance satisfaction, comparison level of the alternatives, adaptation, nonretrievable investment, shared technology, summate constructs, structural bonds, social bonds, intimacy, and passion) that were used in qualitative research with members of key publics in three focus groups in order to identify the variables that seemed most important in the organization–public relationship. Based on the responses of those participants, the list was narrowed to five dimensions (trust, openness, involvement, investment, and commitment). Finally, group participants were asked to help operationalize each of the organization–public relationship dimensions. The components of the survey reported in this investigation used a 1–10 point Likert-type scale and examined respondent perceptions of the relationship variables of trust (I feel that I can trust *company name* to do what is says it will do), investment (*Company name* seems to be the kind of company that invests in the community), commitment (I think *company name* is committed to making my community a better place to live), involvement (I am aware *company name* is involved in my community), and openness (*Company name* shares its plans for the future with the community). The behavior of public members was measured by asking respondents to indicate whether they would stay, leave, or were undecided regarding their provider of local telephone service (If another company could provide the same service at a 10% discount, would you sign up with them or stay with *company name* for local residential telephone service?).

Gathering of Benchmark Data

For the benchmark, the authors developed a survey questionnaire designed to gather information to help determine the influence that organization–public relationships have on the behavior of public members, as well as issues such as competition, company image, consumer media diet, advertising recall, and demography. Survey interviewers were trained and provided with a script that allowed for a conversational tone in administering the survey and the instrument was pretested with 25 subjects. A list of random telephone numbers was generated and prefixes were weighted to match their occurrence within the population of Relationville prefixes. Approximately 20% of the telephone numbers that were dialed resulted in a completed survey. Although completed interviews averaged approximately 30 minutes in length, 448 (98.25%) of the 456 people who initially agreed to be involved in the study completed the interview.

Intervention

The telecommunications company then implemented a managed communication program in which the company increased its communication with the local community. The company received extensive local press coverage regarding its investment in the infrastructure of the city's communication system, its commitment to the community, and its involvement in the community. Moreover, public relations personnel were frequent guests on radio talk shows during this period. The organization also utilized mailers and billing inserts as a part of the campaign.

Gathering of Postintervention Data

Approximately four months after the benchmark was established, and one month after the intervention, an effort was made to recontact the original 448 respondents to ask them to participate in the retest portion of the analysis. Of the 448 original respondents, 136 (30%) agreed to be interviewed again. The follow-up survey centered around respondent perceptions of the organization–public relationship and their intended behavior regarding selection of a telephone service provider. The average interview in the retest component of the survey lasted approximately 10 minutes.

RESULTS

T tests were computed comparing the pretest condition with the posttest condition on the relationship variables and significantly higher scores were reported in the posttest condition on the variables of trust ($t[248]$ = 3.74, p .001), openness ($t[241]$ = 2.41, p .05), investment ($t[240]$ = 4.71, p .001), and commitment ($t[242]$ = 2.20, p .05). There also were shifts in the intended behavior of respondents, with a 10% increase (from 50% to 60%) in those who said they would stay, a 4% reduction (from 25% to 21%) in those who said they would leave, and a shift among the undecided group, from 25% to 19%. Table 3.1 reports the pretest and posttest relation mean scores, as well as a comparison of the respondent pretest and posttest purchasing behavior.

DISCUSSION

As noted earlier, it was previously argued that relationship dimension ratings can be used to predict the behavior of public members. The results of the research reported here demonstrate that when a managed communication program centered around the relationship dimensions was implemented, the data revealed a corresponding 10% increase in public members who indicated they would stay with the current provider of local telephone service. Hon (1998) has called for research to explore causal inferences between public relations activities and specific outcomes. Although we do not claim a causal inference be-

TABLE 3.1

Relationship Dimensions

Condition	Trust ***	Openness *	Involvement	Investment ***	Commitment *
Pretest	6.95	6.74	6.81	6.41	6.90
Posttest	7.69	7.48	7.14	7.77	7.59

* $p < .05$ ** $p < .01$ *** $p < .001$

Purchasing Behavior

Condition	Stay	Leave	Undecided
Pretest	50%	25%	25%
Posttest	60%	21%	19%

tween organization–public relationship initiatives and the behavior of public members, the research certainly supports the notion that managed communication programs can influence perceptions of the organization–public relationship and, in that way, can impact the behavior of public members. This supports our earlier thesis concerning the strategic role communication plays within the relational perspective to help achieve relationship goals.

This investigation also provided an empirical test of J. E. Grunig's (1993) notion of the interplay of symbolic and behavioral relationships. As noted earlier, the managed communication intervention in this study included news stories generated through press contacts, appearances on radio talk shows, mailers, and billing inserts. The content of the managed communication intervention centered around the organization's actions in the community, including support for local education, community activity sponsorship, and investment in the infrastructure of the community. The results of the intervention are reflected in the significant increase in the ratings of 4 of the 5 relationship dimensions and in the 10% increase in the decision to stay with the current provider of local telephone service. Therefore, when the organization engages in action and communication that facilitates a sense of openness, trust, commitment, involvement, and investment it builds the symbolic and behavioral relationships with key publics that J. E. Grunig (1993) contends are critical to effective organizations.

Benefits generated by the organization's behaviors and communication of those behaviors were accrued by both the organization and its publics. Public benefit took the form of support for local community activities and for the infrastructure of the community. Organizational gain was seen in increased fidelity toward the organization. Thus, the research implies that there are economic as well as corporate social responsibility reasons for organizations to practice two-way symmetrical public relations.

Conclusions

This research underscores the value for organizations and for publics alike of a two-way symmetrical approach to public relations—an approach that emphasizes building and maintaining relationships that benefit not only the organization but also public members. The research indicates that practicing public relations within this framework can result in benefit for publics (through organizational support for community activities) and for the organization (in increased loyalty toward the organization). Thus, the research adds credence to our earlier observations that "organizational ...support of the community in which it operates can engender loyalty toward an organization among key publics when that (support) is known by those key publics" (Ledingham & Bruning, 1998c, p. 63).

The research also supports our earlier thesis that public relations is "a two-step process, in which organizations must (1) *focus on the relationships* with their key publics, and (2) *communicate* involvement of those activities/programs that build the organization–public relationship with members of their key publics" (Ledingham & Bruning, 1998c, p. 63). It is within this process that the role of communication becomes clear regarding relationship building. The organization must engage in behaviors that benefit its publics as well as serving the interests of the organization. Communication should be utilized to inform key publics about the organization's behaviors. As J. E. Grunig (1993) has noted: "Communication—a symbolic relationship—can improve a behavioral relationship, but a poor behavioral relationship can destroy attempts to use communication to build a symbolic relationship or to improve a behavioral relationship" (p. 123). This research supports the notion that organizations must engage in both symbolic and behavioral initiatives in order to effectively manage the organization–public relationship.

The research results have implications for organizational behavior, theory building, public relations practice, and education. Organizations that practice relationship management within a model of two-way symmetry both generate and receive benefits. In the process, their initiatives help build community, while providing social and economic return on their investment.

In terms of theory building, the relational paradigm offers alternatives to traditional measures of communication efficiency or programmatic output. It also supports an argument that models of the organization–public relationship should include relationship dimensions as both building blocks of organization–public relationships and as indicators of relationship quality.

The implications for public relations practice are varied. First, constructing public relations communication around organizational behaviors in support of community interests can engender loyalty toward the organization among some public members. Secondly, "talking the talk" (symbolic relationship) will not result in a positive organization–public relationship unless the organization is also willing to "walk the walk" (behavioral relationship). Additionally, public relations practitioners must overcome the tendency to view the production of communication vehicles as the solution to every public relations problem and embrace the concept of public relations as the management of organization–public relationships if public relations is to have value within organizational structures. Moreover, the paradigm of relationship management implies that public relations education needs to move away from an often near-compulsive concentration on communication and entry-level *production skills* to include a higher order view of public relations as the *management* of organization–public relationships.

Finally, the corporate social responsibility advocate may wish that organizations engage in community-building behavior not because they expect to benefit economically, but because they feel a responsibility to do so as members of their immediate community and of the larger society in which they operate. A rationalist, on the other hand, might advocate two-way symmetrical public relations purely for bottom-line economic gain. Whatever the motivation for engaging in a relational-based, mutually beneficial approach to the practice of public relations, it seems to us that both approaches ultimately lead to the same result—benefit for publics and for their communities, as well as benefit for the organization.

Future Research

Single measurements of relationship dimensions were employed in this study. There is a need to develop a relationship scale that includes several measures of each of the relationship dimensions to ensure greater reliability. There is also a need to develop corresponding scales that measure relationship quality as well as loyalty toward an organization. Moreover, the research needs to be replicated among different industries with different publics to determine the influence of these dimensions in diverse settings as well as to gauge the generalizability of the relationship dimensions identified in this chapter. The research also suggests the usefulness of a model of organization–public relationships that provides for different types of organizations, the nature of key publics (organization-to-public, organization-to-organization), environmental settings, relationship longevity, the presence and strength of competition, and other variables that may influence the relationship. Such a model could serve as the basis for greater understanding of organization–public relationships and their impact both on organizational and on public behavior.

A Final Note

This research demonstrates that organizations that utilize the two-way symmetrical approach, constructed around the organization–public relationship, may gain a competitive advantage that can serve as an additional organizational incentive to "do well by doing right." In that way, the relational approach represents opportunities for managing public relations for the benefit of both organizations and for the publics they serve.

REFERENCES

Botan, C. (1993). Introduction to the paradigm struggle in public relations. *Public Relations Review, 19*, 107–110.

Broom, G. M., & Dozier, D. M. (1990). *Using research in public relations: Applications to program management.* Englewood Cliffs, NJ: Prentice-Hall.

Broom, G. M., Casey, S., & Ritchey, J. (1997). Toward a concept and theory of organization–public relationships. *Journal of Public Relations Research, 9*, pp. 83–98.

Bruning, S. D., & Ledingham, J. A. (1998a, August). *Organization and key public relationships: Testing the influence of the relationship dimensions in a business to business context.* Paper presented at the annual meeting of the Association for Education in Journalism and Mass Communication, Baltimore, MD.

Bruning, S. D., & Ledingham, J. A. (1998b). Public relations as relationship management: Ten guidelines for effectively managing the organization–public relationship. In J. Biberman and A. Alkhafaji (Eds.), *Business research yearbook, 5* (pp. 776–780). Saline, MI: McNaughton & Gunn.

Bruning, S. D., & Ledingham, J. A. (1998c, November). *Public relations in the marketing mix: Relationships and the "bottom line."* Paper presented at the annual conference of the National Communication Association, New York.

Bruning, S. D., & Ledingham, J. A. Organization–public relationships and consumer satisfaction: The role of relationships in the satisfaction mix. *Communication Research Reports.*

Cutlip, S. M., Center, A. H. & Broom, G. M. (1987). *Effective public relations* (6th ed.). Englewood Cliffs, NJ: Prentice-Hall.

Cutlip, S. M., Center, A. H., & Broom, G. M. (1994). *Effective public relations* (7th ed.). Englewood Cliffs, NJ: Prentice-Hall, Inc.

Ehling, W. P. (1992). Estimating the value of public relations and communication to an organization. In J. E. Grunig, D. M. Dozier, W. P. Ehling, L. A. Grunig, F. C. Repper, & J. White (Eds.), *Excellence in public relations and communication management* (pp. 617–638). Hillsdale, NJ: Lawrence Erlbaum Associates.

Ferguson, M. A. (1984, August). *Building theory in public relations: Interorganizational relationships.* Paper presented at the annual convention of the Association for Education in Journalism and Mass Communication, Gainesville, FL.

Grunig, J. E. (1992). Communication, public relations, and effective organizations: An overview of the book. In J. E. Grunig, D. M. Dozier, W. P. Ehling, L. A. Grunig, F. C. Repper, & J. White (Eds.), *Excellence in public relations and communication management* (pp. 1–28). Hillsdale, NJ: Lawrence Erlbaum Associates.

Grunig, J. E. (1993). Image and substance: From symbolic to behavioral relationships. *Public Relations Review, 19*, 121–139.

Grunig, L. A., Grunig, J. F., & Ehling, W. P. (1992). What is an effective organization? In J. E. Grunig, D. M. Dozier, W. P. Ehling, L. A. Grunig, F. C. Repper, & J. White (Eds.), *Excellence in public relations and communication management* (pp. 65–90). Hillsdale, NJ: Lawrence Erlbaum Associates.

Hon, L. C. (1998). Demonstrating effectiveness in public relations: Goals, objectives, and evaluation. *Journal of Public Relations Research, 10*, 103–135.

Ledingham, J. A., & Bruning, S. D. (1997). Building loyalty through community relations. *The Public Relations Strategist, 3*(2), 27–29.

Ledingham, J. A., & Bruning, S. D., (1998a, November). *The impact of relationships in the management of media relations.* Paper presented at the annual convention of the National Communication Association, New York.

Ledingham, J. A., & Bruning, S.D. (1998b). A management approach to media relations. In J. Biberman & A. Alkhafaji (Eds.), *Business research yearbook, 5* (pp. 752–756). Saline, MI: McNaughton & Gunn.

Ledingham, J. A., & Bruning, S. D. (1998c). Relationship management and public relations: dimensions of an organization–public relationship. *Public Relations Review, 24*, 55–65.

Ledingham, J. A., Bruning, S. D., Thomlison, T. D., & Lesko, C. (1997). The applicability of interpersonal relationship dimensions to an organizational context: A qualitative approach. *The Academy of Managerial Communications Journal, 1*, 23–43.

Ledingham, J. A., Bruning, S. D., & Wilson, L. (1998, August). *Time as an indicator of the perceptions and behavior of members of a key public: A work in progress.* Paper presented at the annual convention of the Association for Education in Journalism and Mass Communication, Baltimore, MD.

Toth, E. L. (1995, November). *Interpersonal communication and organizational communication: Contributions to the study and practice of public relations.* Paper presented at the annual meeting of the Speech Communication Association, San Antonio, TX.

Toth, E. L., & Trujillo, N. (1987). Reinventing corporate communications. *Public Relations Review 13*, 42–53.

Wilson, L. J. (1994a). Excellent companies and coalition building among the Fortune 500: A value- and relationship-based theory. *Public Relations Review, 20*, 333–343.

Wilson, L. J. (1994b). The return to Gemeinschaft: A theory of public relations and corporate community relations as relationship building. In A. F. Alkhafaji (Ed.), *Business research yearbook: Global business perspectives, 1* (pp. 135–141). Lanham, MD: University Press of America.

Wilson, L. J. (1996). Strategic cooperative communities: A synthesis of strategic, issue management, and relationship-building approaches in public relations. In H. Culbertson and N. Chen (Eds.), *International public relations*. Mahwah, NJ: Lawrence Erlbaum Associates.

II

Applications of the
Relational Perspective

4

Crisis Management: Advantages of a Relational Perspective

ಬಿ ✧ ೞ

W. Timothy Coombs
Illinois State University

A minor theme running through the crisis management literature is the need to cultivate pre-crisis relationships with stakeholders (Birch, 1994; Couretas, 1985; Fearn-Banks, 1996; Seitel, 1983). Implicit in this precrisis-relationship concern is the assumption that crises are episodes in the ongoing relationship between an organization and its stakeholders. Viewing crises as one episode embedded in a larger relationship can be a valuable perspective for crisis managers. The ongoing relationships with stakeholders provide a practical context from which to analyze a crisis episode. In turn, this relational perspective helps crisis managers to develop effective responses to the crises. A relational approach can yield new insights into the crisis-management process.

This chapter explores three points that will allow readers to develop an appreciation for a relational approach to crisis management. First, the concept of relationship and its relevance to crisis management needs to be developed. It is important to understand what is meant by the term relationship when it is applied to the activities of an organization and how it fits with crisis management. Second, a framework for applying a relational approach to crisis management must be articulated. To be useful to crisis managers, a relational approach must provide a coherent perspective from which to analyze crisis episodes. Finally, the potential contributions of a relational approach to crisis management should be enumerated, and a research agenda based on the relationship approach should be advanced.

RELATIONSHIPS AND CRISIS MANAGEMENT

Any discussion of a relational approach to crisis management demands that two initial concerns be addressed. First, what is meant by the term relationship? Because the concept of a relationship is pivotal to a relational approach, it is imperative to begin by defining the term. Second, how does the concept of relationship fit with crisis management? *Relationship* is primarily a concept associated with interpersonal communication. A relational approach to crisis management assumes that the concept can be applied equally to public relations and crisis management. The exact nature of how relationship meshes with crisis management must be explained.

Relational Definitions

One useful definition of relationship is "the interdependence of two or more people." (O'Hair, Friedrich, Wiemann, & Wiemann, 1995, p. 10). The strength of this definition is its breath and its focus on interdependence. People have a relationship when they are linked together in some way. This link could be family, school, work, church, a club, or any other number of factors. The key is that the people are somehow interdependent with one another—they need one another for some reason. Along with the term relationship comes a constellation of related concepts. Relational history is a collection of events in a relationship (O'Hair et al., 1995). Relationships are dynamic and change over time. One influence on relationships is relational damage. Relational damage tends to be a result of either incongruency between the public and private definitions of a relationship or the people involved in the relationship having different expectations of each other (O'Hair et al., 1995). With the basics of relationship defined, attention now shifts to its applicability to crisis management.

Relevance to Crisis Management

To understand the role of relationships in crisis management, it is instructive to first discuss stakeholder theory and neoinstitutionalism. Both have been important influences on recent conceptualizations of crisis management (Allen & Caillouet, 1994; Coombs, 1995) *Stakeholder theory* explains how organizations interact with various groups that populate the organization's environment—it addresses relationships with stakeholders. *Neoinstitutionalism* provides a mechanism for understanding the development of the relational history between an organization and its stakeholders and where crises fit into this relational history.

Stakeholder Theory. It is taken for granted in the management literature that organizations have stakeholders and that the management of these stakeholders affects the organization's viability (Clarkson, 1991; Freeman, 1984; Wood, 1991). *Stakeholders* are any person or group that has an interest, right, claim, or ownership in an organization (Clarkson, 1995). Stakeholders are more precisely conceptualized as two distinct variants: primary and secondary. *Primary stakeholders* are those whose actions can be harmful or beneficial to an organization. Without the continued interaction of primary stakeholders, an organization would cease to exist. Common primary stakeholders include employees, investors, customers, suppliers, government, and the community (Donaldson & Preston, 1995). *Secondary stakeholders*, or influencers, are those who can affect or be affected by the actions of an organization. Common influencers include the media, activist groups, and competitors (Clarkson, 1995; Donaldson & Preston, 1995).

Both primary and secondary stakeholders are interdependent with an organization. Stakeholders and the organization have a connection that binds them together, whether it be grounded in economic, political, or social concerns. Hence, it is appropriate to talk about relationships between an organization and its stakeholders. In fact, the idea of stakeholder management is nothing more than managing the relationship between an organization and its various stakeholders (Carroll, 1989; Donaldson & Preston, 1995). Neoinstitutionalism is a popular perspective for understanding how to manage the stakeholder-organization relationship.

Neoinstitutionalism.   The centerpiece of neoinstitutionalism is organizational legitimacy. Stakeholders perceive an organization to be legitimate when they believe an organization has conformed to certain social rules or expectations (Bedeian, 1989). Stakeholders believe that legitimate organizations have a right to continue operating and those lacking legitimacy do not (Allen & Caillouet, 1994). Such judgements do matter to an organization. Legitimacy has been linked to the successful operation of an organization (DiMaggio & Powell, 1991). Neoinstitutionalism distills stakeholder management down to the meeting of the social rules or expectations of stakeholders (Allen & Caillouet, 1994). The stakeholder–organization relationship is then defined in terms of social rules or expectations—the stakeholders' perceptions that the organization is meeting their expectations. Moreover, the relational history becomes composed of events related to those social rules or expectations. In essence, relational history is functionally equivalent to reputation. A reputation is based on a stakeholder's experiences with an organization. Both reputation and relational history are built from past interactions between the organization and the stakeholder.

One dimension of a crisis is that it is a threat or challenge to an organization's legitimacy. A crisis can lead stakeholders to question whether or not an organization is meeting the social rules or expectations. A few examples will clarify this point. PepsiCo was boycotted for operating its business in Burma (Myanmar). Some stakeholders felt that PepsiCo violated expectations about protecting human rights through the operation of facilities in a country known for human rights abuses. The Sears scandal over malfeasance in its automotive repair departments violated expectations of fair treatment of customers and basic honesty. A crisis can be viewed as a violation of the social rules or expectations held by stakeholders and, thus, a disruption to the relationship. Allen and Caillouet (1994) argued that a driving force in crisis management is a desire to re-establish adherence to the violated expectations—to repair the relationship.

Relationships and Crisis: A Review.   It is consistent to apply the term relationship to the connection between stakeholders and organizations. By definition, stakeholders and organizations are interdependent. One form of that interdependence is based on social norms and expectations—does the organization's performance meet the stakeholders' expectations. The relational history becomes a function of events related to either meeting or failing to meet stakeholder expectations.

Again, the failure to meet the social norms and expectations of stakeholders is one dimension of a crisis. Other dimensions include financial damage and injuries and loss of life. Failure to meet expectations results in the organization sustaining reputational damage (Allen & Caillouet, 1994). Consider boycotts as an example of this dynamic. The primary damage inflicted by a boycott is reputational, not financial. Organizations suffer reputational damage from media reports that detail the organization's failure to meet social norms and expectations. The direct economic impact of most boycotts is minimal at best (Mueller, 1990; Snyder, 1991). However, the reputational damage can be translated into financial damage (Barton, 1993; Coombs & Holladay, 1996). It follows that crises are a form of reputational damage. Relational damage is a form of reputation damage because the reputation arises from the relational history. Any threat to the relational history is a threat to the reputation.

Crises can reveal that an organization and stakeholders have different expectations or that the organization is acting inconsistently within the relationship. A crisis serves to damage the stakeholder–organization relationship (Allen & Caillouet, 1994; Barton, 1993). Thus, those writing about concerns over precrisis relationships have a valid point. A crisis can be understood in terms of the ongoing stakeholder–organization relationships. These relationships should impact on how stakeholders perceive the crisis, the organization in crisis, and options for addressing the crisis.

FRAMEWORK FOR APPLYING A RELATIONAL APPROACH TO CRISIS MANAGEMENT

Crisis management is a heavily applied field. Crisis managers want tools they can use in the heat of a crisis. Therefore, it is not enough to claim a relational approach has value for crisis management. Crisis managers must be shown how they can apply a relational approach to crisis management. This section explores how attribution theory can be used as an organizing framework for a relational approach to crisis management. The exploration begins with an explication of the basic tenets of attribution theory. This is followed by a discussion of how attribution theory can be used to: explain the type of relational damage caused by a crisis, understand how past relationships shape perceptions of current crisis events, and suggest strategies for repairing the relationship.

Attribution Theory

Attribution theory is based on the assumption that people spontaneously search for the causes of events—people want to know why an event occurred (Weiner, 1985a; Wong & Weiner, 1981). Research in a wide array of domains has proven this assumption (Weiner, 1985a; Weiner, Perry, & Magnusson, 1988). Although people do search for the causes of events, certain conditions help to prompt such searchers. Events that are unexpected or failures serve to stimulate causal thinking. This could be an adaptive function. People want to find the causes for the failures or unexpected events in order to cope with them effectively (Weiner, 1985a). People naturally attribute causes to events, particularly failures or unexpected events.

Attributions are important because they affect how people feel and behave toward the actor involved in the event (Weiner, 1985b; Weiner et al., 1988; Wilson, Cruz, Marshall, & Rao, 1993). Understanding how people make attributions about events allows for the anticipation of their emotional and behavioral responses to events. Typically, greater attributions of individual responsibility for a negative event leads to stronger feelings of anger and a more negative view of the actor (Weiner, Amirkan, Folkes, & Verette, 1987). It is behooving us to understand the attributional process.

McAuley, Duncan, and Russell (1992) have isolated four causal dimensions people use when they engage in their searches. These dimensions help to determine if the cause of the event is attributed to the actor involved in the event (strong individual responsibility) or to factors external to the actor (weak individual responsibility). The four causal dimensions are: stability, external control, personal control, and locus of causality. Stability refers to the frequency of an event. If a person is involved in an event repeatedly it is stable but if their involvement is infrequent it is unstable. People are more likely to attribute the cause of the event to the actor for a stable rather than for an unstable event. External control refers to whether or not some other person can control the cause of the event. Strong external control indicates that someone other than the actor could control the event, whereas weak external control suggests an absence of some outside controlling force. The greater the perceived external control, the less people should attribute the cause of an event to the actor.

Personal control refers to whether or not the actor could control the cause of the event. Strong personal control indicates that the actor controlled his or her own fate in the event. The stronger the perceptions of personal control, the more likely people are to attribute the cause of the event to the actor. Locus of causality refers to whether the cause of the event is something about the actor or something about the situation. The locus is internal when the cause is something about the actor and external when it is something about the situation. An internal locus should lead to stronger attributions that the actor is responsible for the event (McAuley et al., 1992; Russell, 1982; Wilson et al., 1993).

Measures have been developed for all four causal dimensions (McAuley et al., 1992). However, research has consistently demonstrates a substantial overlap between personal control and locus of causality. Research has indicated that personal control and locus should be treated as a single dimension (Wilson et al., 1993). The overlap stems from the fact that both dimensions reflect the intentionality of an act. For instance, high personal control and an internal locus create perceptions of an intentional act by the actor whereas low personal control and an external locus foster perceptions of an unintentional act. Functionally, there appear to be only three causal dimensions: stability, external control, and locus/personal control.

Attribution Theory and Relationships

With a basic understanding of attribution theory in place, attention now shifts to how attribution theory fits with a relational approach to crisis management. The first step in that move is to place attribution theory in the relational framework. This requires an explanation of how attribution theory can help to explain potentially disruptive events in a relationship.

Interpersonal Application. A negative event can disrupt a relationship. An embarrassing event at a company function would be such a negative event. The impact of the negative event on the relationship is a function of how the event is interpreted. Relational history is one factor that influences the interpretation of events in a relationship (O'Hair et al., 1995). Stability is an aspect of relational history. An event should be perceived as more negative if that event is part of a pattern—a stable event. Does the actor have a history of embarrassing acts at public events? Furthermore, strong attributions of intentionality and lack of external control should intensify the relational damage. Did the actor intentionally commit the embarrassing act with no outside interference? People will be angrier when the actor was either in control of the event (strong personal control) or the event was not precipitated by outside influences (weak external control). Conversely, anger is lessened when the actor could not prevent the event (weak personal control) or external forces were responsible for the event (strong external control). Attribution theory provides some insights into how people will interpret and react to potentially disruptive events in a relationship. The implications of such insights for communication are forthcoming.

Crisis Application.   These same attribution dimensions can help to explain how stakeholders interpret crisis events or disruptions in the stakeholder–organization relationship. This information can then be used to develop appropriate responses to the crisis. In this instance, "appropriate" refers to a response that will limit or repair the relational damage wrought by a crisis. The initial step in unpacking attribution theory's utility to crisis management is to translate the theory into crisis management terminology. That provides the foundation for understanding how attribution theory can aid in relational repair work.

A crisis is an ideal event for triggering an attributional search. A crisis is typically unexpected (but not unanticipated) and reflects some form of failure (Barton, 1993). A train derailment illustrates this point. Although it is known that trains do derail, it cannot be predicted when a train might do so, thus, a derailment is unexpected. In addition, the goal of a train safely reaching its destination is not met meaning there has been a failure. Stakeholders should search for causes of a crisis because an unexpected or failure event is a strong prompt for people to make attributions. The crisis attribution will revolve around organizational responsibility for the crisis. Organizational crisis responsibility is the amount of blame for the crisis that the stakeholder attributes to the organization. As perceptions of organizational responsibility increase, so should the reputational damage and the anger felt by stakeholders (Coombs & Holladay, 1996).

The three causal dimensions of attribution theory provide a mechanism for understanding the amount of organizational responsibility generated by a particular crisis. External control refers to whether an actor or group outside of the organization was in control of the crisis. For example, a terrorist attack against an organization would reflect strong external control. Strong external control should weaken perceptions of organizational crisis responsibility because the organization was at the mercy of external agents. Internal locus/personal control refers to whether the organization was in control of events that precipitated the crisis. Knowingly placing a defective product on the market, for instance, reflects a strong internal locus/personal control. Organizational crisis responsibility strengthens as attributions of internal locus/personal control intensifies. Strong attributions of internal locus/personal control indicate that the organization could have prevented the crisis and knew that preventative measures could have been taken.

Stability can have two different forms. First, stability can refer to past crises. In this sense the term stable reflects an organization with a history of crises whereas unstable reflects an organization with infrequent crises. Stable crises indicate a pattern of problems. The pattern suggests that the organization is responsible for the problems because they have done nothing to break the pattern (Coombs & Holladay, 1996).

Second, stability can refer to the general reputation of an organization—the relational history with stakeholders. A favorable reputation is built by consistently going beyond the normal requirements when dealing with stakeholders. These exceptional actions foster a favorable relationship with stakeholders. Typical elements of a favorable reputation include cutting edge treatment of customers, open access to the media, and extensive involvement in the social fabric of the community. In each instance, the organization would have a history of doing more than just the minimum in its interactions with stakeholders. In contrast, an unfavorable reputation results from ignoring or abusing the stakeholder–organization relationship. Ignoring customer complaints, lack of community involvement, and disregard for employee safety are actions that can contribute to an unfavorable reputation. In these cases the organization would have a history of doing less than is expected in its interactions with stakeholders. Reputations also can be neutral. A neutral reputation is a result of either no meaningful interaction between organization and stakeholder or the organization doing just the minimum in maintaining the relationships with stakeholders. Either way, the organization generates no strong effect for stakeholders. For instance, although people receive and pay bills from the water utility company, they rarely have meaningful interactions with the water utility.

The two forms of stability reflect different levels of specificity. Past crisis stability is very specific as it concentrates only on crisis events, a narrow segment of the relational history between the stakeholder and organization. While narrow, past crises deal directly with the event at hand. This direct connection is a powerful influence on the interpretation of the current crisis. Repeated crises are qualitatively different from isolated crises (Coombs, 1998).

Reputational stability is broad and encompasses the entire range of events that comprise the relational history between a stakeholder and an organization. Although not as dramatic, the reputation still colors perceptions of the crisis. A strong, favorable reputation provides a variety of benefits to an organization in crisis. First, a favorable reputation can create a halo effect. Stakeholders perceive the organization in a positive way even in a crisis. The reputation leads stakeholders to give the organization the benefit of the doubt and perhaps to reduce perceptions of organizational-crisis responsibility. Second, a favorable reputation builds positive credits with stakeholders. These credits can be used to offset a crisis. Stakeholders forgive a crisis because of the past good works of the organization. Third, a favorable reputation is a source of initial credibility (McCroskey, 1966). Credibility is the receiver's attitude toward a communicator. Researchers find two dimensions for credibility: expertise and trustworthiness. Expertise is knowledge about the subject, whereas trustworthiness is good will toward, or concern for, the receivers. Initial credibility is the credibility that the source has before he or she speaks. This is different from derived credibility, which is the credibility produced by the speaker's messages. These two forms of credibility combine to create terminal credibility, the credibility a speaker has after the message is delivered. Credibility can significantly affect the degree of attitude change produced by a message (McCroskey, 1966). Background is a part of initial credibility, hence, organizational spokespersons are more believable during a crisis if there is a strong, favorable reputation prior to the crisis.

Crisis stability directly influences attributions of organizational crisis responsibility. The more stable the crisis, the stronger the attributions of organizational crisis responsibility. Reputational stability influences the negative affect generated by a crisis. A positive reputation should lessen the negative affect whereas a negative reputation should intensify it. Attribution theory helps crisis managers to anticipate stakeholder attributions of crisis responsibility. These perceptions of organizational crisis responsibility are related to the selection of appropriate crisis responses.

Attribution Theory and Crisis Responses

Crisis managers must respond—say or do something—in a crisis. Silence and "no comment" are deadly options because they foster perceptions of guilt (Maynard, 1993). A variety of sources have begun to identify possible crisis responses. The list of crisis responses range from lists of 6 to 20 (Allen & Caillouet, 1994; Benoit, 1995; Hearit, 1994). Table 4.1 provides a list and definition of the strategies common in the literature. Benoit (1995) rightfully argued that the exact number of crisis strategies varies according to the level of abstraction used by the researcher. Consequently, debate over the exact number of crisis responses is counterproductive. One productive approach is to select some level of abstraction based on some underlying connection between the strategies.

· Marcus and Goodman (1991) offered a potential connection when they divided crisis responses into accommodative and defensive. Accom-

TABLE 4.1

Crisis Response Strategies Defined

---

1. Attack Accuser: The crisis management team confronts those who claim a crisis exists and maintains that there is no crisis. Requires the stakeholder to believe the organization more than the accuser.

2. Denial: This claims that there is no crisis. There are two forms: simple denial which states nothing has happened and clarification which extends the simple denial by explaining why there is no crisis. Requires the stakeholders to believe the claim of no crisis.

3. Excuse: Minimizes the organization's responsibility for the crisis. Stakeholders must be willing to believe organization's claim of limited responsibility.

4. Justification: Minimizes the damage associated with the crisis. Stakeholders must be willing to believe the organization's claim that there is minimal damage.

5. Ingratiation: Seek to gain public approval of the organization. This includes reminding stakeholders of past good works by the organization.

6. Corrective Action: Some form of compensation of help is offered to victims and/or the damage is repaired.

7. Full Apology: The crisis management team takes responsibility for the crisis, asks for forgiveness, and reports actions taken to prent a repeat of the crisis.

modative strategies accept responsibility or take remedial action whereas defensive strategies claim there is no problem or deny responsibility for the crisis (Marcus & Goodman, 1991). A similar array of crisis strategies was offered by Siomkos and Shrivastava (1993). Their strategies range from denial to corrective action. A continuum of crisis responses can be extracted from these discussions. The continuum is anchored by endpoints of denial and corrective action. Figure 4.1 places a combined list of the Benoit (1995) and Allen and Caillouet (1994) crisis responses on an accommodative-defensive continuum.

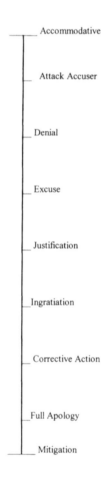

FIG. 4.1. Accommodative–defensive continuum.

A crisis manager must be strategic in his or her crisis response (Barton, 1993). Careful thought must be put into the selection of the words and actions taken to address the crisis, what I term as the crisis response strategies (CRS). An improper response will only compound the damage created by a crisis (Barton, 1993). An important element to factor into the selection equation is the nature of the crisis situation. Specific aspects of the crisis situation should suggest the use of certain CRS and eliminate the use of other CRS (Benoit, 1995; Hobbs, 1995).

The logic behind analyzing the situation is deeply rooted in the communication literature. Public speaking and rhetoric have long recognized the need to consider the situation when making communicative choices. The effective speaker matches his or her communication strategies to the exigencies of the situation (Bitzer, 1968). Similarly the need to consider the situation has been documented in interpersonal communication. Research consistently finds that the nature of the situation influences the selection of communication strategies in predictable ways (Metts & Cupach, 1989). CRS should be subject to situational influences as well. Attribution theory, applied within a relational approach, offers some useful insights into the match between crisis situation and CRS.

As previously noted, attribution theory helps to explain how people assign responsibility for the crisis. The nature of the crisis situation influences the degree of organizational crisis responsibility that is assigned. Research has identified internal locus/personal control as the driving factor in assignment of organizational crisis responsibility. Contrary to predictions, external control was unrelated to attributions of crisis responsibility. Research did find a very strong relationship between organizational crisis responsibility and internal locus/personal control (Coombs, 1998). It appears that internal locus/personal control is a primary factor, whereas stability is secondary. Because people always have some grounds for evaluating internal locus/personal control, it emerges as the primary factor. However, there are times when people lack the information necessary to evaluate stability, thereby reducing it to a secondary factor.

Although there are a wide array of different crises, a cluster analysis has revealed a set of four crisis families: natural disasters, tampering/terrorism, accidents, and transgressions. Natural disasters include hurricanes, tornadoes, severe storms, and so forth. Tampering/terrorism is comprised of product tampering and terrorist attacks such as kidnapings or bombings. Accidents include industrial or transportation mishaps, workplace violence, and product recalls resulting from a technical or mechanical error. Transgressions represent actions in which organizations knowingly place stakeholders at risk or knowingly commit improper acts (e.g., violate laws or regulations). Dow Corning marketing breast implants when their data indicated dangerous side effects is an example of a transgression (Coombs, Hazleton, Holladay, & Chandler, 1995). These crises can be arrayed in terms of crisis responsibility from natural disaster (the least) to terrorism/tampering, to accidents to transgression (the most). Furthermore, crisis stability intensifies perceptions of organizational crisis responsibility. A history of repeated crises leads people to judge the most recent crisis more harshly (Coombs & Holladay, 1996). Crisis stability serves to intensify perceptions of crisis responsibility.

Assessment of organizational crisis responsibility helps in the selection of CRS. As attributions of organizational crisis responsibility intensify, the crisis manager should utilize more accommodative strategies. Strong attributions of organizational responsibility create deeper reputational damage. The greater the reputational damage, the more people will come to expect and demand more accommodative strategies (Coombs, 1998). By taking responsibility and action to resolve the crisis, the organization is actively trying to repair the reputational damage. It is reasonable to expect that defensive strategies become less effective as attributions of organizational crisis responsibility strengthen. Stakeholders are offended when organizations ignore crises of their own making (Maynard, 1993). Defensive strategies would be more effective when the crisis lacked control, such as natural disasters or tampering/terrorism. Table 4.2 provides a summary of potential matches between crisis events and crisis response strategies.

Relational Frame

From a relational perspective, the attribution-based assessment of organizational crisis responsibility is helpful but incomplete. The reputational stability (relational history) must be taken into consideration. Crisis managers must anticipate how the ongoing relationship with a stakeholder group might affect how they perceive the crisis and its impact on the organization. For reasons of simplification, three basic categories of reputation are used: strong favorable, neutral, and strong unfavorable. These categories were previously defined so only their

TABLE 4.2

Matching Crisis Response Strategies and Crisis Situations

Natural Disaster	
One Time Crisis:	Ingratiation. Stakeholders know the organization had no control so remind them of past good works—the organization's favorable image.
	Excuse only. If the are no past good works.
Repeated Crisis:	Excuse and Ingratiation. Remind stakeholders there is still no organizational control event when the crisis happens frequently.
Product Tampering	
One Time Crisis:	Excuse and/or justification with ingratiation. Remind stakeholders there was organizational control.
Repeated Crisis:	Corrective Action: repeated acts makes appear as thought the organization has some responsibility for the crises.
Accident	
One Time Crisis:	Excuse and/or justification with ingratiation. Remind stakeholders there was limited organizational control.
Repeated Crisis:	Corrective Action: repeated accidents suggest the organization has some responsibility for the crises.
Transgression	
One Time Crisis:	Full apology and corrective action. Organization must Take responsibility and work to fix the crisis situation.
Repeated Crisis:	Full apology and corrective action. Organization must Take responsibility and work to fix the crisis situation.

implications will be reviewed now. A strong favorable reputation generates positive affect toward the organization, a weak reputation generates no real affect, and a strong unfavorable reputation generates negative affect. Stakeholders use the relational history as a lens through which to view the current crisis situation. This section outlines some possible ways in which relational history might affect crisis attribution and, thus, impact the stakeholder organizational relationship itself.

Favorable Relational History.   Crisis researchers have assumed that a favorable relational history is always an asset. This tends to be a safe assumption given the benefits of strong credibility, positive credits, and the halo effect. All of these factors help to deflect the potential relational damage associated with most crises. Hence, crises might have less of an impact on the stakeholder–organization relationship when the reputation is favorable.

It is dangerous, however, to conclude that the favorable relational history has no downside. Two potential pitfalls must be considered: the higher standard of organizational performance and the shattering of a reputation. A favorable relational history is derived from an organization going beyond the ordinary when interacting with stakeholders. For example, an organization might be known for excellent customer service or devotion to the community. This exceptional behavior may inflate expectations for how the organization should perform in all circumstances. Stakeholders may expect the organization to use accommodative strategies in all crisis situations. Thus, an organization may not be able to utilize less accommodative strategies, even when attributions of organizational crisis responsibility are low.

An industrial accident will illustrate this point. Consider a small steel manufacturing facility that has a minor gas leak. The gas cloud is nontoxic but does irritate some people living near the plant. The crisis in unintentional, caused no real damage, and was an isolated event indicating the use of the minimization response strategy. However, a justification strategy might not be enough because it is not at the exceptional level the stakeholders have come to expect. Although the halo might lessen the reputational damage from the crisis itself, the stakeholders might develop a negative attitude from the failure to meet expectations—using a justification strategy rather than a more accommodative strategy. The favorable relational history might require the organization to use some accommodative strategies, like apologies and corrective action, directed toward those irritated by the crisis. The high-behavioral standard associated with a favorable relational history could demand more accommodative strategies be used in any type of crisis situation.

The second pitfall is even more dangerous. A crisis that strikes at the core of the relationship can shatter the relationship. Such a crisis contradicts some fundamental premise of the relationship. Consider an organization that has built its reputational/relational history on improving the environment. If a crisis reveals that the organization is harming the environment, the potential damage is multiplied. The organization looks like a hypocrite. The very foundation of the relationship has been breeched. Once more, stakeholders might come to expect more from the organization because it professes to protect the environment. Crises that violate a core belief of the relational history are more intense and damaging than other types of crises (Barton, 1993). The crisis itself

inflicts greater reputational damage and will require highly accommodative strategies to repair that damage.

Neutral Relational History.   A neutral relational history provides
a clear lens for viewing the crisis. In the neutral relational condition, the
precepts of attribution work unabated. The relational damage predictions derived from the application of attribution theory should be
accurate when people hold no strong feelings about the organization.

Negative Relational History.   A negative relational history reflects a below-average set of expectations for organizational performance. It follows that enacting the minimal crisis response strategies
should be enough to meet or exceed expectations. Doing the minimum
is more than the organization has done in the past. However, a negative
relational history may erode the effectiveness of some CRS. Strategies
relying on credibility (i.e., attack accuser, denial, excuse, justification,
and ingratiation) are less effective because the organization lacks initial
credibility. Weak initial credibility also leads stakeholders to question
the sincerity of an apology. Organizations must act to build credibility
in order to prove they are sincere. Reparation or repair strategies are
needed to build credibility. A negative relational history may establish
low expectations as well as limit what types of CRSs an organization
can use.

Summary of Relational Approach and Attribution Theory

Attribution theory provides a strong foundation for evaluating the
potential effect of a crisis on the stakeholder–organization relationship.
Understanding the potential damage allows the crisis manager to select
the appropriate crisis response strategies—those that will match the level
of reputational damage generated by the crisis. A relational approach
adds depth to the attributional analysis of the crisis. The relational
history of the stakeholders and organization provide a value context for
interpreting the current crisis. The relational history may color the
current crisis so that the appropriate CRSs differ from those suggested
by attribution theory. The potential effect of the relational history is
reviewed in the following section on future research.

FUTURE RESEARCH

The relational approach can build on the existing research from attribution theory and crisis management. The attribution theory-based crisis management research has uncovered three important findings. First, there are the anticipated links between internal locus/personal control, organizational crisis responsibility, and reputational damage. Second, there are the anticipated links between crisis stability, organizational crisis responsibility, and reputational damage. Third, more accommodative strategies are more effective at reducing reputational damage when there are strong attributions of organizational crisis responsibility (Coombs, 1998; Coombs & Holladay, 1996). Although the attribution theory-based research represents the neutral relationship condition, there lacks insight into the exact effects of the favorable and unfavorable relationship conditions.

Although a favorable relationship should impact crisis management, one can only speculate on how that will happen. In fact, there is reason to hold contradictory beliefs about the effect of a favorable relationship when organizational crisis responsibility is low. On one side is the halo effect. If stakeholders carry the positive aspects of the relationship into the crisis, stakeholders may dismiss the crisis as an aberration. In this case the crisis would have no impact on the reputation or the relationship and would require only the use of mildly defensive strategies such as minimization. On the other hand, a positive relationship may inflate expectations for organizational behavior. As a result, a mildly defensive strategy may be viewed as falling short of expectations and may intensify reputational damage. Stakeholders may demand more accommodative strategies and be disappointed with mildly defensive strategies. Research is needed to determine which of these explanations is the most accurate.

The halo effect implies the potential for reducing reputational damage for any crisis. The halo effect should act as a buffer. Stakeholders remember the favorable relationship when interpreting the crisis. Thus, stakeholders may perceive less reputational damage for the same crisis when they have a favorable precrisis relationship or reputation with the organization. Research is needed to determine if a favorable relationship can act as a buffer in any or in all types of crises.

Finally, there is the issue of initial credibility and a favorable relationship. Certain crisis response strategies are built around credibility—strong credibility should enhance their effectiveness. For example, clarification is more effective when the stakeholder believes the organization. Research is needed to determine if the credibility-based crisis response strategies are more effective at protecting the reputation in the favorable relationship condition verses the neutral and unfavorable relationship conditions. Moreover, an unfavorable relationship erodes the effectiveness of the credibility-based strategies. This means that the credibility-based strategies should be more effective in the neutral condition than in the unfavorable condition.

The unfavorable relationship may lead to lower expectations of organizational performance. Potential stakeholders can be asked how they would expect organizations with both favorable and unfavorable reputations to respond to the same crises. The results could be analyzed to determine if there are differences in expectations. Finally, an unfavorable reputation requires that an organization build its credibility through its responses. Research is needed to determine which CRSs are most effective in building credibility and if that varies by crisis type.

CONCLUSION

There is no doubt that an organization is enmeshed in ongoing relationships with its various stakeholders. This fact suggests that public relations practitioners should consider the impact of these ongoing relationships. One such application is in the area of crisis management. The value of the relational approach to crisis management is that it affords additional insight into how stakeholders perceive the crisis situation. Perceptions of the crisis situation helps crisis managers to select the CRSs that will be most effective in terms of rebuilding the stakeholder–organization relationship—protect the reputation. This chapter has speculated on some ways that the existing stakeholder–organization relationship might influence the selection of CRSs. Research, similar to the aforementioned, is needed before it is known whether these speculations are true. Extant research from the attribution line of crisis management research serves as a base for these predictions. However, until additional research, specifically designed for the relational approach, is performed, it can only be speculated on the value of viewing a crisis event as one episode within the larger stakeholder–organization relationship.

REFERENCES

Allen, M. W., & Caillouet, R. H. (1994). Legitimation endeavors: Impression management strategies used by an organization in crisis. *Communication Monographs, 61,* 44–62.

Barton, L. (1993). *Crisis in organizations: Managing and communicating in the heat of chaos.* Cincinnati, OH: South-Western.

Bedeian, A. G. (1989). *Management* (2nd ed.). Chicago: Dryden.

Benoit, W. L. (1995). *Accounts, excuses, and apologies: A theory of image restoration.* Albany, NY: SUNY Press.

Birch, J. (1994, Spring). New factors in crisis planning and response. *Public Relations Quarterly, 39,* 31–34.

Bitzer, L. F. (1968). The rhetorical situation. *Philosophy and Rhetoric, 1,* 165–168.

Carroll, A. B. (1989). *Business and society: Ethics and stakeholder management.* Cincinnati, OH: South-Western.

Clarkson, M. B. E. (1991). Defining, evaluating, and managing corporate social performance: The stakeholder management model. In L. E. Preston (Ed.), *Research in corporate social performance and policy,* vol. 12 (pp. 331–358). Greenwich, CT: JAI Press.

Clarkson, M. B. E. (1995). A stakeholder framework for analyzing and evaluating corporate social performance. *Academy of Management Review, 20*(1), 92–117.

Coombs, W. T. (1995). Choosing the right words: The development of guidelines for the selection of the "appropriate" crisis response strategies. *Management Communication Quarterly, 8,* 447–476.

Coombs, W. T. (1998). An analytic framework for crisis situations: Better responses from a better understanding of the situation. *Journal of Public Relations Research, 10,* 177–192.

Coombs, W. T., Hazleton, V., Holladay, S. J., & Chandler, R. C. (1995). The crisis grid: Theory and application in crisis management. In L. Barton (Ed.), *New avenues in risk and crisis management volume IV* (pp. 30–39). Las Vegas, NV: UNLV Small Business Development Center.

Coombs, W. T., & Holladay, S. J. (1996). Communication and attributions in a crisis: An experimental study of crisis communication. *Journal of Public Relations Research, 8*(4), 279–295.

Couretas, J. (1985, November). Preparing for the worst. *Business Marketing, 70,* 96–100.

DiMaggio, P. J., & Powell, W. W. (1991). The iron cage revisited: Institutional isomorphism and collective rationality in organization fields. In W. W. Powell & P. J. DiMaggio Eds.), *The new institutionalism in organizational analysis* (pp. 63–82). Chicago: University of Chicago Press.

Donaldson, T., & Preston, L. E. (1995). The stakeholder theory or the corporation: Concepts, evidence, and implications. *Academy of Management Review, 20*(1), 65–91.

Fearn-Banks, K. (1996). *Crisis communications: A casebook approach.* Mahwah: NJ: Lawrence Erlbaum Associates.

Freeman, R. E. (1984). *Strategic management: A stakeholder approach.* Boston: Pitman/Ballinger.

Hearit, K. M. (1994, Summer). Apologies and public relations crises at Chrysler, Toshiba, and Volvo. *Public Relations Review, 20*(2), 113–125.

Hobbs, J. D. (1995). Treachery by any other name: A case study of the Toshiba public relations crisis. *Management Communication Quarterly, 8,* 323–346.

Marcus, A. A., & Goodman, R. S. (1991). Victims and shareholders: The dilemmas of presenting corporate policy during a crisis. *Academy of Management Journal, 34,* 281–305.

Maynard, R. (1993, December). Handling a crisis effectively. *Nation's Business,* 54–55.

McAuley, E., Duncan, T. E., & Russell, D. W. (1992). Measuring causal attributions: The revised causal dimension scale (CDII). *Personality and Social Psychology Bulletin, 18,* 566– 573.

McCroskey, J. C. (1966). *An introduction to rhetorical communication.* Englewood Cliffs, NJ: Prentice-Hall.

Metts, S., & Cupach, W. R. (1989). Situational influence on the use of remedial strategies in embarrassing predicaments. *Communication Monographs, 56,* 151–162.

Mueller, W. (1990, September). Who's afraid of food? *American Demographics,* pp. 40–43.

O'Hair, D., Friedrich, G. W., Wiemann, J. M., & Wiemann, M. O. (1995). *Competent communi- cation*. New York: St. Martin's press.

Russell, D. (1982). The causal dimension scale: A measure of how individuals perceive causes. *Journal of Personality and Social Psychology, 42*, 1137-1145.

Seitel, F. P. (1983, May). 10 myths of handling bad news. *Bank Marketing*, 12-14.

Siomkos, G. & Shrivastava, P. (1993). Responding to product liability crises. *Long Range Planning, 26*(5), 72-79.

Snyder, A. (1991, April 8). Do boycotts work? *Adweek's Marketing Week*, (pp. 16-18).

Weiner, B. (1985a). An attributional theory of achievement motivation and emotion. *Psychology Review, 92*, 548-573.

Weiner, B. (1985b). "Spontaneous" causal thinking. *Psychological Bulletin, 97*(1), 74- 84.

Weiner, B., Amirkan, J., Folkes, V. S., & Verette, J. A. (1987). An attribution analysis of excuse giving: Studies of a naive theory of emotion. *Journal of Personality and Social Psychology, 53*, 316-324.

Weiner, B., Perry, R. P., & Magnusson, J. (1988). An attribution analysis of reactions to stigmas. *Journal of Personality and Social Psychology, 55*, 738-748.

Wilson, S. R., Cruz, M.G., Marshall, L. J., & Rao, N. (1993). An attribution analysis of compliance-gaining interactions. *Communication Monographs, 60*, 352-372.

Wong, P. T. P., & Weiner, B. (1981). When people ask "why" questions, and the heuristics of attributional search. *Journal of Personality and Social Psychology, 40*(4), 650-663.

Wood, D. (1991). Corporate social performance revisited. *Academy of Management Review, 16*, 691-718.

5

Issues Management:
A Relational Approach

ဆဝ✧ဝ

Janet A. Bridges
Department of Communication,
University of Southwestern Louisiana

Richard Alan Nelson
Manship School of Mass Communication,
Louisiana State University

This chapter seeks to accomplish three purposes: to place issues management firmly within the sphere of public relations practice; to provide an overview of major concepts, issues, and authors; and to draw some conclusions about developments in the field.

For many organizations, issues management often begins as reactions to a crisis or an event that has thrust its problem into the mass media or onto a legislative agenda. The implication is a focus on containment of or diffusion of a situation that is expected either to have a negative effect on the organization or to result in unfavorable regulation or litigation. This connotation of issues management presumes attempts to remove an issue—a potential problem—from the public agenda.

Two problems are evident in this problem removal approach to issues management: First, issues can be beneficial as well as problematic for organizations, and second, when an issue reaches the containment point, the management of issues management in reality is a failure or becomes a lobbying effort. As J. F. Coates, Coates, Jarratt, and Heinz (1986) remind us, the National Association of Manufacturers' "Life Cycle of a

Public Policy" demonstrates that an organization has decreasing ability to influence an issue as it develops to the legislative or litigation stages (p. 22). Grunig and Repper (1992) indicated that publics form around issues; only by proactively focusing on building and maintaining relationships with publics and potential publics can issues managers begin to protect their organizations from unwanted legislation and litigation. As McCombs (1977) warned, "Once an issue is highly salient and opinions are largely shaped, public relations may be limited to a defensive posture or a redundant 'me too-ism'" (p. 90).

This proactivity should extend as well to building favorable issues for the organization, and by extension to creating opportunities for favorable regulation or resolution of issues. Not all organizational regulation has unfavorable results. For example, J. A. Bridges and Bridges (1998) found that of the 66 corporate-related bills introduced into the 105th Congress, 60.6% were identified as procorporate. Building favorable issues is a development perspective on issues management, and the development perspective sees the issue as an opportunity. However, the term used to describe development of an opportunity issue may be programming or campaign management (see, for example, Hendrix, 1998, and general public relations textbooks).

Van Leuven and Slater's (1991) model presents a comprehensive discussion of media interest and the development of an opportunity issue to a result favorable to the organization. Their model of issue development suggests that an organization shepherds the issue through five stages: awareness, elaboration, understanding, attitude crystallization, and action.

The concept of managing issues appears in the literature from both the diffusion and the opportunity perspectives. For example, one criterion to determine whether an issue should be placed in an organization's issues-management system is that the issue presents *either* a threat *or* an opportunity for the organization (Heath, 1997); Renfro (1993) also indicated that an issues management system both promotes opportunities and avoids or mitigates threats. However, applied discussions do not seem to recognize this duality. Most discussions of issues management from the perspective of a practitioner's responsibility focus on diffusing negative situations before they attract media interest.

Both issues perspectives require early and continual attention to stakeholder relations, early identification of potential issues, and willingness of the organization to understand and accommodate stakeholder points of view. Both perspectives also require understanding of three political theories: schema theory, agenda-setting theory, and framing theory. Schema theory helps explain how media audiences and organizational stakeholder publics respond to media coverage and other information about an issue. Schema theory is discussed both as a moderating factor in agenda setting and in framing and as the focus of the relational perspective of issues management. Agenda-setting and framing theories are presented in the following paragraphs as explanations for the influence of media coverage on the development of an issue.

Issues management is a continuous process that emphasizes monitoring the environment and making adjustments to feedback from both the external and the internal environments. Effective issues management involves 10 functions:

1. Integrating public policy process issues analyses and audits into the organizational leadership's strategic planning;
2. Monitoring standards of organizational performance to discover the opinions and values key publics hold that may affect operations;
3. Developing and implementing ethical codes of organizational social accountability;
4. Assisting senior management in decision making, particularly in readjusting goals and operating policies vis-à-vis public opinion;
5. Identifying, defining, prioritizing, and analyzing empirically those issues of greatest operational, financial, and political significance to the organization;
6. Creating multidimensional proactive and reactive institutional response plans from among the range of available issue-change strategy options;
7. Establishing grassroots contact with potential cooperators (including the media);
8. Communicating on those issues identified as most important to the organization and its various key publics to establish an agenda and build external support;
9. Directing opinion to stall or mitigate the development and effects of undesirable legislation or regulation; and
10. Evaluating the impact of these efforts to determine whether objectives were achieved, direct ongoing improvements, and make further recommendations to management.

Underlying all 10 of these functions is the need for continual two-way communication with stakeholders before they become issues-oriented publics. This includes the need to act responsibly, to communicate this responsible behavior to appropriate stakeholders, to assess the effects of organizational behavior, and to secure commitments by upper management for these activities. No communication program can begin without research, and it is interesting to note that only 4 of the 10 functions involve actual communication behavior.

DEVELOPMENT OF AN ISSUE

Issues managers presume that their activities will affect issue development, but they need to understand that there is evidence that issues have a life cycle of their own (Downs, 1991; Heath, 1997). Issues develop through predictable patterns. These patterns include a step when the media become interested and move the issue from stakeholder tensions to public interest. Media coverage of an issue legitimizes that issue for the public, and media interest has been identified by both practitioners and theorists as a critical point in development of an issue (see for example, Cook & Skogan, 1991; Downs, 1991; Heath, 1997; Heath & Nelson, 1986; and Foote & Harte [as cited in Price, 1992]). Van Leuven and Slater (1991) suggest that the media perform two roles in the issue process. The media provide "running accounts of developing issue dimensions and events prompted by the issue," and the media provide "a description of how publics are organizing around an issue." Van Leuven and Slater cite Price and Roberts' use of the term "polltaking" to describe these reports of public response (p. 166).

The media are attracted to conflict about an issue. Corporate attention to an issue must be associated with a minimum of one identifiable group, which could well be a competing interest that provides conflict for the media. At least in the short term, media interest can also be attracted by an event, such as a protest, a public hearing, or a legal filing (for the latter, see Newsom, 1998; Roschwalb & Stack, 1995); or it can be attracted to conflict between competing interests, such as the organization and its relevant stakeholders. (For more stakeholder theory background and a useful bibliography, see the "Redefining the Corporation: An International Colloquy" web site, 1998)

AGENDA SETTING

Another criterion for whether an organization decides to focus on officially managing an issue is that the issue begins to appear in indexes, indicating legitimization by journalists (Heath, 1997). Heath has not said here that a specific organization is identified with the issue. The implication is that organizational issues managers should be alert enough to realize when an issue has potential impact on their organization. Entman (1993) also suggested that in the political process frames (see the following information) identify power by the sources and source positions included. No tobacco industry executive should have been surprised when public hearings began concerning the responsibility of the industry and public health. The media in the United States for years have been publicizing research supporting the relationship between smoking and both cancer and heart disease. Media coverage of the link between smoking and health as an issue was accompanied by media and political attention to containing the rising costs of health care. However, the industry developed a siege mentality that has resulted in considerable financial losses. Were it not for the dependency of tobacco industry workers on the revenue generated, these financial losses would probably have been greater (see Kasindorf, 1998). The issue of tobacco's contribution to health care costs and public health in general had become salient on the media agenda and also on the political agenda. Agenda setting is a process that suggests "the pattern of news coverage influences public perception of what are the important issues of the day" (McCombs, 1992). In his essay, McCombs explains that the theory, or "metaphor" (p. 815), presumes that coverage of and attention to issues by the mass media create a perception that the media-covered issues are important, or salient.

This salience may apply to the individual or to the individual's community. Additionally, some tests of the agenda-setting hypothesis have tied the agenda-setting effect to either an awareness of these issues or a belief that the media-covered issues are a priority, among a set of salient issues, for the individual or the community. McCombs (1992) notes two studies that have tied the agenda-setting effect to audience behavior (see Brosius & Kepplinger, 1992; Roberts, 1992), and one of these included advertising. Yet agenda setting as a concept implies a link with public opinion, as perception of salience of an issue implies mental attention to the issue. Thus agenda-setting re-

search specifically relates media effects to issues, and McCombs indi-
cates that in 20 years nearly all of these issues have been public issues.
(For other discussions of agenda setting, see Protess & McCombs, 1991;
Shaw & McCombs, 1977).

Agenda-setting researchers suggest, then, that media interest can
create public interest in an issue or make the issue important to the
general public. Heath (1997) reminds us that politicians and other
political communicators have their own agendas. They not only shape
but also respond to public opinion; therefore, issue salience has the
potential to move an issue onto the political agenda as well. In agenda-
setting terms, media interest can place an issue on the public agenda,
and that public agenda can be adopted as an agenda of politicians.

FRAMING

Not only *whether* the issue appears in the media, but *how* the issue appears
will be very important to an organization. If agenda setting affects *what*
the public thinks about, the frames around an issue can affect *how* the
public thinks about a topic (Maher, 1997; McCombs, 1992). The concept
of framing applied to issues management suggests that what is said, what
is omitted, and the terminology related to media coverage define an
issue for media audiences. For example, is NAFTA a way to increase
trade opportunities for American business or is it a potential drain on
jobs for American workers? The same treaty can be framed in several
different ways. Framing theorists suggest that the way an issue is presented—the frame—especially through the media, can affect public perceptions of the issue. As Entman (1993) explained:

> Framing essentially involves selection and salience. To frame is to select some
> aspects of a perceived reality and make them more salient in a communicating
> text, in such a way as to promote a particular problem definition, causal
> interpretation, moral evaluation, and/or treatment recommendation ...(p. 52)

He suggested that media frames can "define problems," including costs
and benefits; "diagnose causes"; "make moral judgments"; and "suggest
remedies," and that these frames are related to cultural values of the
time (p. 52). More important, Entman (1989) suggested a link between
media coverage and attitudes: "The way to control attitudes is to provide
a partial selection of information for a person to think about, or process.

The only way to influence what people think is precisely to shape what they think about" (p. 349).

Frames in issues campaigns could be seen as analogous to appeals. Davis's (1995) experiment with environmental communication found that the students who received varying definitions or appeals associated with the problem of environmental pollution were more willing to use environmentally responsible behavior if they received messages that emphasized negative consequences for their own generation. He had formed appeals in terms of environmental gains and environmental losses, both short and long term.

Entman (1989) also demonstrated effects of media framing, this time in relation to political attitudes, where some political targets reacted differently to the media messages based on their political leanings. Although not tied directly to issue framing, Dozier and Ehling (1992), Price (1992), and Nelson (1995, 1996) brought Lippmann's (as cited in Price, 1992, pp. 31–32) definitions to public opinion, suggesting that political activists are actors, a relatively small group that actually participates in resolving a problem. Price identified a larger group of "spectators" who provide the audience for these actor-activists. The larger the spectator group that focuses attention to an issue, the larger the issue becomes. This spectator group, and by extension public opinion or perceived support for the activist actors, can be both influenced and attracted, first by media coverage of an issue and even more important by the frame, or spin, presented with an issue. Although characteristics of the issue affect the influence of the media on an issue (see Yagade & Dozier, 1990; Zucker, 1978), media coverage can increase the size of this spectator group and by extension perception of the importance of the issue. However, neither placement on the public agenda nor effects of framing are absolute. Both Wanta and Wu (1992) and Weaver, Zhu, and Willnat (1992) have found that interpersonal communication can affect the agenda-setting process. The implication for issues managers is that communication in the relationship that an organization has built and maintained with its potential publics can influence the publics' reaction to media coverage.

J. Nasi, Nasi, Phillips, and Zyglidopoulos (1997) suggested that Sethi's legitimacy gap theory is one explanation of problems in issues management that create a need to diffuse an issue. Sethi (1994) explained that gaps in society's expectations of an organization and society's perceptions of the organization's behavior can create a problem with perceptions of the legitimacy of the organization itself. When the organization is no longer seen as being legitimate or behaving legitimately, the relationship of publics with the organization can break down (see also Nelson, 1990; Sethi & Falbe, 1987). An obvious reaction to legitimacy gap theory would be building a reputation for accuracy and legitimate behavior with target publics, in anticipation of mitigating the effects of media-created expectations. The focus is on mental perceptions of the organization, or, as is discussed in the following section, individual schemata.

PROCESSING INFORMATION

Grunig's situational publics theory suggests that an individual's information-seeking behavior could explain some of these differences in media effects. Grunig (1997) and Grunig and Repper (1992) segmented publics into four groups based on their likelihood to communicate with the organization. Definitions of these segments seem to have been refined over time; for example, in 1992, Grunig and Repper defined publics as stakeholders who have recognized the consequences of organizational activity or organizational policy as a problem and have organized to do something about it. They classified publics on their recognition of the problem itself, their perception that they can do something about the problem, and their perception that the organization's behavior involves them. Those who fit none of the three conditions were classified as a nonpublic; those who recognize the problem but see little involvement or ability to do something about the problem were identified as latent publics. In more recent works, nonpublics are defined as those who are not affected by the problem, whereas those who are affected but are not aware of the effect are classified as latent publics (Dozier, 1995).

Regardless of definition, neither the nonpublics nor the latent publics are expected to communicate about an issue, and media attention to the issue should have minimal effect. Even so, latent publics may become more active as an issue becomes more public. As the three conditions change—recognition of the problem grows, perceptions of involvement increase, and perceptions of constraints decrease—publics are expected to move into the aware and the active stages, similar to Lippmann's (as cited in Price, 1992) spectators and actives. At the aware and active stages, communication is expected to be more intense. Active publics, "who generate consequences" for the organization, are expected to seek information about the problem and the organization and to critically evaluate organizational messages (Dozier & Ehling, 1992, p. 171). If these actives oppose organizational policy, they may find their own sources of information, discount organizational communication, or do both. Other levels of publics may process rather than seek information, a more passive activity than information seeking (Dozier, 1995; Dozier and Ehling, 1992). Heath's (1997) discussion suggested that activist groups should be viewed as potential allies as well as potential adversaries, depending upon the issue and the mutual interests of the activists and the corporation.

Organizations could help create active publics by showing members of aware groups of potential allies how to remove constraints or even by creating feelings of personal involvement. Grunig's (Grunig, 1997; Grunig & Repper, 1992; Dozier & Ehling, 1992) situational theory of publics can help identify which groups may respond to organizational overtures. In dealing with adversarial activist groups, attention to Grunig's situational publics hierarchy can help generate two-way dialogue that can result in mutually favorable resolution of issues. Research should show what types of messages would be of interest to these groups. Problematic issues may thus be diffused before they reach the litigation, legislative or regulatory stage, coalitions may be formed to mutually take advantage of issue opportunities, or both events may occur. The type of information behavior displayed by a public group may affect reactions to media coverage of an issue.

Entman (1989), as noted previously, found variation in public reaction to framed media messages. He based his research on information-processing theory and concluded that exposure to diverse points of view can override some political ideology or "cognitive structure," the schemas used as organizational tools for thought. Schema theory can also serve as one explanation for the varying behaviors of stakeholders toward media coverage of an issue. According to Neuman, Just, and Crigler (1992), schema theory explains how individuals cope with political information within the broader "constraints and distractions" of life (p. 15).

In her extensive work on news processing, Graber (1988) explained how an individual's schema, or information-processing mechanism, helps that individual cope with the massive amounts of information produced by the mass media. She describes a schema as a "cognitive structure" that includes all of a person's "organized knowledge" about both "situations and individuals" that has been acquired from past experiences (p. 28). This knowledge includes factual information, information about relations among these facts, and anticipated sequences of events in a variety of situations. Both abstract and concrete information are included in schematas. If we visualize schemata as a series of mental file folders, specific examples are filed mentally with more general or abstract patterns of events. Individuals may organize their schemata, or mental file folders, under a broad ideological umbrella in which most information is related, or they may organize their personal schemata in several higher level mental files that may be only slightly related.

Graber (1988) effectively summarized characteristics of the use of schemata in processing information as follows:

1. The individual can "mentally restructure" the information by "adding, subtracting, or altering features so that the situation fits the established mental image more readily."
2. The individual may use thinking that "progresses readily from one schema to the next. ... Many schemata may overlap so that the same bits of information are stored in different contexts and often represent different perspectives."
3. Individuals have a "limited capacity for dealing with information ... [and] practice 'cognitive economies' by forming simplified [or generic] mental models ... about the world (pp. 28–29)."

Graber said schemata perform four major functions:

(a) They determine what information will be noticed, processed, and stored so that it becomes available for retrieval from memory. (b) They help individuals organize and evaluate new information so that it can be fitted into their established perceptions. This makes it unnecessary to construct new concepts whenever familiar information is presented. (c) Schemata make it possible for people to go beyond the immediate information presented to them and fill in missing information, which permits them to make sense of incomplete communications. (d) Schemata also help people solve problems because they contain information about likely scenarios and ways to cope with them. (p. 29)

These mental file folders allow individuals to react without having to reorient themselves every time a new piece of information is presented.

There may be preexisting evaluations, and even imagined scenarios, waiting to be accessed (Graber, 1988).

An understanding of schema theory and of the particular schemata associated with stakeholders should enable organizations to relate their communication to schemata-available material, making organizational communication more understandable and hopefully both acceptable and useful to the stakeholder. Using an example from the political arena, U.S. House Speaker Newt Gingrich (R–GA) in 1995 very carefully structured the Medicare debate around the terms "preserve, protect and strengthen" Medicare "for the next generation" (Weisskopf & Maraniss, 1995). The word "cut" was forbidden. Gingrich's trilogy of terms evolved from trials of "protect, improve, and preserve" and "preserve, protect, improve." The final trilogy has alliterative impact, even though "strengthen" has no alliterative relationship with "preserve" and "protect." Even more important, it taps into a public safety schemata associated with the "preserve, protect and defend" slogans painted on police cars in countless communities and, as Weisskopf and Maraniss noted, parallels the presidential oath of office. These terms were proposed after research with potential constituencies isolated expectations and concerns about pending Medicare legislation.

Issues can be dealt with at any stage of development, but the legislative and regulatory arena also involves public opinion that can be influenced when an issue becomes a priority for Lippmann's (as cited in Price, 1992) spectators. Issues managers need to understand the mass communication concepts of agenda setting and framing if they are to understand the passage of issues through this arena. Schema theory would suggest that maintaining relationships with stakeholders should provide these potential publics with mental perceptions of the organization that serve as a framework when issues are raised by competing groups. Media coverage should have less influence as pieces of information are tested mentally against information already stored in the minds of stakeholders.

BUILDING RELATIONSHIPS

Issues management requires making difficult decisions regarding relationships. Ironically, in the public relations approach to issues management, there has been very little serious attention paid to what is meant by relations, and the attention proposed is generally assumed to be at best communication by the organization's management to various constituent groups accompanied by evaluative research to determine the effects of this outreach. At its worst, no research is conducted and communication is reserved for clean up or crisis-type management.

Since the 1900s, farsighted companies have striven to develop policies that correspond to the standards of behavior expected by society. Moreover, leaders of innovative organizations have worked to implement these guidelines and audit the behavior of their employees toward others. These "others" make up the stakeholders whose relationships can have a major effect on the organization.

Eight publics or stakeholder groups comprise the publics with whom organizations need to maintain relationships: employee publics, member publics, community publics, government publics, investor publics, consumer–client publics, media publics, and special publics that don't fit into the other categories (Hendrix, 1998). Hendrix also included international publics as a separate category.

Dozier and Ehling (1992) applied Esman's (as cited in Dozier & Ehling, 1992, p. 170) linkage typology to stakeholders; Esman had identified four linkages to an organization's environment. The first two are organized or collective groups that Dozing and Ehling said are critical for an organization's survival:

1. Enabling linkages provide organizations "the right to exist and pursue their goals" (Dozier & Ehling, p. 170). These enabling linkages would include regulatory agencies and government sources.
2. Functional linkages provide the needed inputs and outputs. Inputs would be investors, who provide capital, suppliers of raw materials, and labor such as employees; outputs would be customers or clients.
3. Normative linkages provide links that "assist collective efforts to solve shared problems" (p. 170). These linkages include other organizations such as professional associations and industry or trade associations.
4. Diffused linkages are ties to "groupings of individuals who are not themselves part of an organization" (p. 170).

Individuals in these diffused linkages can organize into a cohesive active public or interest group whose activities influence members of the enabling linkage publics. Members of the media as individuals could be considered a diffused linkage, because they do not have a direct effect on the organization's survival. However, members of the media serve as a conduit for information, as noted previously, and must be considered as an important public.

Enabling Linkages

Linkages with the regulatory and governmental environments are commonly the responsibility of public affairs offices. Public affairs programs are communication efforts specifically designed to influence public policy, or affect legislation, regulations, political activities or even candidacies at the local, state, federal, or international levels (or both) so that the entity funding the program benefits.

In order to build and maintain relationships, public affairs communication programs must be continual rather than reactive. As indicated previously, politicians are sensitive to public opinion. If an organization has become part of a negative regulatory effort that is public, prior attitudes or knowledge about the organization may influence members of the process. The organization may also be given an opportunity to propose a solution, become part of the solution, or do both. Associations have been the most publicized actors in this type of endeavor. Both the National Association of Broadcasters (NAB) and the Chemical Manufacturers Association (CMA) have proposed and agreed to programs that have replaced potential regulative strictures.

During public hearings about children and television, the NAB proposal for program ratings avoided proposals that could have mandated timing of broadcast content and other restrictions. The CMA has mandated behavior for members and requires members to demonstrate their behavior as a condition of membership. The CMA provides communication about the industry's attempts to operate safely. For a discussion of the CMA activities, see Center and Jackson (1995).

Normative Linkages

The NAB and the CMA are examples of normative linkages for an organization. They are examples of associations that represent their members' interests and are often an organization's visible association with the government and with regulatory publics. Associations include trade and industry groups, professional societies, and chambers of commerce, for example.

Organizations can rely on these associations to represent their industry's best interests, but they cannot be certain that the association or its positions are best for a single organization. Heath (1997) reminded us that different corporations may have competing interests that can force an issue into the regulatory environment; if so, each organization must be alert to its own interests. Active membership and alliances within the appropriate associations create an excellent source of information about proposed regulatory problems and about industry developments, and they provide an opportunity to influence these developments. Even in a competitive environment, these organizations are also an excellent source of information and support for relations tied to functional linkages, especially with input linkages such as suppliers. They may also be very useful in providing information about output linkages, such as customers and clients. Employees and other internal groups, an input linkage, require a special type of relationship building. Although associations may be helpful in providing general guidance, organizations have to deal with each of their own internal groups as a special group affected by local conditions as well as by national norms.

Media Relations

As indicated previously, the mass media are often one link between an organization and many publics and can be critical in developing an issue that positively affects an organization. Media personnel are generally very wary of being manipulated, and those in an organization responsible for media relations should carefully cultivate and develop these relationships by acquiring a reputation for both truth and availability.

Media relations can establish the credibility of the organization so media writers contact the organization as a source when relevant problems or issues are in the news. If an organizational representative is perceived as a credible source, the organization has an opportunity to place its position forward. If the organization has established a reputation for credibility with the relevant media, a schemata has been created that should be activated when negative information reaches the media writer or reporter. Individuals attempting to establish media relations have an obligation to provide accurate and timely information and to respond to inquiries in the same manner, even when the truth is unpleasant. They also have an obligation to avoid flooding the media with time-wasting, self-serving material that has no news value. See Frazier (1992) for a discussion of faxes and flooding.

Functional Linkages

The largest and most diverse grouping of established publics is the functional linkages. If we use the list of eight publics, the functional linkages include three input linkages: investors, employees and members. Output publics would be consumer–clients.

Investor Publics. Investor relations, especially in large organizations, are commonly the responsibility of specialized public relations personnel who understand the investment environment and the investment community. Investor relations programs are directed to share owners, other investors, and the investment community as a whole. Some individuals are very active in their own investment decisions, but the primary public in investor relations is usually not the individual shareholder but an intermediary such as a fund manager or broker who advises, represents, or acts in behalf of groups of individual shareholders (or provides all three services). Writers who specialize in the investment market are also an important public. Because some large corporations are setting up mechanisms through which single investors may purchase stock individually, this primary public may expand to include these individuals. Regardless of the specific public identified, relationships with these publics must be honest. The investor public must have enough trust in the organization to wait out short-term downward trends with the organization's stock.

Employees or Members. Employees and member publics may be the responsibility of a specialized human relations practitioner who develops internal communications programs, but relationships with employees and members are the responsibility of all members of management. Internal communication programs are targeted specifically to special publics directly allied with an organization, and this alliance could include not only employees and members, but also franchisees, affiliated dealers, and other associated groups. Members and volunteers may be one common or two separate publics, especially for nonprofit organizations or for associations. Employees and members need to feel that they are part of the organization, that their contributions are recognized, and that the organization is a good citizen both locally and geographically beyond the local community. See Allen (1992) for a discussion of communication and employee perceptions of support.

Several trends in the corporate environment may make employee relations more difficult. First, corporate downsizing has affected employee loyalties, and an organization that has reached its optimum size will have to rebuild employee trust. Second, outsourcing, or contracting out work that had previously been done by employees, creates two problems. One is the same as the effects of downsizing; the second is that contractors are not really members of the organization, will be harder to reach with two-way communication, and have loyalties to themselves and to their entrepreneurial activities rather than to the organization. Third, the workforce is diversifying and will continue to diversify, in terms of gender, age, and ethnic composition. Relationships with this diverse public will require sensitive attention to the needs and even the cultures of diverse groups to reach compatible mutual goals (see Neher, 1997).

Tensions exist between the needs of two important input publics, investors and employees. One cannot benefit without the other, yet when resources are allocated, one takes from the other. Issues managers must deal with the tension.

Consumer–client Publics.   Consumers and clients will probably be a shared responsibility of marketing and public relations or issues managers. Marketing communication programs are designed to publicize and promote new products and services produced by the organization. However, marketing communication programs are not sufficient for consumer or for client relations (see Grunig, 1989.) A broader interactive or two-way communication program is needed to be certain that customers are satisfied, that their needs are being met, and that they perceive the organization as capable of meeting these needs.

Community Publics.   Community publics could be diffused linkages and could be enabler linkages as they regulate the community conditions that permit an organization to operate, but more likely they overlap the Esman (as cited in Dozier & Ehling, 1992) categories. Community publics establish and grant variances on zoning codes and tax districts and establish environmental and nuisance regulations, serving as enablers. Community publics could also be sources of employees, of consumers–clients, or of both. They could also form the basis for interest groups. Because of this diversity, community publics are considered a separate, unique category.

Community relations efforts seek to win the support or cooperation of or aim to improve relationships with people or organizations in communities in which the sponsoring organization has an interest, need, or opportunity. The organization must maintain a visible, positive profile in the community. Organizational members can serve on boards of nonprofit community organizations; organizations can donate funds to appropriate functions and causes; and they can provide release time for employees to provide community service. The organizational logo present on the ubiquitous t-shirts at community events, for example, quietly demonstrates an organization's participation in these types of community activities.

Organizations can ask community members to serve on their public service committees or boards and to participate in decisions to donate funds. Local media representatives should be part of these commit-tees—not for the organization's self-serving publicity, but because these media representatives will then have more knowledge about positive activities of the organization in their schemata.

DISCUSSION

Proper attention to the interpersonal aspects of various public relations efforts are of increasing importance given the liabilities associated with organizational miscues. Uncertainty is a reality. We live in a litigious society where financial opportunities often transcend relationships. Just as biological families experience tension and dissolution when the financial stakes reach critical levels or are perceived to be potentially high, so too there are simply no guarantees that organizational attention to stakeholder relationships will avoid all unfavorable legislation and litigation. However, effective commitment to ongoing stakeholder rela-tions certainly may help mitigate the outcome of conflicts tied to financial rewards.

Those caveats stated, organizations and public relations researchers committed to professional practice must conceptualize issues manage-ment in two ways: as resolving potential threats to and as providing potential opportunities for the organization. Organizations should not expect to manipulate issues, but instead should expect to use issues management principles to analyze and adapt to issues in ways that enhance conflict resolution. If an organization can identify and work with the affected public to determine and work toward mutual interests and goals, the organization has a good probability of ending organizational–public conflict.

This means, however, that organizations and those who run them have to be willing to integrate legitimate requests and prove sensitive to the genuine needs of various publics residing in the institutional environment. Managers also have to be certain that these publics are aware of changes being made on their behalf. An organization that expects to singularly change the environmental publics is on a direct path to regulation or litigation. Negotiation doesn't have to be a win–lose situation, and indeed organizations who negotiate from a win–lose framework take great risk.

Regardless of the conceptual framework employed by issues managers, attention to building and maintaining relationships with stakeholders can establish a dialogue and framework of mental relationships with the organization. This framework could be mobilized when an issue presents an opportunity for the organization or could be activated when an issue presents a threat. If an issues manager is systematically scanning the environment, few surprise threats or missed opportunities should arise. Publics who have been part of positive, continuing relationships that were established before a conflict develops will be more willing to understand the organization's position, to accept organizational overtures and changes as dependable, and to negotiate to a win–win solution. Management's commitment to the activities required for issues management is critical, as management determines financial allocations that support the issues management effort. Review of the 10 functions of issues management reveals that research identifying potential problems and then monitoring organizational behavior is critical.

Issues that never reach a crisis are difficult to document, even though it may have been the use of effective issues management that avoided the development of conflict. Issues managers need to learn to effectively evaluate the results of their activities if they are to present a credible argument to management to support their efforts. Documenting activities is not sufficient if their benefit to the organization cannot be documented. Without documentation, the time and other resources required to maintain positive relationships with publics may not be made available by management. If issues managers do not have good relationships with the organization's dominant coalition and become part of the decision structure, issues management will not be supported appropriately.

Developing and maintaining real relationships is hard work. The trials and tribulations found in establishing interpersonal connections can also be found within and without organizations. Organizations, including corporate and government entities, are simply collectives of people. Just as selfish behavior is often encountered in day-to-day interactions with others, so too can the field of public relations fall into the trap of being perceived as only the self-interest of the company, to the disadvantage of consumers and other stakeholders. Complex judgments are often based on available, incomplete information. Despite these limitations, experience shows that companies with good management seek to frame their issues campaigns around topics that also have relevance to others. Once corporations seek public support, take a stand on policy issues, or otherwise speak out, they need to reach and inform constituencies who are willing to serve as supporters. In such battles, the corporate interest must be conjoined with the self-interests of the targeted audience for a solid alliance.

REFERENCES

Allen, M. W. (1992, fall). Communication and organizational commitment: Perceived organizational support as a mediating factor. *Communication Quarterly, 40,* 357–367.

Bridges, J. A., & Bridges, L. W. (1998). Issues management and managing issues: Refining the concept. In J. Biberman, and A. F. Alkhafaji (Eds.), *Business research yearbook: Global business perspectives* V. (pp. 741–745) Saline, MI: McNaughton & Gunn in cooperation with the International Academy of Business Disciplines.

Brosius, H. B., & Kepplinger, H. M. (1992, winter). Beyond agenda setting: The influence of partisanship and television reporting on the electorate's voting intentions. *Journalism Quarterly, 69,* 893–901.

Center, A. H., & Jackson, P. (1995). *Public relations practices: Managerial case studies and problems* (5th ed.). Englewood Cliffs, NJ: Prentice Hall.

Coates, J. F., Coates, V. T., Jarratt, J., & Heinz, L. (1986). *Issues management: How you can plan, organize and manage for the future.* Mt. Airy, MD: Lomond.

Cook, F. L., & Skogan, W. G. (1991). Convergent and divergent voice models of the rise and fall of policy issues. In D. L. Protess & M. McCombs, (Eds.), *Agenda setting: Readings on media, public opinion, and policymaking* (pp. 189–206). Hillsdale, NJ: Lawrence Erlbaum Associates.

Davis, J. J. (1995, summer). The effects of message framing on response to environmental communications. *Journalism & Mass Communication Quarterly, 72,* 285–299.

Downs, A. (1991). Up and down with ecology: The "issue-attention cycle." In D. L. Protess & M. McCombs, (Eds.), *Agenda setting: Readings on media, public opinion, and policymaking* (pp. 27–33). Hillsdale, NJ: Lawrence Erlbaum Associates.

Dozier, D. M. (1995). *Manager's guide to excellence in public relations and communication management.* Mahwah, NJ: Lawrence Erlbaum Associates.

Dozier, D. M., & Ehling, W. P. (1992). Evaluation of public relations programs: What the literature tells us about their effects. In J. E. Grunig (Ed.), *Excellence in public relations and communication management* (pp. 159–184). Hillsdale, NJ: Lawrence Erlbaum Associates.

Entman, R. M. (1993). Framing: Toward clarification of a fractured paradigm. *Journal of Communication, 43*, 51–58.

Entman, R. M. (1989, May). How the media affect what people think: An information processing approach. *Journal of Politics, 51*, 347–370.

Frazier, L. D. (1992, winter/spring). The fax news flood: Editors grapple with technology's benefits, burdens. *Newspaper Research Journal, 13*, 100–111.

Graber, D. A. (1988). *Processing the news: How people tame the information tide* (2nd ed.). New York: Longman.

Grunig, J. E. (1989). Publics, audiences and market segments: Segmentation principles for campaigns. In C. T. Salmon (Ed.), *Information campaigns: Balancing social values and social change* (pp. 199–228). Newbury Park, CA: Sage.

Grunig, J. E. (1997). A situational theory of publics: Conceptual history, recent challenges and new research. In D. Moss, T. McManus, & D. Vecric (Eds.), *Public relations research: An international perspective* (pp. 3–48). London: International Thomson Business Press.

Grunig, J. E., & Repper, F. C. (1992). Strategic management, publics, and issues. In J. E. Grunig (Ed.), *Excellence in public relations and communication management* (pp. 117–157). Hillsdale, NJ: Lawrence Erlbaum Associates.

Heath, R. L. (1994). Issues management: The unfinished agenda. Paper presented to the International Communication Association, Sydney, Australia.

Heath, R. L. (1997). *Strategic issues management: Organizations and public policy challenges.* Thousand Oaks, CA: Sage.

Heath, R. L., & Nelson, R. A. (1986). *Issues management: Corporate public policymaking in an information society.* Newbury Park, CA: Sage.

Hendrix, J. A. (1998). *Public relations cases* (4th ed.). Belmont, CA: Wadsworth.

Kasindorf, M. (1998, April 23). Minnesota takes tobacco debate to another level: Persistence brings secrets out into open. *USA Today*, 6A.

Maher, T. M. (!997). Framing: A possible paradigm for communication research. In J. Biberman & A. F. Alkhafaji (Eds.), *Business research yearbook* IV (pp. 797–801). Slippery Rock, PA: International Academy of Business Disciplines.

McCombs, M. (1977, winter). Agenda setting function of mass media. *Public Relations Review, 3*, 89–95.

McCombs, M. E. (1992, winter). Explorers and surveyors: Expanding strategies for agenda-setting research. *Journalism Quarterly, 69*, 813–824.

Nasi, J., Nasi, S., Phillips, N. & Zyglidopoulos, S. (1997, September). The evolution of corporate social responsiveness: An exploratory study of Finnish and Canadian forestry companies. *Business and Society, 36*, 296–321.

Neher, W. W. (1997). *Organizational communication: Challenges of change, diversity, and continuity.* Boston: Allyn and Bacon.

Nelson, R. A. (1995). Activist groups and new technologies: Influencing the public affairs agenda. In L. B. Dennis (Ed.), *Practical public affairs in an era of change: A communications guide for business, government, and college* (pp. 413–422). New York: Public Relations Society of America/Public Affairs and Government Section, copublished with the University Press of America.

Nelson, R. A. (1990, spring). Bias versus fairness: The social utility of issues management. *Public Relations Review, 16*(1), 25–32.

Nelson, R. A. (1996). *A chronology and glossary of propaganda in the United States.* Westport, CT and London: Greenwood Press.

Newsom, D. (1998). Defining litigation in the marketplace of public opinion. In J. Biberman, & A. F. Alkhafaji (Eds.), *Business Research Yearbook: Global Business Perspectives* V (pp. 716–720). Saline, MI: McNaughton & Gunn in cooperation with the International Academy of Business Disciplines.

Neuman, W. R., Just, M. R., & Crigler, A. N. (1992). *Common knowledge: News and the construction of political meaning.* Chicago: University of Chicago Press.

Price, V. (1992). *Public Opinion.* Newbury Park, CA: Sage.

Protess, D. L., & McCombs, M. (Eds., 1991). *Agenda setting: Readings on media, public opinion, and policymaking.* Hillsdale, NJ: Lawrence Erlbaum Associates.

Redefining the Corporation: An international colloquy (1998). [On-line]. Available: http://www.mgmt.utoronto.ca:80˜stake/CCBE/Bibliography.html.

Renfro, W. L. (1993). *Issues management in strategic planning.* Westport, CT: Quorum Books.

Roberts, M. S. (1992, winter). Predicting voting behavior via the agenda-setting tradition. *Journalism Quarterly, 69*, 878–892.

Roschwalb, S. A., & Stack, R. A. (Eds., 1995). *Litigation public relations: Courting public opinion.* Littleton, CO: Fred B Rothman & Co.

Sethi, S. P. (1994). *Multinational corporations and the impact of public advocacy on corporate strategy: Nestle and the infant formula controversy.* Boston: Kluwer Academic.

Sethi, S. P., & Falbe, C. M. (Eds., 1987). *Business and society: Dimensions of conflict and cooperation.* Lexington, MA: Lexington Books.

Shaw, D. L., & McCombs, M. E. (Eds., 1977). *The emergence of American political issues: The agenda-setting function of the press.* St.Paul, MN: West Publishing.

Van Leuven, J. K., & Slater, M. D. (1991). How publics, public relations, and the media shape the public opinion process. *Public Relations Research Annual, 3*, 165–178.

Wanta, W., & Wu, Y. C. (1992, Winter). Interpersonal communication and the agenda-setting process. *Journalism Quarterly, 69*, 847–855.

Weaver, D. H., Zhu, J. H., & Willnat, L. (1992, Winter). The bridging function of interpersonal communication in agenda setting. *Journalism Quarterly, 69*, 856–867.

Weisskopf, M., & Maraniss, D. (1995, November 6–12). Gingrich's war of words: How he and his legions marshaled the forces of rhetoric to change medicare. *The Washington Post National Weekly Edition*, 6–8.

Yagade, A., & Dozier, D. M. (1990). The media agenda-setting effect of concrete versus abstract issues. *Journalism Quarterly, 67*, 3–10.

Zucker, H. G. (1978). The variable nature of news media influence. In B. D. Ruben (Ed.), *Communication Yearbook, 2*, 225–240.

6

Relationship Management: A New Professional Model

ಬಿ ✧ ಛ

Susan L. Dimmick
University of Tennessee
with
Traci E. Bell
SCI Publications

Samuel G. Burgiss
University of Tennessee Medical Center

Caroline Ragsdale
*Tennessee Department of Economic
and Community Development*

In pursuing the notion of public relations as relationship management, numerous scholars have identified the dimension of trust as critical. In a seminal article on public relations models, Leichty and Springston (1993) described the process of building trust in an interpersonal relationship: "One party takes a small risk by disclosing a small piece of personal information. ... If the other party reciprocates the self-disclosure, then the first party is likely to self-disclose again ... (and) mutual trust emerges from a positive feedback spiral" (pp. 180–188). Leichty and Springston (1993) noted that "building trust between an organization and its publics probably follows a similar cycle" (p. 335).

This notion is reinforced by Grunig (1993, p. 135) in his article concerning symbolic and behavioral relationships. Grunig wrote of " ... two concepts that are stalwarts of theories of interpersonal communication, trust and credibility, and the concept of reciprocity" (p. 135). Grunig notes that researchers and practitioners "could use any of these concepts to measure the quality of behavioral relationships of organizations, but the following seem to be the most important: reciprocity, trust, credibility, mutual legitimacy, openness, mutual satisfaction, and mutual understanding" (p. 135). In addition, Ledingham and Bruning (1998) have demonstrated that programs developed around the relationship dimensions identified in their research of openness, trust, investment, involvement and commitment "can engender loyalty toward an organization among key publics when that involvement is known by key publics" (p. 63).

This chapter examines transcripts from a case study conducted with health care providers, physicians, and patients. This case study was a needs assessment concerning the introduction of a patient-held health record (PHHR) for use by patients, physicians, and providers at a mid-South hospital. Neither the physician–patient relationship, nor the dimensions that may impact that relationship, were the central foci of the original investigation. However, to ignore the connection between the results in this case study and the research and models cited in the literature would be to miss an opportunity, for no good reason, to further the development of general relationship models in what is clearly an important stream of research for the study and practice of public relations.

Physicians' and providers' discussions about a PHHR revealed relationship issues related to trust, openness, reciprocity, and mutual understanding. Such dimensions play an important role in the physician–patient setting, and insights about them are gleaned through a number of in-depth, qualitative interviews with representatives of a number of perspectives in the provider–patient relationship. For the purposes of this study, *trust* is defined as a willingness to self-disclose and a willingness to have that self-disclosure known to another. *Openness* is a willingness to "consult the relationship partner" (Grunig & Grunig, 1992, citing Fisher & Brown, 1988, p. 315). Reciprocity is characterized by cooperation, collaboration and coordination rather than domination, power and control (Broom, 1997, citing Oliver, 1990, pp. 243–246). Mutual understanding is the degree to which two or more individuals feel that their perspectives have been taken into account.

The results of this case study provide clues into ways both physicians and patients might forge a new relationship based on mutual understanding and benefit. They also demonstrate the folly of continued reliance on the well-documented asymmetric communication model that dominates health care relationships in the United States. (Research documentation of both the power and communication asymmetry in physician–patient relationships is extensive. A good recent overview is Roter & Hall, 1992).

SETTING AND METHOD

The health card study was conducted at a 602-bed acute care facility. Focused small group discussions with physicians, patients, and medical center administrators who might play a critical role in making a card available were conducted. Participants were asked to focus on the advantages and disadvantages of patients having an electronic PHHR. The original transcripts were reexamined to study trust, openness, reciprocity, and mutual understanding issues from the points of view of patients, physicians, and other health care providers. Physicians, nurses, and administrators associated with those departments that would be contact points for using a PHHR were interviewed in focused small groups and in key informant interviews. Cancer patients and patients registering in the outpatient department during April 1997 were interviewed individually about the advantages and disadvantages of a PHHR. Cancer patients were chosen because of the repetitive nature of their visits and the role a PHHR might play in facilitating those visits. Outpatients were interviewed to understand the viewpoints of a variety of patients. Forty-three patients were interviewed and access to them was granted on the condition that their hospital or physician visit not be disrupted. Patients were interviewed to the point of redundancy and no new information was captured after the 43rd interview.

RESULTS

Patients

Patients reacted very favorably toward the idea of having a portable health record. In doing so, they clearly indicated a willingness to make things easier for themselves and for their health care providers by helping to keep track of their own medical data. Excessive paperwork, repetition of medical histories, and waiting were identified by 51% of cancer patients and 25% of outpatients as problems that could be solved by the PHHR. Patients also indicated very strongly that they trusted their doctors and the medical center. Comments recorded in the open-ended sections of the patient interviews indicated a strong sense of trust. For example, one patient said

> I'm not one to switch doctors. I've been here for 4 years and they take good care of me. If I have any problems with the hospital, I just tell my doctor and he sees (that) it gets taken care of.

Patients trusted that the medical information on a potential PHHR would be correct and used for their benefit: "This is good for [the hospital]. You know, this is really a progressive hospital, and they've made many advances within the past 10 years. They never stop trying new things and this is another way to help patients."

Feelings of openness were evident: "If it [the information on the card] was wrong, I would know it and tell them." Feelings of being understood were evident as well: "I'd feel like they knew me. They would have all your information and know you on a regular basis; and, I would feel more familiar with what they were doing." "I don't know if anyone has mentioned the word 'secure.' People would feel more secure because it [the health card] gives them a sense of belonging to [the medical center]. They're a preferred customer. I'm a PC [preferred customer]." Additionally, there were indications that reciprocity was expected: "I don't tolerate them (problems). If I go to the hospital, it's for a purpose and I want to be waited on. I'm very nice to people, too. That makes them want to help you."

The most common complaints in the open-ended question section were about waiting, paperwork, and answering questions. Typical comments were "Paperwork. I have to fill out the same thing ... the same information at each doctor's office. I have to carry a list of medications," and "I requested lab work results be sent to two doctors and one doctor never got it. I always have to fill out extensive forms in the lab and then they end up chasing the results down anyway."

None of the patients interviewed said that they would forget their PHHR if it were ever issued, and none of them said that they would need an incentive to remember it. "Reducing the paperwork would be incentive enough" was a typical opinion. The majority of patients could not think of any information that they did not want on the card. This indicates a strong willingness on the part of patients to risk revealing themselves by making their medical life histories very accessible to medical personnel and to their doctors. Additionally, all patients said that they were willing to assume the responsibility of carrying the PHHR with them, without the need of an incentive to remember it. This indicates a clear willingness to assume more responsibility in health care relationships, by helping to make the relationship more cooperative and collaborative.

In summary, the closed- and open-ended answers related to the PHHR demonstrated strong sentiments of trust, openness, feeling understood and reciprocity. The medical center was viewed as "progressive" and "caring" because patients believed that it was going to return some autonomy to them by allowing them to have a portable health record that was perceived to make their access to medical care easier (100%); more convenient (94.7%); more time efficient (94.7%) and less anxious (57.9%). These interpersonal relationship dimensions remained as "trace elements" in a dialogue that was initiated to talk about another topic, the PHHR. Patients were never asked directly about their health care relationships, yet their feelings about important aspects of relationships were left like footprints in the snow to interpret without fear of their having given the polite or socially correct answer.

Physicians

In contrast to patient perspectives, physicians were much more guarded about the prospect of patients having a portable health record. The objections that physicians raised were related to the accuracy and currency of the medical information on the PHHR. They were concerned that those who had access to the PHHR might not correctly interpret the information. There was a strong sense of mistrust. One physician said that he would always check a patient's blood type, even if it was recorded on a PHHR, or on a military dog tag, for that matter.

Physicians agreed that the less medical information there was on the PHHR, the better, "or there will never be agreement about what information should be on it." This is an indication that there is little sharing of medical information, either between physicians and other health care providers or between patients and physicians. (A long and extensive body of health communication research on doctor–patient relationships bears this out. There are many citations, but for an overview and summary, see Roter & Hall, 1992.)

Two physicians agreed that limited information could be put on a PHHR without causing too much "damage." This information would be "static," such as previous surgeries, illnesses, and allergies.

> I think static facts could be there. So, if you had your uterus out, it's not going to grow back. If you had pneumonia that you recovered from last year, well, that's not going to change. The most static facts will be the medical history. If you're allergic to green beans, you're always allergic to green beans.

However, the other physicians thought that static medical information would be a problem precisely because it was static and not up-to-date: "I guess I kind of have doubts about the reliability of medical information on the card because it's static, and things happen between the time it was last updated."

> I would be uncomfortable if it could not access whatever type of encounters I could have, not just acute therapy, like outpatient or lab work or physical therapy. What good is the card going to do if it can't access that information for all of those patient encounters?

Without the ability to update medical information, physicians said that they could not trust the content of the PHHR. One physician said such out-of-date information would be "very harmful." However, physicians also were reluctant to trust those who would access the PHHR to update it. Both they and other administrators wanted an assurance that the date and identification of the person who last accessed the PHHR would be readily apparent. The most acceptable application of the PHHR would be within the medical center, making the PHHR a simple identification card that would trigger access to medical records already on file within the institution. The following is an example of the ambivalence that one doctor felt:

> When I talked to Sam about this project early on I was, I mean it is a great idea, but knowing what we have now, the mess we have now, and how fragmented the medical information is already, my thoughts were that we either had to use the card for some very basic patient registration, identification issues, or we had to choose a population that was small and easily identified to test …the more sophisticated application on, and then I became concerned just thinking about money, about what we are doing already with our computerized patient records, and God knows we don't want another system out there.

This remark prompted other participants to reach the beginning of a consensus that the best use of a PHHR might be as an identification tool to trigger access to internal medical records: "Well, if it is a card that is used for patient identification that accesses what we already have in our system, that makes it infinitely more functional and more attractive."

This option would allow providers to retain control of the medical record and have it contain only identifying information, such as name, address, date of birth, and social security number. One other doctor was willing to add "sociologic data," such as "what church I go to, what minister needs to be notified if things go bad, my caretaker or next-of-kin to be notified. ... " He was also willing to have permanent medical facts included, such as allergies, although "as soon as you start putting any sensitive data on the card, you're going to get into trouble." He added, "There won't be any agreement about what to put on the card. Some doctors will want all kinds of information, and some won't want anything on there."

This physician, and others in the focus group, also were mistrustful of patients' use of the PHHR. They wanted a photograph on the PHHR because "that's a real good guard against fraud." He, like other physicians, felt that patients would need an incentive to remember a PHHR. "Parking. People would absolutely adore that. ... Bring in your card and get a 10% discount on parking." Physicians did not indicate in their talk about the PHHR that they thought patients would be sufficiently interested in their own medical records to remember to bring them. This is in contrast to what patients actually said. The patients interviewed said unanimously that they would not need an incentive to remember to bring their PHHR.

One of the physicians was asked whether he had any qualms about patients carrying around their own records. The physician responded, "I don't really have a lot of qualms about people carrying around the record I'm talking about. I think you have a right to have that information written down. I don't think there is anything wrong with that."

This physician, who was in the initial focus group, was reinterviewed at some length because he was retired and had been with the medical center for a very long time. He noted that he would support a PHHR if it was "the kind I'm talking about," meaning an identification tool with a minimum number of static medical facts. He also noted that the PHHR really wasn't as useful to the patient as it was to the medical center: "I think [it should be] the one buck card with the rest of the information readily available. It doesn't do any good if it's in the patient's pocket. Where it's needed is at the interface [in the medical institution.]"

One other physician was interviewed as a key informant. He could not attend the focus group and was chosen because he was a respected opinion leader in the medical center. He said that a "disease-oriented card" would work better for patients "because they would keep up with that." He favored a PHHR if it was embedded within a medical record system that would allow providers to "talk to one another."

> I could see where this would very easily be applicable to oncology patients, and I think they would have a high buy-in because of the way oncology is delivered. It is like multiple specialties, like they may go to one doctor on Monday and another on Wednesday and another doctor on Friday. There is no way the information could transfer that rapidly in a nonintegrating information system. ... Now I could see that smart card putting it [medical information] into the computer, transferring the data onto the smart card, going off and when the patient comes back three weeks later for their next check, there it is.

This physician saw the PHHR as a way to reduce the cost of medicine by helping to avert redundant testing.

> Well, it happens all the time. People go see other doctors. They come to see me and they have seen other doctors. I ask them, " when have you seen Dr. X last?" "Well, he said he would send you a note or a copy of the lab." It happens all the time—over and over. That drives the cost of medicine up because there is so much duplication because I can't get Dr. X's records. "You've got to have this test. I am sorry you've got to do it again, sorry."

This physician also saw the PHHR as a way to reduce the number of times that patients had to give their medical history: "You could take this comprehensive medical history that is on the screen that everybody agrees upon instead of asking those questions 47 times. ..."

In answer to the question of what benefit the PHHR might have for patients, he said, "Three words: continuity of care. It's just less hassle." He added that the PHHR could:

> Give them a sense of ownership. This is where I go to get my care. This identifies me as a patient in that facility. And the other thing is it saves a lot of time because they won't have to fill out forms and answer questions.

This physician's perspective about the PHHR was different from the other physicians' perspectives. His talk reflected far more empathy with patients and his remarks were more reflective of the actual problems and benefits about the PHHR expressed by patients in their interviews. Empathy, of course, appears to be a necessary condition for the creation of mutual understanding in a relationship. This particular physician had longer term relationships with patients, and more intense ones, because he is a cancer specialist engaged in the management of chemo and radiation therapy. These are longer term treatments that usually require more physician–patient involvement over a period of time. The implications of that longer term involvement for the management of physician–patient relationship is discussed in the section on Conclusions.

In summary, physicians' remarks were characterized mainly by mistrust, both of the information provided by other health care providers and by the patients themselves. Most physicians were willing to entertain the idea of the PHHR as an identification tool, again an indication that patients can't be trusted to represent themselves as who they are or to represent their conditions correctly. Most of the physicians were concerned about losing control over the creation of and access to medical information. This indicates a definite tendency toward lack of openness, not only with patients but with other providers as well. Physicians' remarks also indicated that they did not have an accurate understanding of patients' stated desires to take responsibility for the PHHR without need of an incentive to bring it or to not lose it. Allowing portability of a health record was considered to be harmful even though patients said portability would be beneficial. In the majority of physicians' remarks, there was no real sense that reciprocity of any kind was necessary. This absence of commentary about reciprocal obligations and benefits may reflect physicians' views that the physician–patient relationship is a professional one, and one that confers upon the physician the status of medical authority. This medical authority is buttressed by formal licensure, which involves control of the knowledge base and practice of medicine in all its forms, including pharmaceuticals. Medical authority is vertically integrated so that health problems invariably require professional consultation. Therefore, in professional consultations "stress is placed on the necessity of faith or trust in the practitioner" because the patient is "captive in a closed universe of practitioners established in an official position in society" (Friedson, pp. 116, 119). A faith-based trust

requires no dialogue; in fact, deference forms the basis for a professionalized view of reciprocity.

Other Providers

The comments of other service providers were chiefly those of inpatient
and outpatient registration managers, as well as those of two managers
of satellite physicians' groups. Mistrust was a significant barrier to a
portable medical record. These providers felt even more strongly than
physicians that patients weren't to be trusted with a PHHR because they
would "swap" the cards around:

> Particularly in the clinic they will swap them. A picture might be helpful there.
> I think in the long run it is going to be a thumbprint or eyeball scan. There
> would have to be something on it that would let you know that it really
> belonged to the person holding it.

Another disadvantage cited was that patients would either lose their
PHHR or forget it:

> You've got to think of it from the patient's perspective and when they come
> in the last thing they want to do is to take out their driver's license and their
> insurance card, and now you've given them another card. Half of them won't
> have it. The [low-income] population, I can just about guarantee you, they
> won't bring these things and we have massive experience with that. They just
> don't bring them.

and:

> They'll lose it. Fifty percent lose their card. The Medicare patient will get
> flustered and upset—the older Medicare patient 75 and above—will get upset.
> What does it look like? Where is it? That is what they go through. They get
> very aggravated. The current managed care situation in this town is such that
> people are changing their insurances very frequently. I can't take your card if
> it has insurance on it because I can't trust that it is going to be right.

There also were significant trust problems related to physician's
medical information: "If I felt like I could trust the information in the
physician's offices, I probably would be more open to the idea. It's just
that their information is usually not very good. They don't put much
emphasis on it."

The reason that accuracy about the diagnosis is important is because
the medical center cannot be reimbursed for services unless there is

precertification that the patient's illness and its treatment is reimbursable. The registration people are the "front line people" for making sure that collection on the hospital bill is possible: "The ability to collect an account totally depends on these two guys and if they don't do it right, I don't collect. It's pretty cut and dry, if they don't do their job right, we don't collect the money."

Like physicians, control was important:

> If I made the card, then I wouldn't have a problem at all with that because I've got control of the data. ... the database was just useless, you try to pull information out of it and it doesn't tell you anything and here in the hospital you really need that information to collect insurance money.

There was a sense among a few providers that a PHHR could create better accessibility, at least institutionally. There was frustration that the mass of medical information out there could be valuable if it were accessible.

> Outpatient records are extremely obscure, difficult to obtain, and impossible to read, very incomplete. Work done in the hospital hardly ever makes its way to the outpatient department, and I think anything that would improve access to records would be tremendously cost effective because we waste an awful lot of time, and we cannot get any information.

This kind of remark indicates a willingness to share and be open and that the PHHR might play a role in facilitating at least information exchange. Providers also said that other advantages of a PHHR would be time savings on the front end, access to accurate information, and "theoretically, it will allow one provider to communicate with another provider." However, the willingness to be open seems to be limited to communication with other providers. Most of the administrators thought that patient involvement with a PHHR would be problematic: "Creating a card for clinic patients with their past medical history on it would be, well that is a labor intensive thing...."

Providers thought that patients would need some kind of incentive to make the PHHR worthwhile: "I guess, too, you have got to make it worth something to them, say, save them time in line. We can't even get employees to do things that aren't worth something to them."

Providers were asked whether they thought patients wanted a PHHR: "If they think it will get them something, if they think it will get them in there quicker. If they perceive it, whether it is or it isn't, but it is not going to get things done quicker...."

However, one provider did seem to understand the patient's point of view and how a PHHR might resolve a common patient complaint:

> You give it [the card] to a patient who is being sent to the hospital for specific tests, and you make it a nonpainful experience for the patient. That will impress them, especially if they have been in places where they have had painful experiences before. A painful experience is being there all day for a 20-minute test.

Like most physicians in the case study, most providers did not have an accurate understanding of why patients wanted a PHHR and that their desire for a PHHR wasn't something that would have to be cultivated with incentives. Again, the difference in perspectives about the PHHR illuminated differences in how providers and patients viewed their relationship, with providers wanting to retain control.

Most providers viewed reciprocity as an economic exchange, or a payment for services rendered. Most of them viewed the PHHR and patients' involvement with it as a potential obstacle to payment because payment is contingent on a physician's determination of illness. Therefore, physicians, and only physicians with medical center privileges, should have access to the patient's health record so the system of services and payment would not be upset by outside interference. However, one provider did note that a PHHR as a "preregistration card could have competitive advantage in the healthcare marketplace." He said that within 3 to 5 years the competition among hospitals was going to break down into "hand-to-hand combat" and that the difference would be "service."

> You are always going to have a degree of competition. It's just been reduced. And I can see two people talking, comparing their experiences, "Well, my doctor gave me this card and I went to the hospital and there was no hassle. They just took my card and I was pre-registered." And someone else says, "Well, I went to the hospital and it took all day." I think it's going to come to just a small difference in the future. Costwise we have got to be competitive with one another. The doctors, they are pretty much the same. The differential is going to be customer service. I think anything has the potential if it gives the customer value. What is value? Value is a discount, saving money or saving time. Save me aggravation.

In summary, most providers, much like most physicians, had similar feelings of mistrust toward patients and physicians' offices outside of the medical center network, they were suspicious about sharing information and lacked openness, and they seemed to misunderstand what patients wanted and why. Providers did not want a portable health record, as patients wanted, but could support the PHHR as an identification card. This would permit providers to retain control of medical information but would address patients' concerns about paperwork and repeating their medical histories. Providers' understanding of reciprocity was construed as an economic exchange based on services rendered and on the understanding that patient relationships needed to be structured to facilitate that economic exchange.

DISCUSSION AND CONCLUSIONS

Although the results of this case study cannot be generalized to larger populations of patients, physicians, or other health care providers, their indirect reflections on relationship dimensions are a step toward understanding the meaning and importance of those dimensions in relationships as they are perceived by the interactants. The necessity of understanding how important publics perceive their relationships takes on greater urgency when change occurs in an industry, as Ledingham and Bruning (1997) found in their study of competition in the telecommunications industry. Similar competitive struggles have consumed the health care industry and the "hand-to-hand combat" that one provider identified in this study is a significant catalyst for a better understanding of how health care relationships are created, developed, and maintained. Additionally, physician groups are becoming larger and are affiliating with integrated medical centers. Therefore, the management of the provider–patient relationship can be conducted at the organization–public level.

Results from this case study indicate that patients are more interpersonally oriented in their view of their relationships with health care providers. They appear to trust their physicians and the medical center, and that's important to them. In fact, even though they have problems with waiting and paperwork and repeating their medical histories, they are willing to carry a PHHR to help minimize these problems. They value openness and speak in terms of the importance of being known and understood. They want more responsibility in making their relationship with their physicians and their medical center more productive by being responsible for carrying a PHHR. They appear ready, willing, and able to collaborate with providers to solve problems.

Both physicians and providers were more professionally oriented in their view of what relationships should be like with patients. For physicians, professional prerogative dictates that there should be a faith-based trust and for that reason, sharing a health record with the patient is problematic and harmful. Control of medical information is considered critical. Openness disrupts the system of service and the repayment that the professionalization of medicine has accorded them. Their understanding of patients' desire to have a PHHR was predicated on the belief that patients wanted something that they didn't really need to have, unless it was to better identify them as patients who were entitled to insurance benefits and as a check on fraud.

The significance of the difference between what patients valued in their relationships with health care providers and what health care providers valued in that relationship is that a competitive environment exacerbates the need for loyalty. Loyalty can be cultivated by paying attention to interpersonal relationship dimensions (Ledingham and Bruning, 1997, 1998). In the case of health care, what patients value is trust, openness, mutual understanding, and collaboration (reciprocity). What physicians and other providers deliver is medical expertise in an impersonal, professionalized relationship.

What is in need of continued exploration are ways to modify the professionalized relationship between health care providers and patients to permit the development of a more personalized one, one that we know patients would value. To that end the following model is proposed, based on this case study, on an extensive review of the health communication literature (see references), and on the work of the following communication researchers. Leichty and Springston (1993) advised that dynamic public relations models should be situational and developmental and should identify a sequence of relational stages in an evolving organization–public relationship. Broom, Casey, and Ritchey (1997) addressed the need to identify antecedents and consequences of a relationship, and also noted the preeminence of the communication linkage for understanding the state of the relationship. Ledingham and Bruning (1998) identified the interpersonal relationship dimensions that distinguish those who remain or leave an organization–public relationship in a competitive environment. L. A. Grunig (1987) addressed the need to vary relationship strategies according to the nature of the public involved. J. E. Grunig (1993) identified concepts that can be used to measure the quality of behavioral relationships of organizations.

Following Broom et al. (1997), antecedents are those characteristics upon which a relationship depends, and there are two sets of antecedents for each actor in the health care provider–patient relationship. Antecedent conditions can be measured at Time 1, the current state, and reassessed at Time n, the desired state, as can be seen in Fig. 6.1. Additionally, antecedents can be further categorized at the individual, professional, and institutional levels for health care providers and at the individual level for patients. For providers, individualistic antecedents include social and cultural norms, communication competence and individual expectations about the provider–patient relationship. For providers, there also are professional norms developed through education and licensure that shape collective perceptions and expectations about patient relationships. Case study data indicate that professional norms are a significant predictor of relationship behavior. Professional specialty also affects behavior. Institutional antecedents include legal and voluntary necessity, perceptions of an uncertain environment, and the need for resources, including the need for third-party reimbursement arrangements. Antecedents for patients include social and cultural norms, communication competence, expectations about the relationship, disposition toward loyalty or willingness to stay in the relationship, the need for medical resources, and type of resources sought (e.g., acute care; chronic, long-term care; routine, short-term care). Providers relate differently to these patient publics as was suggested in the case study. For example, oncologists have more frequent contact of a longer duration with their cancer patients. The level of intensity is higher because of the frequent life-or-death nature of cancer and its treatment. Additional research may confirm an association between specialty and differential relational strategies with health care publics, and can add to our understanding of exhaustive and mutually exclusive categories of antecedents.

The relationship between providers and patients is created through interaction prescribed by antecedent conditions. This is accomplished through communication linkages. The state of that linkage can be assessed by measuring the qualities identified by Broom et al. (1997), including the communication linkage's degree of symmetry, its intensity, its content, its frequency and duration, and its valence (positive or

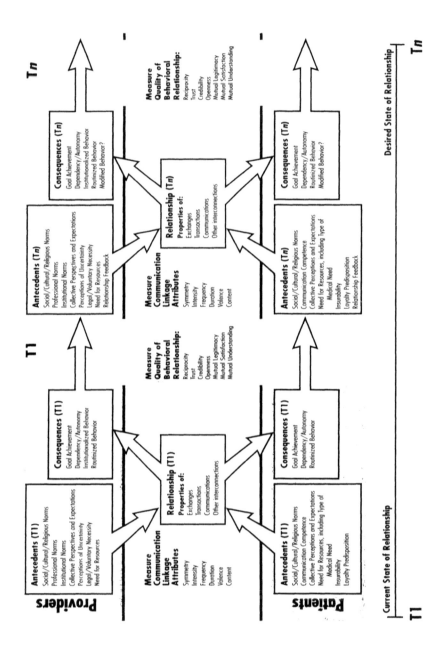

FIG. 6.1. Antecedents and Consequences in a Developing Health Care Relationship.

132

negative attitude toward the linkage). The health communication research literature allows the construction of a general picture of the "typical" relationship between providers and patients in the U.S. health care industry. The relationship is characterized by asymmetry, with dominance and control exerted by the provider, chiefly due to professionalization measures that restrict knowledge and practice to a small group of practitioners while cutting off problem solving alternatives for patients in need of traditional medical resources.

The consequences of the relationship result in changes in goal states, and in behavior changes in both interactants. When the consequences of the relationship are felt, the quality of the behavioral relationship can be assessed using Grunig's (1993) criteria. These qualities include the level of reciprocity, trust, openness, credibility, mutual legitimacy and understanding. An assessment of relationship quality can be done formally or informally by any of the interactants. Consequences feed back to antecedents, thus reconfiguring, to some degree, the antecedent conditions that guide interaction and the reformation of the professional relationship over time.

This model permits the measurement of important indicators of the nature, strength, and quality of the relationship over time. An assessment of these indicators would permit an organization to adapt its public relations strategy to a particular stage of the relationship. It also permits an assessment of how to move an organization toward a more symmetrical relationship by benchmarking the state of the communication linkages (symmetry, intensity, frequency, duration, valence, and content) and the quality of the behavioral relationship (reciprocity, trust, credibility, openness, mutual legitimacy, satisfaction, and understanding) at different points in time. Additional research is necessary to field test these lineage and quality attributes, and the model as it may apply to assessing the development of organization–public relationships over time.

REFERENCES AND SELECTED READINGS

Allman, R. M., Yoels, W. C., & Clair, J. M. (1993). Reconciling the agendas of physicians and patients. In J. M. Clair & R. M. Allman (Eds.), *Sociomedical perspectives on patient care* (pp. 29–46). Lexington: The University Press of Kentucky.

Amatayakul, M. K., & Wogan, M. J. (1992). Record administrators' needs for computer-based patient records. In K. J. Hannah & M. J. Ball (Eds.), *Aspects of the computer-based patient record* (pp. 57–64). New York: Springer-Verlag.

Ballard-Reisch, D. S. (1990). A model of participative decision making for physician–patient Interaction. *Health Communication, 2*(2), 91–104.

Beisecker, A. E. (1990). Patient power in doctor-patient communication: What do we know? *Health Communication, 2*(2), 105–122.

Bell, T. E. (1997). *A needs assessment of patient health card technology at a university teaching medical center*. Unpublished master's thesis, University of Tennessee, Knoxville.

Bronson, D. L., Costanza, M. C., & Tufo, H. M. (1986). Using medical records for older patient education in ambulatory practice. *Medical Care, 24*, 332–339.

Broom, G. M., Casey, S., & Ritchey, J. (1997). Toward a concept and theory of organization-public relationships. *Journal of Public Relations Research, 9*(2), 83–98.

Buckley, W. H. (1992). Patients' needs for computer-based patient records. In K. J. Hannah & M. J. Ball (Eds.), *Aspects of the computer-based patient record* (pp. 36–39). New York: Springer-Verlag.

Cassell, E. J. (1985). Talking with patients. *The theory of doctor-patient communication, Vol. 1, and Clinical technique, Vol. 2*. Cambridge, MA: Massachusetts Institute of Technology.

Cegala, D. J., McGee, D. S., & McNeilis, K. S. (1996). Components of patients' and doctors' perceptions of communication competence during a primary care medical interview. *Health Communication, 8*(1), 1–27.

Cegala, D. J., McNeilis, K., McGee, D. S., & Jonas, A. P. (1995). A study of doctors' and patients' perceptions of information processing and communication competence during the medical interview. *Health Communication, 7*(3), 179–203.

Cicourel, A. V. (1983). Hearing is not believing: Language and the structure of belief in medical communication. In S. Fisher & A. D. Todd (Eds.), *The social organization of doctor-patient communication* (pp. 221–239). Washington, DC: The Center for Applied Linguistics.

Clair, J. M. (1993). The application of social science to medical practice. In J. M. Clair & R. M. Allman (Eds.), *Sociomedical perspectives on patient care* (pp. 12–28). Lexington: The University of Kentucky Press.

Fisher, S. (1983). Doctor talk/patient talk: How treatment decisions are negotiated in doctor-patient communication. In S. Fisher & A. D. Todd (Eds.), *The social organization of doctor-patient communication* (pp. 135–157). Washington, D.C.: The Center for Applied Linguistics.

Fisher, R., & Brown, S. (1988). *Betting together: Building relationship that gets to yes*. Boston, MA: Houghton Mifflin.

Friedson, E. (1970). *Professional dominance*. New York: Atherton Press, Inc.

Glaser, B. G., & Strauss, A. L. (1965). *Awareness of dying*. Chicago: Aldine Publishing Co.

Gouldner, A. W. (1960). The norm of reciprocity: A preliminary statement. *American Sociological Review, 25*(2), 161–178.

Greenfield, S., Kaplan, S., & Ware, J. E. (1985). Expanding patient involvement in care: Effects on patient outcomes. *Annals of Internal Medicine, 102*, 520–528.

Grunig, J. E. (1993). Image and substance: From symbolic to behavioral relationships. *Public Relations Review, 19*(2), 121–139.

Grunig, J. E., & Grunig, L. A. (1992). Models of public relations and communications. In J. E. Grunig, D. M. Dozier, W. P. Ehling, L. A. Grunig, F. C. Repper, & J. White (Eds.) *Excellence in Public Relations and Communication Management*. (pp. 285–325). Hillsdale, NJ: Lawrence Erlbaum Associates.

Grunig, L. A. (1987). Variation in relations with environmental publics. *Public Relations Review, 13*, 46–58.

Hall, J. A., & Dornan, M. C. (1988). Meta-analysis of satisfaction with medical care: Description of research domain and analysis of overall satisfaction levels. *Social Science Medicine, 27*, 637–644.

Karlberg, M. (1996). Remembering the public in public relations research: From theoretical to operational symmetry. *Journal of Public Relations Research, 8*, 263–278.

Kreps, G. L. (1987). The pervasive role of information in health and health care: Implications for health communication policy. *Communication Yearbook, 11*, 238–276.

Kreps, G. L., & Thornton, B. C. (1992). *Health communication: Theory and practice, 2nd Ed.* Prospect Heights, IL: Waveland Press, Inc.

Ledingham, J. A., & Bruning, S. D. (1998). Relationship management in public relations: dimensions of an organization-public relationship. *Public Relations Review: 24*(1), 55–65.

Ledingham, J. A., & Bruning, S. D. (1997). Community relations and loyalty: Toward a relationship theory of public relations. *Business Research Yearbook*, Vol. IV, pp. 772–776.

Leichty, G., & Springston, J. (1993). Reconsidering public relations models. *Public Relations Review, 19*(4), 327–339.

Littlejohn, S. W. (1992). Theories of human communication, 4th Ed. Belmont, California: Wadsworth Publishing.

McLeod, J. M., & Chaffee, S. R. (1972). The construction of social reality. In J. T. Tedeschi (Ed.), *Social influence processes* (pp. 50–99). Aldine Atherton.

National Research Council. (1997). *For the record: Protecting electronic health information.* Washington, DC: National Academy Press.

O'Hair, D. (1989). Dimensions of relational communication and control during physician-patient interactions. *Health Communication, 1*(2), 97–115.

Oliver, C. (1990). Determinants of interorganizational relationships: Integration and future direction. *Academy of Management Review, 15*, 241–265.

Pierloot, R. A. (1983). Different models in the approach to the doctor-patient relationship. *Psychotherapy, Psychosomatics, 39*, 213–224.

Quill, T. E. (1983). Partnerships in patient care: A contractual approach. *Annals of Internal Medicine, 98*, 228–234.

Quint, J. C. (1965). Institutionalized practices of information control. *Psychiatry, 28*, 119–132.

Ray, E. B., & Miller, K. I. (1990). Communication in health care organizations. In E. B. Ray & L. Donohew (Eds.), *Communication and Health: Systems and Applications* (pp. 92–107). Hillsdale, NJ: Lawrence Erlbaum Associates.

Ritchey, F. J. (1993). Fear of malpractice litigation, the risk management industry and the clinical encounter. In J. M. Clair & R. M. Allman (Eds.), *Social Medical Perspectives on Patient Care.* Lexington, KY: The University Press of Kentucky.

Robinson, E. J., & Whitfield, M. J. (1985). Improving the efficiency of patients' comprehension monitoring: A way of increasing patients' participation in general practice consultations. *Social Science Medicine, 21*, 915–919.

Roter, D. L., & Hall, J. A. (1992). Doctors talking with patients/patients talking with doctors: Improving communication in medical visits. Westport, CT: Greenwood Publishing Group.

Rubin, B. D. (1990). The health caregiver-patient relationship: Pathology, etiology, treatment. In E. B. Ray & L. Donohew (Eds.), Communication and health: Systems and applications (pp. 51–68). Hillsdale, NJ: Lawrence Erlbaum Associates.

Scherz, J. W., Edwards, H. T., & Kallail, K. J. (1995). Communicative effectiveness of doctor-patient interactions. *Health Communication, 7*(2), 163–177.

Schenkin, B. N., & Warner, D. C. (1973). Sounding board—giving the patient his medical record: A proposal to improve the system. *New England Journal of Medicine, 289*, 688–692.

Shortliffe, E. J., Tan, P. C., Amatayakul, M. K., Cottington, E. Jencks, S. F., Martin, A., MacDonald, R., Morris, T. Q., & Nobel, J. J. (1992). Future vision and dissemination of computer-based patient records. In K. J. Hannah & M. J. Ball (Eds.), *Aspects of the computer-based patient record* (pp. 273–293). New York: Springer-Verlag.

Smith-Dupre, A. A., & Beck, C. S. (1996). Enabling patients and physicians to pursue multiple goals in health care encounters: A case study. *Health Communication, 8*(1), 73–90.

Speedling, E. J., & Rose, D. N. (1985). Building an effective doctor-patient relationship: From patient satisfaction to patient participation. *Social Science Medicine, 21*, 115–120.

Stevens, D. P., Staff, R., & Mackay, I. R. (1977). What happens when hospitalized patients see their own records. *Annals of Internal Medicine, 86*, 474–477.

Street Jr., R. L. (1991). Information-giving in medical consultations: The influence of patients' communicative styles and personal characteristics. *Social Science Medicine, 32*, 541–548.

Suchman, A. L., & Matthews, D. A. (1988). What makes the patient-doctor relationship therapeutic? Exploring the connexional dimension of medical care. *Annals of Internal Medicine, 108*, 125–130.

Thompson, T. L. (1994). Interpersonal communication and health care. In M. L. Knapp & G. R. Miller (Eds.), *Handbook of interpersonal communication*, 2nd Ed. Thousand Oaks, CA: Sage Publications.

Thornton, B. C., & Kreps, G. L. (1993). *Perspectives on health communication.* Prospect Heights, IL: Waveland Press.

Waitzkin, H. (1984). Doctor-patient communication: Clinical implications of social scientific research. *Journal of the American Medical Association, 252,* 2441–2446.

Watzlawick, P., Beavin, J. H., & Jackson, D. D. (1967). Pragmatics of human communication: A study of interactional patterns, pathologies and paradoxes. New York: W. W. Norton & Co.

West, C. (1983). "Ask me no questions ..." An analysis of queries and replies in physician-patient dialogues. In S. Fisher & A. D. Todd (Eds.), *The Social organization of doctor-patient communication* (pp. 75–106). Washington, DC: The Center for Applied Linguistics.

Wilmot, W. W. (1995). Relational communication. New York: McGraw-Hill, Inc.

Wood, J.T. (1996). Everyday encounters: An introduction to interpersonal communication (pp. 180–188). Belmont, CA: Wadsworth.

Young, M., & Storm Klingle, R. (1996). Silent partners in medical care: A cross-cultural study of patient participation. *Health Communication, 8*(1), 29–53.

7

Building Employee
and Community Relationships
Through Volunteerism:
A Case Study[1]

ℬ ✧ ℭ

Laurie J. Wilson
Brigham Young University

The recent studies of relationships and the dimensions contributing to their strength and success identify both characteristics and behavioral outcomes. Wood's (1995) extensive review of the interpersonal relationship literature isolates four essential relationship dimensions: investment, commitment, trust, and comfort with relationship dialectics. Elsewhere, this author's theory of strategic cooperative communities postulates eight characteristics to determine the strength of relationships with organizational publics: trust, credibility, predictability, mutual interest, mutual gratification or benefit, proximity, spillover, and immediacy of collective need (Wilson, 1996).

Even more recently, Ledingham's and Bruning's (1997) study of relationship dimensions between regional telephone companies and subscribers yielded results that support the behavioral significance of the dimensions of openness, trust, commitment, and investment. Per-

[1]Special thanks goes to BYU graduate students Linda Linfield and Cory Cook who did extensive research on Novell's community relations and employee volunteerism programs, respectively.

137

haps more important, they discovered that as awareness of corporate support of the community increased, the positive perception of these relationship dimensions increased. With the increase of positive perceptions came a behavior identified as loyalty on the part of the subscribers. According to Ledingham and Bruning, "Public relations activities that create positive perceptions of relationship dimensions can engender loyalty to an organization when those activities are known by significant publics" (p. 25).

Although more research is needed to replicate the tests, validate the results, and extend the reach of their research, the findings are nevertheless encouraging and provide a point of departure for practical relationship development. Furthermore, practitioners have long operated under the assumption that building trust in relationships with an organization's publics resulted in some level of loyalty to the organization. What is particularly significant is that Ledingham and Bruning (1997) have tied a public's trust to the openness (and honesty) of communication and the organization's commitment to and investment in that public's community.

An attitude of trust expressed behaviorally as loyalty must be one of the primary goals in relationship building with organizational publics. In fact, a community relations plan developed by an organization that consciously takes the relationship-building approach in its public relations would of necessity identify loyalty as one of the desired outcomes. If the research cited previously is accurate, that loyalty would be the result of known organizational activities that demonstrate openness, trust, commitment, and investment.

THE CASE OF NOVELL, INC.

Building loyalty within the community and among employees was a primary objective of Novell, Inc., the fifth largest software developer in the world, when it developed its community relations plan in 1995 (for fiscal 1996) after the earlier purchase of software giant WordPerfect. At that time, the community relations function was relocated under the senior vice president of corporate marketing, where responsibility for corporate public relations and internal communications also resided. Through several years of upheaval—management changes, mergers, cutbacks, and layoffs—Novell seemed anxious to focus on community relations as both a public relations and an employee relations tool to build confidence and loyalty. Guiding values for the new organization included employee satisfaction, timely employee communication, and company participation in the local community (Linfield, 1998). The mission statement for community relations was to

> create a positive impact on the quality of life in the communities where a significant number of Novell employees live and work by focusing corporate philanthropy, software donations, and employee volunteer efforts in areas of education, critical community needs, and cultural development.... (Cook, 1997, pp. 46–47)

The 1996 mission statement and guiding values certainly imply the existence of the relationship dimensions of openness, commitment, and investment. By involving employees in the mission of its community relations efforts, the mission further provides for awareness among the employee public. The trust dimension of the company's relationship with the employee and community publics is more difficult to identify, though the desire to foster trust is apparent in the stated mission and guiding values. Whether or not trust was a factor in the relationship may only be determined through a study of the implementation of the plan that was developed to reach Novell's community relations mission, and of the employees' and the communities' response.

Prior to the preparation of this mission statement, Novell had no strategic policy for corporate giving, and no employee volunteer program (Linfield, 1998). The community relations staff assessed the process of software donation to be slow, bureaucratic, and underused. They did have a couple of programs in local areas that the corporation supported, but the employees had not been incorporated into the community relations effort or decision making.

Novell's Community Relations Strategic Plan

The community relations plan for fiscal 1996 (beginning in 1995) focused on creating a perception of Novell as being "socially aware and giving back to its community" (Linfield, 1998). The three goals of the plan were

- To target philanthropy to support and enhance corporate image and marketing;

- To create the best working environment in the industry through community involvement of which employees could be proud, and to involve them in donation and volunteer efforts; and
- To raise visibility of Novell as socially responsible and innovative.

Key publics of the plan included community organizations, state governments, and Novell employees and executives. To accomplish these goals as they pertained to employee loyalty, some key recommendations of the community relations plan included that Novell should

- Establish an employee volunteer program;
- Establish a 100% matching funds program for employee contributions to charities of their choice;
- Establish local employee committees to determine where local monies should be donated; and
- Publicize community relations programs internally and externally.

As a result of the assessment of the community relations staff that the community relations effort should follow the lead of employees in philanthropic decisions and employee volunteerism in the communities surrounding their San Jose and Utah offices, the function was relocated to report to human resources. According to one employee, the move indicated a shift in the perception of community relations from purely external relationship building to internal as well (Cook, 1997).

Employee Volunteer Program.   Based on the recommenda-tions, Novell implemented a generous and extensive employee volunteer program. Although release time was not adopted as official policy, unit manager's were given the authority to approve release time for volunteer efforts with no limitation on the amount of time granted. The company communicated its trust in unit managers to make sound decisions on allowed release time for community volunteerism within the parameters of expected unit contribution to organizational objectives.

To enhance the Novell team spirit, the company provided t-shirts for their employee volunteers. Differing designs for summer and for winter still identified the wearer as a "Novell volunteer." Further, volunteer opportunities were well publicized within the company by e-mail, news-letter and voice mail. Nevertheless, the community relations staff be-lieved that the most effective publicity is word of mouth. Former volunteers spread the word quickly and more and more employees participated with each new opportunity.

The employee volunteer program has firmly established itself in the local communities through cooperative activities like the United Way's Day of Caring, the annual Corporate Games, Utah's Make a Difference Day, and Utah's annual Freedom Festival. But more significant, the employees have become involved in suggesting their own community projects that Novell undertakes unilaterally. Typical of such projects is the annual food drive for the local food banks, the renovation of Clover House (a safe house for children in San Jose), the California site's Net Day, which supports computer resources and education in local schools, and computer engineer training in conjunction with a local community college in Utah. The projects cited here are but a few of the long and impressive list of projects supported by Novell through its employee volunteer program.

Employee and Matching Charitable Contributions.   In keeping with the recommendations, Novell established a matching program for employee charitable contributions. Although it was initially recommended that employee committees determine the recipients of corporate giving, further research indicated that such committees in other companies did not work well because the committees became dominated by employees pursuing personal agendas rather than community priorities. Accordingly, the matching program was established with a commitment of one third of the corporate philanthropic budget being dedicated to match employee charitable contributions up to $520 per employee per year.

In addition, employees were given access to the company's nationwide software donation program. Whereas previously, software donations were made primarily to agencies certified as sound and effective by the United Way in local communities, employees can now request software donations to any bona fide charity. Their requests are given priority processing to ensure that the company supports those efforts in a community to which its employees are most committed.

Internal and External Publicity.   In keeping with its goals, the community relations staff began a more systematic effort to publicize the company's commitment to and investment in the community. In addition to the volunteer opportunities being well publicized, results of efforts were communicated through internal channels such as e-mail and newsletters. Further, the effort at external communication, already fairly effective, was intensified through partnerships with local community organizations. Novell let the community and beneficiary charitable organizations spread the word, but also made sure they enhanced their own publicity efforts. They also joined the Community Communications Resource Consortium (CCRC) in California, an organization that assists companies in creating partnerships to address a community's most pressing needs. A secondary function of the CCRC is to help companies spread the news of their community involvement.

Evaluation of Novell's Community Relations Efforts

Although evaluation of the effort has not been systematic or quantified, there are some strong indicators of the positive impact of the community relations function on employees and on the local communities over the past 3 years:

• The corporate and employee community relations effort at Novell has been recognized in its Utah community with the United Way Caring Company of the Year award, the Outstanding Partner in Education in 1997 (simultaneously awarded from all three local school districts), and the Utah State Helping Hands Award (Cook, 1997). In San Jose, the local food bank awarded the company the Golden Harvest Award.

• A Utah community survey conducted by another local business rated Novell first among the major local corporations for investment in the community (Linfield, 1998).

• The communities continue to maintain favorable business and tax climates.

• Although the company experienced a 20% reduction in force in 1997, the number of employees participating in the annual employee charitable giving campaign rose by 8%. The annual employee food drive yielded the same per capita contribution, and a new "Angel Tree" program was added to the drive in which virtually all gift requests were filled (Linfield, 1998).

• The number of volunteers for projects has increased with each activity, many being repeat volunteers who bring family, friends, and coworkers. There is virtually no attrition among volunteers who organize projects such as site coordinators for the annual food drive who, with very few exceptions, are eager to repeat their efforts the following year. There has also been a significant increase in employees suggesting volunteer projects for the company to sponsor, and at least one phone call per week from an employee requesting an opportunity to work with community relations (Linfield, 1998).

• In the midst of downsizing and job insecurity, the retention rate of employees has improved in comparison to the industry standard. At the end of 1996, the Saratoga standard for attrition in this industry was 10% and Novell's rate was 14%. By the end of 1997, the Saratoga standard had risen almost seven points to 16.9%, while the Novell rate had risen only 2.9 points to 17.4% (Linfield, 1998).

• Corporate endorsement of the efforts as strategic is reflected in the fact that the community relations budget was the only budget in the human resources group that was not cut in the midst of downsizing (Cook, 1997).

Summary and Conclusions

For the evaluation of Novell's community relations efforts to be accurate, it must include assessment of the program's positive impact on the community and upon the employees. The previously mentioned results demonstrate that impact. It is more difficult, however, to tie that positive impact to enhanced loyalty toward the company measured behaviorally.

Positive perceptions of the relationship dimensions identified by Ledingham and Bruning (1997) in their theory of organizational–public loyalty are unquestionably present in Novell's relationship with two of its key publics: employees and local communities. There can be little doubt that Novell has demonstrated its commitment to and investment in the communities in which its employees reside. The enthusiasm of employees for the program is apparent in the continual increase of employee participation. Openness and trust have also been demonstrated through the process of employee involvement in corporate philanthropy and volunteerism. Certainly the awareness of corporate community involvement by employees and by the host communities is apparent in the approach taken by Novell.

Ledingham and Bruning (1997) were dealing with the customer or stakeholder public, yet Novell's experience would tend to support the application of their theory to the community and employee publics as well. Nevertheless, the short time frame—the program has been in place for only 3 years—may have an effect on the resulting degree of loyalty. (Length of time in the relationship was not identified as a factor by Ledingham and Bruning.)

The more difficult questions can only be answered over time and in the face of adversity. The loyalty of the stakeholder public was demonstrated by Ledingham and Bruning (1997) through anticipated retention in the face of price increases. What behavior measures the loyalty of a community toward a corporation? Certainly the host communities have expressed their appreciation of Novell's efforts through awards and recognitions. Perhaps the maintenance of a favorable business and tax climate is another behavioral measure of a community's loyalty.

However, the loyalty of the employee public comes at a much greater risk than either the stakeholders studied by Ledingham and Bruning (1997), or the community public identified in this case. For employees, behavioral loyalty involves the question of economic survival of the individual and his or her dependents. Behaviorally measured, that would require retention rates to be comparatively better than competitors even in periods of labor force reduction. Do employee-focused community relations programs such as those implemented by Novell in the last 3 years increase employee loyalty in the face of layoffs and downsizing? The preliminary indication is that they do. It will be interesting to see whether that loyalty continues over the difficult times ahead in this very competitive industry.

Whatever the outcome, the theory of organizational–public loyalty based on studies of interpersonal relationships provides an exciting new direction of inquiry in the field of public relations. It is a giant step forward in providing practitioners with concrete principles that lead toward success. It will require further study and testing, and perhaps some reshaping in its application to a diversity of organizational publics. Nevertheless, it reinforces the notion that public relations truly is business—it is the business of relationships.

REFERENCES

Cook, C. (1997). Volunteerism: A strategic approach to community and employee relations. Thesis presented to the Department of Communications, Brigham Young University.

Ledingham, J. A., & Bruning, S. D. (1997, August). Interpersonal dimensions in an organizational–public relationship: Toward a theory of loyalty. Paper presented in the Public Relations Division of the Association for Education in Journalism and Mass Communication in Chicago.

Linfield, L. (1998). Corporate community relations as a strategic communications function: A case study. Thesis presented to the Department of Communications, Brigham Young University.

Wilson, L. J. (1996) Strategic cooperative communities: A synthesis of strategic, issue management, and relationship-building approaches in public relations. In H. M. Culbertson and N. Chen (Eds.), *International public relations: A comparative analysis* (pp. 67–80). Hillsdale, NJ: Lawrence Erlbaum Associates.

Wood, J. T. (1995). *Relational communication*. Belmont, CA: Wadsworth Publishers.

8

Public Relations: Toward a Global Professionalism

৪০ ✧ ଓଃ

Dean Kruckeberg
University of Northern Iowa

In 1988, Kruckeberg and Starck argued in their book, *Public Relations and Community: A Reconstructed Theory*, that public relations is best defined and practiced as the active attempt to restore and maintain a sense of community. They noted: "Only with this goal as a primary objective can public relations become a full partner in the information and communication milieu that forms the lifeblood of U.S. society and, to a growing extent, the world" (p. xi).

Since that treatise was published, communication technology has continued to evolve both dramatically and exponentially, ironically making the authors' admonishment for community building all the more critical. Communication technology has compressed time and space to such an extent that Marshall McLuhan's "Global Village" is an incontestable reality in its technological sense.

However, some scholars question the desirability of technology that allows an economical and readily accessible—but fundamentally changed—means of communication; nor fully appreciated are the ramifications of communication technology that accelerates globalism and its concomitant requisites of multiculturalism and diversity, but does not inherently facilitate community building. Kruckeberg (1995) has observed: " ... *(E)xisting* relationships are being strained, and virtually everyone is being forced into *new* relationships within social systems that are becoming both increasingly diverse and correspondingly divisive."

Communication technology has brought mixed blessings: parents who are prideful of their children's computer literacy and bemused that their offspring can keystroke before they can read are rightly concerned about an enticing virtual reality of electronic pool halls and interactive cyber street corners where innocents can fall prey to various forms of electronic exploitation and social scientists ponder a cyber universe that is capable of psychologically mapping and electronically defining people, places, and things.

These massive technological changes—evolving within an extraordinarily short time frame—have tremendous and little understood implications for society and heretofore unmeasured impact on individuals. At the forefront of those who must understand the societal impact of communication technology are public relations practitioners; they must reconcile their organizations' ongoing relationships with a range of seemingly amorphous publics that are evolving within a global—yet multicultural and highly diverse—society that shows little inclination toward becoming a global community.

NEW CHALLENGES IN RELATIONSHIP BUILDING

As public relations professionals realign their primary attention from communication tactics and techniques to focus more directly upon strategic relationship building, these practitioners will be faced with several unprecedented challenges that are being created by the global technological society in which we are destined to live, but which Bellah, Madsen, Sullivan, Swidler, and Tipton, in *The Good Society* (1992), said we do not adequately understand.

Globalization

The implications of contemporary globalism are far greater than the overlay of an improved communication network on a culturally static world population. Inextricable linkages through communication technology will accentuate the impact of population trends and any corresponding changes in social institutions that will result during a redistribution of demographically derived power. Extreme changes in population ratios favoring rapidly developing and modernizing countries will challenge First World political, economic, and cultural hegemony.

Although the rate of world population growth is decreasing, overall numbers will continue to grow. World population will reach 7.6 billion by the year 2020. Most of this growth will be in the developing countries of Africa, Asia, and Latin America. The combined population of less developed countries grew from 1.7 billion people in 1950 to 4.6 billion in 1996 and is projected to reach 6.4 billion by the year 2020. In contrast, the combined population of the more developed countries increased from 800 million people in 1950 to 1.17 billion in 1996. These countries' populations will only increase to 1.25 billion by the year 2020. The population of more developed countries has declined from 27% of the world total in 1970 to 20% in 1996; in another 25 years, the more developed countries may comprise only 16% of world population (Office of Population, 1996, July).

However, these data do not reflect the potential for rapid modernization of many less-developed countries that may expand their economies and create modern national infrastructures far more quickly than did present First World powers.

A status quo is unlikely when Third World countries' population growth is juxtaposed with unprecedented opportunities for development. Readily available and highly economical communication technology will ensure that these countries can develop productive linkages within a globalized economy, not only in their historic role as providers of natural resources, but particularly as they are perceived as emerging markets as well as potential sources of trained labor by First World powers. However, internal tensions and instabilities resulting from rapid modernization of fast-growing traditional societies may have a deleterious global impact that may particularly affect First World powers. Stephen (1995) noted two characteristics that differentiate modern and traditional societies:

> The first dimension is pluralism. In traditional societies, beliefs are consensual and communication functions mainly to convey information and to coordinate action. Modern societies are highly pluralistic. Beliefs are up for grabs and communication is used to create shared constructions of reality—local pockets of consensus—that provide stability and bridge existentially isolated individuals....

The second dimension is egalitarianism. If a society is predominantly hierar-
chical rather than egalitarian—as may more often be the case in traditional
societies—interpersonal interaction occurs predominantly between individuals of unequal social power. This circumstance makes it more difficult for
communication to operate to create shared constructions of reality. Egalitarianism tends to be characteristic of modern societies. (p. 16)

In addition to the accompanying internal turmoil resulting from less
developed countries' attempt to rapidly modernize, during the interim
misunderstandings will continue in these societies' communication with
the more developed countries. Stephen (1995) said that differences in
the degree of modernity within two cultures increase the potential for
cross-cultural misunderstanding and conflict because of the mutually
incomprehensible methods in which people place themselves within
their social milieu.

Societal Changes Caused by Computer Technology

Further, rapid modernization might take different forms in less developed countries compared to how modernity is presently defined by First
World norms. Innis observed that culture is fundamentally affected by
communication technology that can alter the structure of interests (the
things thought about) by changing the character of symbols (the things
thought with) and by changing the nature of community (the arena in
which thought is developed). Innis distinguished between a space-bind-
ing culture whose predominant interest is in communication as a form
of power and transmission and a time-binding culture that is interested
in history and permanence and whose communities are rooted in place
(Carey, 1989).

Communication technology that may be intended to facilitate modernization will become part of that indigenous society's infrastructure
through social influences as well as through an unpredictable range of
opportunities, constraints, and inducements (Sclove, 1995). Communication technology applied to specific cultures may fulfill unique functions that can differ considerably from the functions such technology
accommodates in First World modern society. Certainly, communication technology need not influence different cultures in the same way
nor to the same extent.

Further, technological developments do not inherently nor necessarily provide meaningful social benefits (Besser, 1995). Technology and any benefits assumed to be accruing from this technology are shaped by social forces that are operating on a broader level; again, communication technology may have different outcomes in culturally distinct, less developed countries. Long-term contributions to national infrastructure remain uncertain. Boal (1995) observed that the largest previous project in the U.S. infrastructure, that is, the railroad system, now lies derelict.

There are those who remain suspicious—if not fearful—of communication technology's role in modern society's infrastructure, let alone its effect on the modernization of less developed countries; they see this technology as not necessarily bettering society, but being psychologically harmful and possibly placing into greater servitude the traditionally downtrodden.

For example, Neill (1995) argued that social alienation intensifies as humans interact via computer, destroying individuals' ability to socialize comfortably with those who are physically present. In inducing this social and physical isolation, the computer becomes the embodiment of the "white man," (p. 191) that is, emotionless and non-nurturing. Neill prophesized:

> ... (T)he computer itself will be used to shape the personality. The model is the computer—the malleable, controllable, programmable "smart machine." Part of the information–technology agenda is to learn how better to control the thinking of humans. At the crudest level, schools will try to do what they have always tried to do, shape students into workers, but the more subtle strategy is to make the mind *want* to be computerized. (p. 190)

Nor will computerization contribute to "good jobs," Neill predicted (1995). Computers in schools are lauded as powerful vehicles for learning; however, such learning will not lead to a universal high wage.

> Computer use in schools *will* fit the economy—not the mythical economy of "high skills and high wages," but the real economy of "the race to the bottom." While following orders, not questioning, being on time, and submitting one's personality to the dictates of the school all prepared workers for jobs in the mass-production era, the schoolwork form directly fit the actual jobs for only a relatively few workers. With computerization, however, form can more closely resemble function. (p. 188)

Popular mythology holds that new technology is driven by the natural expansion of the market system (Drew, 1995). However, Drew maintained that there have been many instances where the market system has worked to impede, retard, or abandon new technologies that would have benefited the public good. Drew observed that engineering decisions are rarely based on public need, nor on a desire to improve consumers' quality of life; further, seldom has the public been allowed to participate in technological decisions that directly affect them. Brook and Boal (1995) liken the work now being celebrated using computers to the routinized work that originated in medieval monasteries.

The existing consumer benefits of communication technology may neither remain inexpensive nor decrease in cost, and privacy will become a greater issue, claims Besser (1995). The information superhighway will likely be billed on a "pay-per-use" basis, such as "pay-per-view" TV is presently billed. Metering that will be needed to accompany pay-per-use can give governmental agencies and service providers unprecedented demographic and consumption information regarding private individuals.

CORPORATIONS AS GLOBAL INSTITUTIONS

Within this context of globalization that is being facilitated by new communication technology in a world of uneven population growth, where the largest numbers of people will be in nations that will be modernizing rapidly (and likely tumultuously) through the use of this same communication technology, the role of corporations is certainly subject to profound consideration.

In many ways, corporations as global institutions may become far more powerful and pervasively influential than will most nation–states—at least in the global arena beyond these nation–states' borders. Critics say the private governments of the great corporations will make unilateral decisions according to their own advantage; government agencies that will be assigned to regulate them may be ineffective because transnational corporations can cross national frontiers with impunity to accomplish their goals and objectives within the most favorable national environment—all the while maintaining their global position of power and influence.

Traditionally, the corporation has been a central institution in American culture, with a historical pattern of rights and duties, powers and responsibilities. The government's parallel role has been to assure national defense as well as to provide the infrastructure needed for business growth; in contrast, the government's function as a provider of social support is a relatively new role traceable barely to the 1930s (Bellah et al., 1992). Other First World powers, albeit some with a greater tradition of social entitlement, have similar histories of corporations as social institutions.

Every indication suggests that this legacy of corporations as institutions will continue, but with corporations increasing their influence to unprecedented levels worldwide. Schiller (1995) reported that, among the 37,000 companies that predominate in the world economic order, it is the largest 100 transnational "megafirms" that are the true global power-wielders:

> This world corporate order is a major force in reducing greatly the influence of nation-states. As private economic decisions increasingly govern the global and national allocation of resources, the amount and character of investment, the value of currencies, and the sites and modes of production, important duties of government are silently appropriated by these giant private economic aggregates. ...(p. 21)

Schiller (1995) said that these corporations are promoting deregulation and privatization of industry worldwide, notably in the telecommunications sector; one effect of this large-scale deregulation and massive privatization is the increasing ineffectualness of national authority.

At one level, corporations that increase their role as global social institutions may further worldwide linkages that will make war untenable, at least beyond a regional scale, and the international economic codependence that will be created by transnational corporations may help equalize nation-states' global power ratios far better than did the Cold War arms race. Bellah et al. (1992) observed that, immediately after World War II, other First World nations were economically dependent on the United States; now this dependence is more nearly mutual.

However, Bellah et al. (1992) warned that world economic interdependence still places the fate of the world's poorest nations into First World hands—generating fierce resentment in the Third World. The world financial system, for instance, tends to protect the richest countries, while placing heavy burdens on the poorest nation-states:

> A purely "rational" international market system would require that when faced with competition from societies where workers are paid low wages and have few social welfare benefits, societies where wages and welfare benefits are high would have to either reduce their wages and welfare or stop competing in the

world market. Yet powerful nations like the United States can, within limits, avoid doing this by manipulating the values of their currencies so that their goods are still competitively priced abroad. Weak and poor governments, like many of those in Latin America and Africa, however, have no such luxury. ... The resultant poverty and resentment constitute potent fuel for violent conflict. (pp. 121–122)

At a macro level, traditionally considered questions concerning corporate power become relatively mundane, for example, whether corporations may impose conditions of employment that are unconstitutional within a given country, whether they may ban employee behavior occurring outside the workplace, and whether they may control behavior affecting health care costs that the corporations pay. More significant are questions of corporations' influence over the cultures, economies, and politics of nation–states.

From this perspective, questions certainly arise about corporate imperialism—cultural and otherwise—that may be undertaken primarily for corporations' economic benefit and for their consolidation of global power. As far back as World War II, U.S. leaders were recognizing the centrality of information control for gaining world advantage (Schiller, 1995).

"Free flow of information" has presently conferred this advantage to U.S. cultural industries, as has the adoption of English as the world's second language. Schiller (1995) argued that private creation and ownership mean that the emerging Global Information Infrastructure (GII) will be of greatest value to those having the financial ability to satisfy their need for instantaneous and voluminous global message flow, that is, the transnational corporations:

> The launching of the global information superhighway project comes at a time when most of the preconditions for a corporate global "order" are in place. There is, first and foremost, the actually existence of a global economy, organized and directed by a relatively tiny number of transnational corporations. (p. 20)

CHALLENGES FOR PUBLIC RELATIONS PRACTITIONERS

Castigating globalism and modern communication technology and seeking regress to a pastoral and isolationist existence can be likened to a Canutian attempt to hold back the tides. There can be no return to a preglobal and pretechnological society, nor is there a desire to do so by most people who are quick to embrace the advantages of contemporary life—despite its accompanying social problems and troubling issues of power differentials.

Demands May Be Made
to Participate in Decision Making

However, there are those who remain watchful of the social cost of globalism and communication technology. In addition, demands may be made by the ultimate consumers of communication technology to participate more fully in the decision-making contributing to its development. For example, Sclove (1995) reported that the Dutch have formed public "science shops" since the late 1970s where citizens receive free assistance in learning to address social issues that have technical components. Sclove argues that technology must become substantively compatible with democracy; procedurally, expanded opportunities must exist for people to participate in shaping technology, which Sclove says is part of social structure. Both technological design and practice, he argues, must be democratized.

Sclove (1995) urged that technology be seen as more than a set of tools for accomplishing narrowly defined objectives; instead, technology must represent social structure, that is, background that helps define and regulate social life.

Brook and Boal (1995) concluded:

> ...(W)e do not object in principle to the introduction of new machinery in the workplace. But like the Luddites of the first industrial revolution, we refuse to cede to capital the right to design and implement the sort of automation that deskills workers, extends manager control over their work, intensifies their labor, and undermines their solidarity. Automation in the name of progress and "inevitable" technological change is primarily to the benefit of that same class that not so long ago forced people off the land and into factories, destroying whole ways of life in the process: "labor-saving" devices have not so much reduced labor as they have increased profits and refined class domination. (pp. vii–viii)

Institutional Role of Corporations
May Come Under Scrutiny

Most nation–states and their citizens would readily relinquish neither the economic, the consumer, nor the employment benefits that corporations bring inside their borders. However, the institutional role of corporations and of their social contributions may come under increasing scrutiny among societies that they impact; nation-states may demand more control over corporations operating within their borders. Bellah et al. (1992) observed:

> The corporations and the world economic system in which they were enmeshed grew up "over the heads," so to speak, of the people and even of their leaders. Misunderstanding these new institutions, and insisting on speaking of them in the older Lockean language, Americans failed to make sense of them and, even more than the citizens of most other modern nations, allowed them to produce whatever unintended consequences they would, some of which were serious indeed. (p. 72)

Public relations professionals representing global corporations—which corporate bodies will increase markedly in a modern era of worldwide opportunity—will face challenges that the public relations literature has only begun to address.

Community building will be an instrumental part of their responsibilities as practitioners are called upon to socially define their corporations within the context of the societies in which they operate (many of these societies will be undergoing rapid population growth and modernization) and must defend why these corporate bodies should be allowed to be part of, not only such traditional societies, but also the increasingly multicultural and diverse modern communities worldwide.[1]

Creedon (1996) referred to the process of "strategic ethics" in international public relations, which means relationship building from a mutually defined sense of values. She argued that strategic public relations should be built upon relationships that are based on mutual respect for—and honesty about—each other's values. A foundation of shared values establishes trust in the relationship, which in turn facilitates the corporation's ability to achieve a strategic objective.

Kruckeberg's (1995–1996) perspective of public relations in the global environment is compatible with this perspective. He warned:

> ...(O)rganizations will need "keepers and reconcilers" of their values and belief systems up to and including their base ideologies. Those professionals will be critically needed who can examine, maintain, and modify as necessary tradi-

---

[1] A comprehensive argument for the primary importance of community building appears in Kruckeberg, D. & Starck, K. (1988). *Public relations and community: A reconstructed theory* (New York: Praeger).

tional organizational and societal values and beliefs that will be challenged in a McLuhanesque "global village" in which the values and belief systems of peoples throughout the world will ideologically confront one another. (p. 37)

Public Relations Practitioners Must "Professionalize" Globally

To address these challenges, public relations practitioners must professionalize on a global scale. Such professionalization is not primarily to enhance practitioners' class, status, and power, but to provide a succinct definition of practitioners' role and function within global society—together with an articulate description of these professionals' worldview, that is, their ideology, values, and belief systems. This professionalization will take practitioners away from the functionary role of a corporate "gunslinger" or Samurai warrior, providing this specialized occupation with the necessary philosophical foundation to develop a "professional" worldview.

Kruckeberg (1995–1996) said that practitioners must first acknowledge their own professional ideology, values, and belief systems before they can address the same for their corporations. Public relations professionals must possess an agreed-upon worldview to address the relationship building, that is, the community building, that must occur between their client corporations and multicultural and diverse societies worldwide:

> There must be recognition among public relations practitioners—as well as by society at large—that public relations not only *represents* ideologies; rather, in its symmetrical models,[2] public relations practice is, *itself,* highly value-laden and ideological with a concomitant set of professional beliefs and worldview. (p. 38)

Grunig and White (1992) said that a *worldview* is a mindset that focuses the attention of a scientist primarily upon theories of observations that fit within that mindset. Bell (1988) said that *ideology* has come to mean a creed held with the will to believe, that is, with dogmatism and stridency. In their book on strategic planning, Goodstein, Nolan, and Pfeiffer (1993) adopted the Rokeach definition of values and value systems, that is

> a *value* is an enduring belief that a specific mode of conduct or end state of existence is personally or socially preferable to an opposite or converse mode

---

[2]This refers to two-way symmetrical public relations as advocated by Grunig et al. (1992) and best described in J. E. Grunig (Ed.), *Excellence in Public Relations and Communication Management.* Hillsdale, N. J.: Lawrence Erlbaum Associates.

of conduct or end state of existence. A *value system* is an enduring organization of beliefs concerning preferable models of conduct or end states of existence along a continuum of relative importance. (p. 147)

Stated simply, public relations practitioners worldwide must know and agree on who they are as a professional body, and these professionals must be able to articulate their worldview before they can perform their professional role and their function for their client organizations, that is, corporations operating within a global milieu. As professionals, public relations practitioners must not blindly take orders or accept their corporations' worldviews without question or challenge; rather, public relations practitioners must be able to apply professional problem-solving methodologies and their own professional body of knowledge to address corporate issues of relationship building and community building across cultures and nations.

Questions remain regarding whether public relations is culturally relative at the strategic level, and its practice certainly will remain culturally sensitive at the tactical and technical levels to accommodate a range of environments. Nevertheless, professionalized public relations must be more directly likened to universally practiced professions, such as medicine and accounting, that is, occupations that share more similarities globally among their professional practitioners than differences—not only in their bodies of knowledge, but also in their worldviews, ideologies, and values that ultimately determine how they conduct their professional practice.

For public relations to make its maximum contribution, not only to its client corporations, but also to a rapidly changing world that demands appropriate relationship building and community building, public relations practitioners must know who they are and what they believe before they can help corporations define themselves and defend their role in a rapidly changing multicultural and diverse global society.

REFERENCES

Bell, D. D. (1988). *The end of ideology*. Cambridge: Harvard University Press.

Bellah, R. N., Madsen, R., Sullivan, W. M., Swidler, A., & Tipton, S. M. (1992). *The good society*. New York: Vintage Books.

Besser, H. (1995). From internet to information superhighway. In J. Brook & I. A. Boal (Eds.), *Resisting the virtual life: The culture and politics of information* (pp. 59–70). San Francisco: City Lights.

Boal, I. A. (1995). A flow of monsters: Luddism and virtual technologies. In J. Brook & I. A. Boal (Eds.), *Resisting the virtual life: The culture and politics of information* (pp. 3–15). San Francisco: City Lights.

Brook, J., & Boal, I. A. (1995). Preface. In J. Brook & I. A. Boal (Eds.), *Resisting the virtual life: The culture and politics of information* (pp. vii–xv). San Francisco: City Lights.

Carey, J. W. (1989). *Communication as culture: Essays on media and society.* Boston: Unwin Hyman.

Creedon, P. J. (1996, December). *The future of strategic public relations practice in the global marketplace: Building a case for strategic ethics.* Paper presented at the Conference on Strategic Planning of the United Arab Emirates University, Dubai, UAE.

Drew, J. (1995). Media activism and radical democracy. In J. Brook & I. A. Boal (Eds.), *Resisting the virtual life: The culture and politics of information* (pp. 71–83). San Francisco: City Lights.

Etzioni, A. (1994). *The spirit of community: The reinvention of American society.* New York: Touchstone.

Goodstein, L., Nolan, T., & Pfeiffer, J. W. (1993). *Applied strategic planning: A comprehensive guide.* New York: McGraw Hill.

Grunig, J. E., & White, J. (1992). The effect of worldviews on public relations theory and practice. In J. E. Grunig (Ed.), *Excellence in public relations and communication management* (pp. 31–64). Hillsdale, NJ.: Lawrence Erlbaum Associates.

Kruckeberg, D. (1995, April). *Public relations as ideology.* Paper presented at the meeting of the Eastern Communication Association, Pittsburgh, PA.

Kruckeberg, D. (1995–1996, Winter). The challenge for public relations in the era of globalization. *Public Relations Quarterly, 40*(4), 36–39.

Kruckeberg, D., & Starck, K. (1988). *Public relations and community: A reconstructed theory.* New York: Praeger.

Neill, M. (1995). Computers, thinking, and schools in the "new world economic order." In J. Brook & I. A. Boal (Eds.), *Resisting the virtual life: The culture and politics of information* (pp. 181–194). San Francisco: City Lights.

Office of Population. (1996, July). *World population profile: 1996.* Washington, DC: Bureau for Global Programs, Field Support, and Research, U. S. Agency for International Development.

Schiller, H. I. (1995). The global information highway: Project for an ungovernable world. In J. Brook & I. A. Boal (Eds.), *Resisting the virtual life: The culture and politics of information* (pp. 71–83). San Francisco: City Lights.

Sclove, R. E. (1995). Making technology democratic. In J. Brook & I. A. Boal (Eds.), *Resisting the virtual life: The culture and politics of information* (pp. 85–101). San Francisco: City Lights.

Stephen, T. (1995). Interpersonal communication, history, and intercultural coherence. In F. L. Casmir (Ed.), *Communication in Eastern Europe: The role of history, culture, and media in contemporary conflicts* (pp. 5–25). Mahwah, NJ: Lawrence Erlbaum Associates.

9

Organization and Key Public Relationships: Testing the Influence of the Relationship Dimensions in a Business-to-Business Context

Stephen D. Bruning
Capital University

John A. Ledingham
Capital University

The notion of public relations as the "function that establishes and maintains mutually beneficial relationships between an organization and the publics on whom its success or failure depends" (Cutlip, Center, & Broom, 1994, p.6) provides a management framework for public relations scholarship and practice. Within the relationship management paradigm, communication is seen as the vehicle that can be used to link organizations and their key publics (Grunig & Huang, chap. 2, this volume). Moreover, the distinction between public relations as a management function and public relations as a communication function can be seen in Thomsen's (1997) definition of public relations as "the building of relationships and the management of communication between organizations and individuals" (p. 12). Thus, many scholars are moving toward the notion that the primary purpose of public relations is to manage the relationship between an organization and the organization's key publics. Communication, then, becomes is a vehicle that organizations should use to initiate, develop, maintain, and repair mutually productive organization–public relationships.

Increasingly, public relations managers are being pressed to account for program expenditures in terms of contribution to market share, financial impact, corporate citizenry, and other organizational goals. In our study of local telephone subscribers, we reported that the perceived relationship between the individual and the organization was an effective predictor of consumer behavior (Ledingham & Bruning, 1998). In a later study, we also reported that the relationship dimensions influence consumer perceptions of satisfaction with the organization (Bruning & Ledingham, 1998). This chapter utilizes the relationship dimensions developed in those studies (trust, openness, involvement, investment, and commitment), and explores the influence those dimensions have on relationships that exist in a different context, that of business-to-business. If this investigation finds that perceptions of organization-to-organization relationships can be used to predict purchasing behavior and satisfaction with the organization, practitioners should be provided with a rationale for public relations expenditures and programs designed to improve organization–key public relationships because relationship outcomes will have been related specifically to two traditional methods of evaluation: consumer behavior and satisfaction with the organization. This, in turn, should make it easier for practitioners to operate within the management framework of analysis, planning, implementation, and evaluation. To better understand relationship management within the practice of public relations, we provide an overview to various relationship management theories, models, and applications.

Relationship Management Theories and Models

Since Ferguson's (1984) call for relationships to be the central unit of study in public relations, scholars increasingly focused research attention on the organization–public relationship. Broom, Casey, and Ritchey (1997) developed a model of organization–public relationships after a wide-ranging review of relationship literature. The model includes antecedents (components of relationships), concepts (properties of relationships), and consequences (relationship outcomes). Broom et al. (1997) contended that relationships consist of patterns of linkages through which the parties pursue and service their independent needs, that relationships are "dynamic," and that relationships can be described at any given point in time. They further suggested that relationship information and maintenance should be a process of mutual adaptation and contingent responses, and that relationships between an organization and key publics are phenomena that can be studied as distinct from the perceptions of the relationship held either by an organization or its key publics. The Broom et al. (1997) model is an outgrowth of concern that impact on relationships is rarely the focus of public relations evaluation. This concern was first noted by Broom (1977) when he stated that

> ...the function of public relations is to establish and maintain communication linkages between an organization and its publics in order to maintain mutually beneficial relationships. This ... calls for measuring the relationships in the social system composed of an organization and its publics. Public opinion surveys ... do not provide all the information needed to adequately describe corporate–public relationships on issues of mutual concern. (p.111)

In this book, Broom, Casey, and Ritchey explore the applicability of their organization–public model through a case study in which the concept of relationship was the central unit of analysis. Perceptions of the relationship were analyzed from a coorientational perspective and compared to documented communication patterns. As a result, Broom, Casey, and Ritchey conclude that relationships are subject to multiple interpretations and concluded that there is value in determining the perceptions of the relationship of all parties involved, separate from their behavior in the relationship.

Broom and Dozier (1990) have suggested that public relations practitioners utilize a coorientational approach to quantify the organization–public relationship as part of a public relations audit. The authors argued that such an approach provides a measure of the level of agreement between the organization and its key public regarding a given topic of interest or concern, as well as an estimation of the accuracy of each group's perceptions. As they noted, public relations programs intuitively affect the relationship between an organization and its publics. However, they contended that measurement of program impact on the relationship itself is rare. Broom and Dozier concluded that the "combination of one-sided measures of program impact and coorientational measures provides the most complete picture of program impact on the organization–public relationship" (p. 86).

Grunig (1993) advocated a two-way symmetrical model of public relations in which the organization and its key publics engage in a process of continual and reciprocal information exchange. The purpose of this exchange is to build a relationship between the organization and its key publics that is mutually beneficial. Grunig argued that by engaging in this type of dialogue, practitioners will be able to develop long-term behavioral relationships between the organization and its key publics, rather than simply symbolic ones that may not impact the long-term behavior of key publics. Similarly, Ehling (1992) argued that when organizations focus public relations efforts on developing long-term behavioral relationships, cost–benefit analyses then can be computed to determine the relative value of the organization–public relationship. Also in this book, Grunig and Huang (chap. 2, this volume) expand the organization–public relationship model of Broom et al. (1998) to include descriptions of the various coalitions that comprise organization–public relationships, strategies for maintaining these relationships, and the consequences of these relationships. Grunig and Huang argued that the model provides a method of predicting the behavioral intentions of the consumer. In doing so, scholars and practitioners could then determine the impact that public relations activities have on consumer behavior, which ultimately can be related to an organization's revenue stream.

Ledingham and Bruning (1998) focused their research efforts on identifying the organization–public relationship variables that influence consumer behavior, and reported that the organization–public relationship indicators of trust, openness, involvement, investment, and commitment differentiated those respondents who were loyal from those who were not. In a later study, Bruning and Ledingham (1998) reported that the organization–public relationship variables likewise impacted consumer perceptions of satisfaction with the organization. The authors contended that the organization–public relationship indicators of trust, openness, involvement, investment, and commitment impact the ways in which organization–public relationships are initiated, developed, and maintained, and ultimately can engender loyalty toward the organization among key publics. Moreover, they argue that public relations practitioners should develop public relations activities, programs, and goals around organization–public relationship indicators. Doing so increases awareness among members of key publics of the organization's desire to establish a mutually productive relationship, and reinforces the notion within the organization that in order for a relationship to have value for both parties, it must provide mutual benefit.

Applications of the Relationship Management Perspective

The relationship management perspective is a relatively new approach to the practice of public relations that has not been applied to many areas of public relations practice. Bruning and Ledingham (1998) adapted Knapp's and Vangelisti's (1996) model of the stages of the coming together and the coming apart of an interpersonal relationship to an organizational setting to construct a diagnostic tool for use in managing agency-client relationships. In this book, Coombs (chap. 4, this volume) suggests that early and continuing attention to a relationship can minimize conflict between an organization and key publics. Dimmick, Bell, Burgiss, and Ragsdale (chap. 6, this volume) explore the relationship dimension of trust in a case study of physician–patient relations. They conclude that there is need for a new, two-way approach to physician–patient relationships. Esposito and Koch's (chap. 12, this volume) analysis of network news logs serves as the basis for their conclusions concerning implications of relationship-based news for the practice of media relations. Kruckeberg (1998) called for attention to the new relationships mandated by accelerated globalism, multiculturalism, and diversity. Wilson (chap. 7, this volume) applies Ledingham and Bruning's (1998) relational dimensions to an analysis of employee and community relationships through volunteerism. Finally, Bridges and Nelson (chap. 5, this volume) indicate that relationships should be at the core of issues management.

What each of these studies demonstrates is the power, impact, and influence that relationships can have when they are managed effectively. The studies, however, tended to focus on the relationship between an organization and an individual, rather than an organization-to-organization relationship. As a result of our prior research with consumers as well as an apparent void in the impact that organization-to-organization relationships have on purchasing patterns, we decided to explore the notion of business-to-business relationships to determine whether the relationship dimensions that predict consumer behavior likewise can be used to predict the purchasing patterns of business owners and managers. Thus the following hypotheses and research questions were posited:

H_1. The organization–public relationship indicators of trust, openness, involvement, investment, and commitment will be positively related to business owners and managers perceptions of satisfaction with the organization.

H₂. The organization–public relationship dimensions of openness, trust, involvement, commitment, and investment will differentiate those business owners and managers who are loyal from those who are not.

METHOD

Setting

The setting for the current investigation was a three-state territory of a telecommunications company that provides both local and business telephone service. The local telephone company also has been a sponsor or co-sponsor of many local events (parades, community events, etc.), has invested millions of dollars in the telecommunications infrastructures of many communities (community development has been a strategy utilized by many utility companies because as communities grow, so does the utility company's opportunity to provide service), and has provided a significant amount of support and technical expertise to both businesses and local school systems.

As was the case with long distance service, local residential and business telephone service is being open to competition. Telephone companies that formerly enjoyed a monopoly now are finding their business subscribers to be the target of other telephone companies, cable television companies, and other providers who are jockeying to provide business telephone service, typically at a discount of at least 10%. This competitive setting provides an excellent opportunity to examine the influence that organization-to-organization relationships have on business decisions, particularly decisions that have a financial incentive attached to them.

Survey Development

After a review of interpersonal communication, social psychology, and marketing literatures, the authors developed a list of 17 relationship dimensions (investment, commitment, trust, comfort with relational dialectics, cooperation, mutual goals, interdependence and power imbalance, performance satisfaction, comparison level of the alternatives, adaptation, nonretrievable investment, shared technology, summate constructs, structural bonds, social bonds, intimacy, and passion) that were presented to business owners and to managers during a series of focus groups in order to identify the relationship dimensions that are important in business-to-business relationships. The focus group participants narrowed the list to 5 indicators of relationships (trust, openness, involvement, investment, and commitment). The relationship questions utilized in the current investigation used a 1–10 point scale and examined respondent perceptions of the relationship variables of trust (I feel that I can trust *company name* to do what is says it will do), investment (*Company name* seems to be the kind of company that invests in its customers), commitment (I think *company name* is committed to its customers), involvement (I am aware that *company name* is involved in my community), and openness (*Company name* makes an effort to be open with its customers). Purchasing behavior was determined by asking the respondents what they would do if offered a 10% discount by a competitor (If a competing company were to offer to provide local business telephone service to you for 10% less than you currently are being charged, would you switch?).

After a series of 4 focus groups with business owners and managers, executive interviews with company officials, and 2 internal roundtables with company employees, a 99-item survey was constructed. The survey was designed to help the organization develop strategies that could be used to combat business telephone service competition, and included questions regarding the relationship indicators, variables that are important in business-to-business relationships, satisfaction with the local telephone company, desirable new product features, the impact of local presence, activities that business owners believed the telephone company should sponsor, advertising recall, community development, local education, the telephone company's competitors for local telephone service, and descriptive information about the businesses.

Data Collection

The survey was administered via telephone to randomly selected business telephone service subscribers in the three-state area. The survey administrators were trained by the authors during a 1 hour preparatory session. Respondents were screened to ensure that owners or managers responsible for telecommunication decisions responded to the survey.

Approximately 40% of the dialed telephone numbers resulted in a completed interview. Of the 132 people who agreed to be involved in the study, 117 (89%) completed the interview. The average completed interview lasted 25 minutes.

Participants

The sample consisted of 117 business telephone subscribers across a three-state region. Survey administrators screened respondents to insure that decision makers responded to the survey. Of the businesses surveyed, 89% had normal business lines, 10% had private branch exchanges, and 1% indicated other forms of business lines. Likewise, 60% of the businesses surveyed had one line, 37% had 2 to 5 lines, and 3% had more than 6 lines. The types of businesses surveyed included 6% that were not-for-profit, 14% that were industrial, 53% that were small businesses, 9% that were retail, 6% that were a hotel or motel, 6% that were food service, and 6% that were a physician or a medical facility. Finally, 36% of the businesses grossed less than $100,000 per year, 24% grossed from $100,001 to $500,000 per year, 11% grossed over $500,001 per year, and 29% did not report yearly gross revenues.

RESULTS

Discriminant analysis was computed to determine whether the relationship indicators of trust, openness, involvement, investment, and commitment would differentiate those business customers who were loyal to the organization from those who were not. The groupings for the discriminant analysis were created as follows: those business owners or managers who indicated they would stay with the historic provider of telephone service, those who would opt for service with a new provider, and those who were unsure. Of the 117 people surveyed, 25% indicated that they would remain with the current provider, 54% would sign up with a new provider, and 21% percent were uncertain. We then used these groupings to determine whether perceptions of the business-to-business relationship could be used to differentiate a consumer's decision regarding the provider of local telephone service (Wilks's Lambda = .70, $X^2 = 29.70$, $df = 10$, p .001). See Table 9.1 for the means, univariate Fs, structure coefficients, and classification results.

TABLE 9.1

Discriminating Variables	Mean Scores of Stayers	Mean Scores of Undecideds	Mean Scores of Leavers	Univariate F	Structure Coefficients
Commitment	7.21	7.50	4.62	11.31***	.93
Trust	7.62	7.00	4.57	10.92***	.92
Openness	7.36	7.36	4.81	8.42***	.81
Investment	6.60	7.20	4.62	7.91***	.75
Involvement	7.32	7.15	4.90	6.55**	.72

* $p < .05$; ** $p < .01$; *** $p < .001$

Classification

	Actual Leavers	Actual Stayers	Actual Undecideds
Predicted Leavers	13	10	4
Predicted Stayers	3	21	5
Predicted Undecideds	4	15	9
Total n	20	46	18
n Correct	13	21	9
Proportion	.65	.46	.50

Overall: $N = 84$ n correct = 43   proportion correct = 0.51

As can be seen in Table 9.1, the organization–public relationship indicators of trust, openness, and commitment are strongly related, and investment and involvement are substantially related. Classification results indicate that stayers, leavers, and undecideds can be predicted at a 61% accuracy rate (prior probabilities were 33%).

A least-squares multiple-regression analysis using a forced entry selection method was computed to determine whether satisfaction scores could be predicted based on the respondent perception of the organization–public relationship, and to determine the relative degree of contribution of each relationship variable to respondent satisfaction scores. The respondent's perception of the organization–public relationship variables of trust, openness, involvement, investment, and commitment served as the independent variables. The respondent's satisfaction with the local telephone company served as the dependent variable. The results indicate that the relationship indicators combine to predict business owner or manager satisfaction with their local telephone company, and the relationship indicators helped to explain 32% of the satisfaction variation. Moreover, the results indicate that the relationship dimension of trust significantly impacts consumer satisfaction. Table 9.2 reports the regression, adjusted R^2, β, and analysis of variance (ANOVA) results.

DISCUSSION

Previous research shows that consumer perceptions of the organization–public relationship differentiates customers who indicated they would stay, leave, or were undecided regarding their provider of local telephone service (Ledingham & Bruning, 1998), as well as impacting consumer perceptions of satisfaction with the organization (Bruning & Ledingham, in press). In the current investigation, we examined the organization–key public relationship in a different context, that of business-to-business. The results from this investigation support the

TABLE 9.2

Regression

Predictor	Standard Error	Beta	t-score		
Constant	.62		6.33***		
Trust	.36	.36	2.47*		
Commitment	.18	.18	.818		
Involvement	.09	.04	.342		
Investment	.15	.16	1.03		
Openness	.16	−.09	−.56		

* p 05   ** p .01   *** p .001

SOURCE	DF	SS	MS	F	p
Regression	5	197.91	39.58	10.07	0.000
Error	92	361.48	3.93		
Total	97	559.39			
Adjusted R^2 = .32					

notion that perceptions of business relationships likewise influence business owner or manager choice of local telephone service provider, as well as influencing business owner or manager perceptions of satisfaction with the telephone company. Thus, the influence of relationships on purchasing behavior and satisfaction should be extended to include the business-to-business context.

Because relationships can be a powerful influence in both consumer decisions and perceptions of satisfaction, public relations practitioners should develop relationship programs grounded in relationship dimensions such as those of trust, openness, involvement, investment, and commitment. These programs must be designed to provide benefit to both the sponsoring organization and the key public. Organizations that develop a relationship management program that focuses on mutual benefit will maximize the influence that relationships can have on consumers while concurrently acting as a good corporate citizen because the organization will be engaging in activities, actions, and communication that are in the best interests of both the consumer and the organization. Moreover, a commitment to trust, openness, involvement, investment, and commitment affects organizational planning in at least two ways. First, it commits the organization to be open and trustworthy in its communication, which inherently is good for consumers, be they individuals, publics, or other businesses. Second, it commits the organization to policies developed around the notion of involvement, investment, and commitment—in this case—toward other businesses. Together, these dimensions suggest a strategy of building and maintaining long-term relationships in which the sponsoring organization is invested in the interests of other businesses in the relationship, is involved in furthering both its own as well as the other businesses' interests, and is committed to not only its own welfare but also that of other businesses in the relationship.

It should be noted that the results from this investigation indicate that trust was both strongly related to the criterion (in the discriminant analysis), as well as significant in influencing perceptions of satisfaction with the sponsoring organization (in the regression analysis). This finding is particularly important because it suggests that the cornerstone on which business relationships are built is trust. Organizations, therefore, should engage in relationship building activities, actions, and communication that build the organization's credibility, reputation, reliability, and dependability; promote honest communication (even if a potentially negative outcome could develop); and actively participate in the relationship. Business relationships that are managed in this manner almost assuredly will build trust between the two organizations, and ultimately should maximize the potential for mutual benefit.

The current investigation also supports the notion that relationships, whether they are between organizations and individuals or organizations and organizations, have the potential to offset financial incentives offered by competing organizations, and demonstrates the importance of public relations to an organization's economic well-being. The data show that respondents who perceive the business relationship more positively are less likely to change their provider of local telephone service when offered a 10% discount. This finding is particularly powerful given the nature of the key public in this particular study. Our focus group research found that, in the abstract, when business owners or managers were provided a scenario in which a comparable product or service was offered for a 10% discount, most focus group participants initially indicated they would receive service from the company that offered the lower price. In general, the focus group participants believed that their primary purpose as a businessperson was, as one participant stated, "to make financial decisions that are in the best interest of my company." Once a specific company was mentioned (in this case it was the local telephone company), however, many business owners or managers indicated they would not immediately switch because of the relationship that existed between the two organizations.

The results from this investigation, coupled with findings from previous research (Bruning & Ledingham, in press; Ledingham & Bruning, 1998), suggest that the practice of public relations should focus on the management of relationships between the organization and its key publics in order to maximize benefit to both the organization and its key publics. It has been estimated that the recruitment of a new customer is five times as costly as maintaining a current customer (Kotler, 1994). Public relations programs that focus on managing organization–key public relationships to ensure maximal benefit for both the organization and the organization's key publics can positively influence customer perceptions and behavior, which, ultimately, will influence the revenue stream of the sponsoring organization. Thus, effectively managed, mutually beneficial relationships can save an organization money by maximizing the number of current customers retained.

Finally, the effective management of an organization–key public relationship always should involve active participation from both parties. Organizations should actively solicit input regarding what can be done to improve the relationship. Likewise, business consumers should provide feedback regarding what they believe is effective in the relationship, what is ineffective, and what could be done to improve the relationship. Finally, and most important, sponsoring organizations should communicate with businesses on an ongoing basis the importance of feedback, the desire of the sponsoring organization to fulfill the wishes of other businesses in the relationship, and the changes that have been made as a result of key public input. Organizations that manage relationships in this manner maximize benefits experienced by both the organization and the organization's key publics.

Future Research

The current investigation supports the notion that relationships are important to a second type of key public, that of business-to-business. This finding, coupled with the finding that relationships play a key role in differentiating loyal from nonloyal customers in an organization–consumer relationship indicates that relationships are important for multiple key publics. Future research should examine additional key publics to determine whether the influence of the relationship between the organization and its key publics transfers to other contexts as well. For example, finding that perceptions of the organization–key public relationship influences the practice of press relations could guide the manner and method in which press relations are practiced by public relations practitioners. Thus, future research that examines the breadth and depth of relationship influence in additional contexts would be useful to both scholars and practitioners to determine the nature and influence that public relations activities have on consumer behaviors.

Because trust appears to be a variable that plays an integral role in business-to-business relationships regarding perceptions of satisfaction and consumer behavior, future research clearly is appropriate in order to clearly define trust. Developing both constitutive and operational definitions of trust would help both scholars and practitioners to better define, measure, and understand what trust is, and how trust can be incorporated into a theory of relationship management.

The current investigation has provided a second context in which perceptions of the relationship can be used to differentiate loyal from nonloyal publics. Because the purpose of public relations is to establish, develop, and maintain relationships, focusing public relations efforts on organizational activities and actions that facilitate relationships should help to demonstrate the value of public relations not only in terms of effective relationship building, but also in terms of public satisfaction and consumer purchasing behavior. Understanding the importance of organization–key public relationships, the impact that they can have on key public behavior, and their nature will continue to be of vital importance to both scholars and practitioners. This study is an attempt to explicate the association between organization–key public relationships and consumer behavior, and is offered as a part of the continued stream of scholarly inquiry attempting to develop a theory that can be used to explain organization–public relationships, understand their influence and determine the outcomes of effectively managed relationships.

REFERENCES

Broom, G. M. (1977). Coorientational measurement of public issues. *Public Relations Review 3*, 110–119.

Broom, G. M., & Dozier, D. M. (1990). *Using research in public relations: Applications for program management.* Englewood Cliffs, NJ: Prentice-Hall.

Broom, G. M., Casey, S. & Ritchey, J. (1997). Toward a concept and theory of organization–public relationships. *Journal of Public Relations Research, 9*, 83–98.

Broom, G. M., & Dozier, D. M. (1990). *Using research in public relations: Applications for program management.* Englewood Cliffs, NJ: Prentice-Hall.

Bruning, S. D., & Ledingham, J. A. (1998). Ten guidelines for managing the organization–public relationship. *Business Research Yearbook, 5*, 776–780.

Bruning, S. D., & Ledingham, J. A. (1998). Organization–public relationships and consumer satisfaction: The role of relationships in the satisfaction mix. *Communication Research Reports, 15*(2), 199–209.

Cutlip, S. M, Center, A. H., & Broom, G. M. (1994). *Effective Public Relations.* Upper Saddle River, NJ: Prentice-Hall.

Dozier, D. M. (1983, November). *Toward a reconciliation of "role conflict" in public relations research.* Paper presented at the meeting of the Western Communication Educators Conference, Fullerton, CA.

Ehling, W. P. (1992). Estimating the value of public relations and communication to an organization. In J. E. Grunig (Ed.), *Excellent public relations and communication management* (pp. 617–638). Hillsdale, NJ: Lawrence Erlbaum Associates.

Ferguson, M. A. (1984, August). *Building theory in public relations: Interorganizational relationships as a public relations paradigm.* A paper presented to the annual meeting of the Association for Education in Journalism and Mass Communication, Gainesville, FL.

Grunig, J. E. (1993). From symbolic to behavioral relationships. *Public Relations Review. 19*, 121–139.

Hon, L. C. (1998). Demonstrating effectiveness in public relations: Goals, objectives, and evaluation. *Journal of Public Relations Research, 10,* 103–135.
Knapp, M. L., & Vangelisti, A. L. (1996). *Interpersonal communication and human relationships.* Needham Heights, MA: Allyn and Bacon.
Kotler, P. (1994). *Marketing Management* (8th ed.). Englewood Cliffs, NJ: Prentice-Hall.
Ledingham, J. A., & Bruning, S. D. (1998). Relationship management in public relations: Dimensions of an organization–public relationship. *Public Relations Review, 24,* 55–65.
Thomsen, S. R. (1997). Public relations in the new millennium: Understanding the forces that are reshaping the profession. *Public Relations Quarterly, 42,* 11–17.

III

Implications of the Relational Perspective

10

An Interpersonal Primer With Implications for Public Relations

ಚಿ✧ಚೆ

T. Dean Thomlison
University of Evansville

This chapter offers a primer on interpersonal communication theories with the potential to contribute to public relations theory generation, model building, and practice. The primary objective of the chapter is to provide a *praxis*—a merging of theory and practice. Praxis leads to theoretically informed application, which is the overall purpose for this entire volume. The chapter contains a brief discussion of the nature of relationships, a review of the evolution of the transactional model of communication, and an examination of selected interpersonal communication theories and models. Suggestions on possible applications and implications for public relations are given throughout the discussion.

The phrase "public relations" is used in this chapter as a general label encompassing a host of activities including investor relations, membership relations, outreach, health advocacy, public affairs, public information, risk communication, strategic marketing, strategic planning, crisis management, constituent relations, community relations, and many others. As Botan (1997) pointed out, such terms are commonly used in advertising, marketing, and health promotion instead of "public relations."

It is hoped that a brief review of interpersonal communication and its potential applicability for public relations theory and practice may serve to create a greater appreciation of their complementary nature. An obvious starting point for this examination is to establish a basic understanding of the fundamental nature of relationships.

THE NATURE OF RELATIONSHIPS

Defining "Relationship"

Public relations and interpersonal communication have a common core—relationships. A *relationship* has been defined as a set of expectations two parties have for each other's behavior based on their interaction patterns. A more extensive definition of a relationship has also been advanced:

> The connection that exists when (1) the interactants are aware of each other and take each other into account, (2) there is some exchange of influence, and (3) there is some agreement about what the nature of the relationship is and what the appropriate behaviors are given the nature of the relationship. (Berko, Rosenfeld, & Samovar, 1997, p. 448)

According to this definition, mutuality of awareness, influence, benefit, and behavior are all part of successful relationships. *Thus, relationship management in public relations settings implies the development, maintenance, growth, and nurturing of mutually beneficial relationships between organizations and their significant publics.*

Dimensions of Satisfying Relationships

It is not enough to simply know *what* a relationship is. Before a public relations specialist can build and maintain a relationship, it is necessary to know the basic elements or building blocks of a healthy, mutually fulfilling relationship. A review of more than 700 articles and books by Wood (1995) isolated four essential dimensions of satisfying interpersonal relationships: investment, commitment, trust, and comfort with relational dialectics.

Investments refers to the time, energy, feelings, effort, and other resources given to build the relationship. The perception of equality of investments influences the level of satisfaction one experiences. For example, research on couples who are most satisfied with their relationships revealed that both partners believe each is investing equally in the relationship (Fletcher, Fincham, Cramer, & Heron, 1987; Hecht, Marston, & Larkey, 1994).

Commitment is the personal choice to continue a relationship. It adds the element of responsibility to a relationship by facing inevitable, relational difficulties together. This means problems are viewed as opportunities to mutually solve and strengthen the relationship rather than as an excuse to terminate the relationship.

Trust essentially refers to a feeling that relational partners can rely on each other. A high degree of predictability exists because each believes their partner is dependable, reliable, forthright, and trustworthy—that is, worthy of being trusted to do what is in the best interest of maintaining their long-term relationship. Each relies on the other to protect the welfare of the relationship. (Brehm, 1992)

Comfort with relational dialectics involves the numerous opposing forces on relationships that generate tensions and require a delicate balance if relational equilibrium is to be maintained. Wood (1996) cites three examples: autonomy/connection, openness/closedness, and novelty/predictability (pp. 185–186). For example, most people feel a natural desire to be connected to others but at the same time require a certain amount of autonomy. In an organizational context, there may be opposing "pulls" in which an individual may expect an organization to act in his or her best interest but, at the same time, may resist the need that organization may have for certain types of private information. Dialectical tension can generate frustration, distrust, and disloyalty in both personal and organizational settings.

THE EVOLUTION OF THE TRANSACTIONAL MODEL OF INTERPERSONAL COMMUNICATION

Transmission Model

As with public relations, the study of interpersonal communication has evolved significantly since the 1970s. Early interpersonal models viewed the communication process as primarily one-way. These simplistic models originally grew out of rhetorical and mass communication perspectives and terminology. These individualistic or *transmission models* viewed messages as emanating from a sender and being directed toward a receiver. According to this stimulus–response model, messages were basically aimed at receivers almost like projectiles (Fig. 10.1). Like the transmission model, the press agentry model (striving for favorable publicity) and the public information model ("journalist in residence" distributing information through various mass media) are one-way models. Grunig (1992) pointed out that both of these public relations models are asymmetrical one-way models because "they try to make the organization look good either through propaganda (press agentry) or by disseminating only favorable information (public information)" (p. 18).

Feedback Model

The addition of feedback to the transmission model resulted in a two-way interaction or *feedback model* in which messages are sent in response to messages received (Fig. 10.2).

The importance of the feedback model is that instead of viewing communication as the one-way aiming of messages as the transmission

FIG. 10.1. The transmission model.

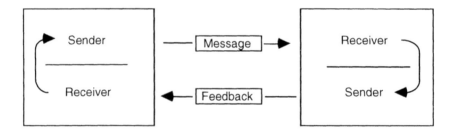

FIG. 10.2. The feedback model.

model did, it is seen as a trading of messages or information. It is similar to the two-way asymmetrical model of public relations that uses the feedback of research "to identify messages most likely to motivate or persuade publics" (Grunig, 1992, p. 289). Although still a linear model, the feedback model recognizes the reciprocal and cyclical nature of communication. However, it still lacks insight about the dynamic process nature of human communication.

Variables Model

Likewise, the SMCR or *variables model* originally suggested by Shannon and Weaver in 1949 and modified by others, including Berlo (1960; Fig. 10.3), simply noted visually the major components of communication without attempting to incorporate the processes operating between the four major variables of his model: source, message, channel, and receiver. A *source* (S) is the person who encodes the message, using such codes as verbal, nonverbal, visual, musical, or any other modality. Sources are influenced by the proficiency of their communication skills, their attitudes, their level of knowledge on the subject at hand, the social

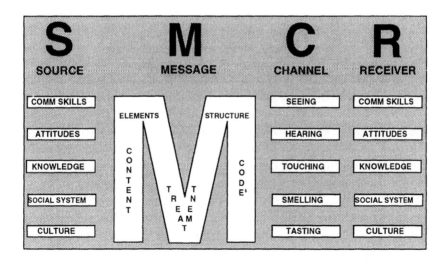

FIG. 10.3. Berlo's variables model.
Note. From *The Process of Communication: An Introduction to Theory and Practice* by David Berlo, copyright © 1960 by Holt, Rinehart, & Winston, Inc. and renewed in 1988 by David K. Berlo. Reproduced by permission of the publisher.

system within which they are operating, and their cultural environment, among others. A *message* (M) is used to convey the source's meaning by means of any of the codes. A *channel* (C) is the method of carrying the source's message using any combination of the basic senses. "Noise," anything that distorts or alters the original intended message, is also inherently part of a channel. A *receiver* (R) is the person who decodes the message, including the filtering of channel noise and the interpreting of the message based on such factors as communication skill level, attitudes, knowledge, social system, and culture.

Transactional Model

The current evolutionary development of basic interpersonal communication models is the *transactional model* of communication, first proposed by Barnlund (1970) and subsequently refined by other theorists (Fig. 10.4). Departing from a linear view of communication that had its rhetorical and persuasion seeds before the time of Aristotle, the transactional model posits that interpersonal communication is a dynamic, process-oriented activity in which the two participants are *simultaneously* sending and receiving messages. Anderson and Ross (1994) summarized the model as follows: "Encoding and decoding are not alternating subprocesses of communication, however, but are mutually dependent, each contributing to the meaning the communicators are building together (pp. 81–82). The two-way symmetrical model identified by Grunig and Hunt (1984) takes a transactional view of public relations because the objective is to gain understanding rather than to persuade.

Furthermore, human beings are too complex to be viewed as simple depositories of information who are trading messages with other depositories; a function that can be met by the simplest computer. We can do much more. As human beings, we have an extraordinary repertoire of communication skills centering around our unique capacity to engage in the mutual creation of meaning when we communicate with another person (Thomlison, 1982, p. 8). The transactional model acknowledges that communication is a delicate process evolving from the joining of two participants into a relationship that is more than the sum of its parts.

The transactional model of communication also views all behavior as having the potential of being meaningful to others, whether intended or not. This is an important distinction because it means that we do not necessarily communicate what we attempt to communicate and we may

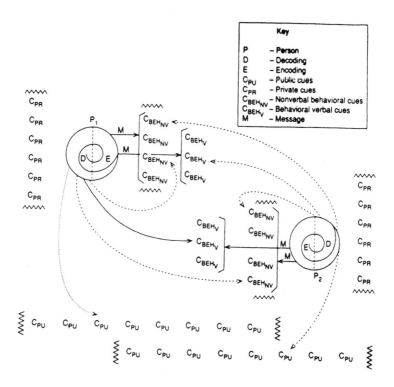

FIG. 10.4. Barnlund's transactional model.

Note. From "A Transactional Model of Communication" by D. C. Barnlund from *Language Behavior: A Book of Readings in Communication,* edited by Akin et al. As presented in K. K. Sereno and C. D. Mortensen (eds.), *Foundations of Communication Theory* (pp. 83–102). Copyright © 1970 by Harper and Row. Used with permission by MOUTON DE GRUYTER, a division of Walter de Gruyter GmbH & Co. Publishers, Berlin - New York.

be communicating even when we are not attempting to do so. Once a transaction is underway we cannot avoid communicating, even when we try. This basic interpersonal axiom can also be applied to the communication between an organization and its individual publics—its "public" relationships. The model sees human communication as much more than a conveyor belt on which messages are traded—arriving in the same basic condition as the message that was sent. The main point of this model is that communication is a dynamic, process-oriented, meaning-creating relationship between the two participating parties.

SELECTED INTERPERSONAL
COMMUNICATION THEORIES AND MODELS

The remainder of this chapter focuses on selected concepts from the discipline of interpersonal communication. Although not exhaustive, these interpersonal theories and models suggest a few of the many implications possible for public relations activities.

Social Exchange Theory

Social exchange theory provides a further extension and elaboration of the relational dimensions of investment and commitment, which were among Wood's (1995) four components of satisfying personal relationships discussed earlier. It is one of the most useful interpersonal theories for explaining why and when relationships begin, are maintained, and end. Social exchange theories, first advanced in the disciplines of psychology and sociology, have been applied to relational communication by Roloff (1981) and others with significant success (Liska & Cronkhite, 1995). Sometimes referred to as economic balance theory, social exchange theory states that social relationships involve the exchange of resources such as status, information, goods, services, money, intimacy, friendship, companionship, social acceptance, security, and love (Devito, 1996; Knapp, 1984). In a nutshell, this theory holds that people tend to develop relationships in which profits are maximized. Profit equals rewards minus costs. Rewards are anything that one would incur costs to obtain. Relationships, this perspective suggests, usually are maintained as long as rewards exceed costs, and usually are terminated when costs are greater than rewards.

The giving and receiving of physical and psychological resources can be viewed as costs and rewards. Rewards provide pleasures, satisfactions, and gratifications that reduce a drive or meet a need. Costs are factors that deter a desired sequence of behaviors or deny the meeting of a need. Thibaut and Kelley (1959) explained: "Thus, cost is high when great physical or mental effort is required, when embarrassment or anxiety accompany the action, or when there are conflicting forces or competing response tendencies of any sort" (pp. 12–13).

This "economic model" of relationships says that each person in a relationship has a certain standard or expectation for the behavior of their partner. Individuals enter relationships with a general notion of the types of rewards and profits that can realistically be desired and deserved from the relationship. When this standard or *Comparison Level* (CL) is reached or exceeded, satisfaction with the partner and the relationship results. Perceived rewards or value usually outweigh perceived costs in such cases. Meeting or exceeding a relational partner's expectations for the relationship becomes vital to that relationship's quality and longevity. Littlejohn (1996) cited studies by Taylor and Altman (1973) indicating that "relational partners not only assess the rewards and costs of the relationship at a given moment but also use the information they have gathered to predict the rewards and costs in the future" (Littlejohn, p. 264).

How much cost-over rewards a person will accept and remain in a relationship depends on that individual's *Comparison Level for Alternatives* (CLalt). That is, if there are other equally attractive or more attractive choices available to a person, then there will be less tolerance for anything below the standard for satisfaction (Fig. 10.5). Deterioration of the relationship or movement to an alternate relationship occurs when costs exceed rewards or greater profits are available in another relationship. According to this model, relationship participants compare current relationship profits with the imagined profits from other available relationships. In essence, having other viable choices available will

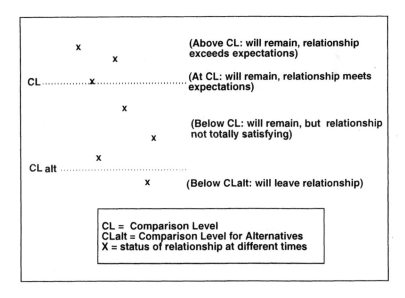

FIG. 10.5. The social exchange model.

reduce an individual's acceptance of anything less than his or her expectation for satisfaction. Of course, level of commitment to that relationship and how much one has invested in the relationship also affects how much attention one pays to other available choices. Having numerous options tends to raise or increase the Comparison Level or standard for satisfaction. As a relationship develops, we tend to build a cumulative balance of costs and rewards (Taylor & Altman, 1973).

In short, if several options are available we tend to be dissatisfied unless our expectation level is met or exceeded, and we may select from the other viable alternatives that will provide more rewards for the same or for less costs. If one can determine the other choices available and thus establish a fairly accurate idea of the CLalt, and if one can determine the CL or standard for satisfaction for a given partner, it is possible to predict when this person will terminate or maintain a particular relationship.

However, this is not simply traditional economic theory applied in an interpersonal context. Richard M. Emerson points out the critical difference:

> At its core, neoclassical economic theory views the actor (a person or a firm) as dealing not with other actors but with a *market*. In economic theory, decisions are made by actors not in response to, or in anticipation of, the decision of another party but in response to environmental parameters such as market price.... By contrast, in the various forms of social exchange theory, the longitudinal *exchange relation* between two specific actors is the central concept around which theory is organized.... Social exchange theory studies person–environment relations (Emerson, 1987, pp. 11–12).

Clearly, social exchange theory is a departure from traditional marketing perspectives in public relations, offering a refreshing interpersonal, relationship-sensitive perspective that has powerful implications and applications for public relations study, research, and practice.

Implications for Relational Management

The research and theories presented in this chapter and throughout this text suggest that relational dimensions such as Wood's (1995) four can be applied to noninterpersonal relationships between an organization and individual members of its publics. We now have quantitative research findings to demonstrate that these relational dimensions can be used to identify the desired level of satisfaction (CL) for individual consumers in their relationship with a specific organization, and thereby predict the amount of rewards necessary to maintain a given relationship. Likewise, it is possible to determine the specific level of rewards offered by alternative choices (competitors) necessary to overcome the commitment a consumer has with their current organizational relationship (Ledingham, Bruning, Thomlison, & Lesko, 1997).

This suggests that the level of expectation for stakeholder satisfaction (CL) is a key component of high quality ongoing relationships and, therefore, of public relations. For example, Heath (1993) likened the relationship between an organization and its significant publics or stakeholders to a courtship.

> "In this courtship, one important organizational prerogative is its marketing effort which can couple with public relations to foster relationships and advance organizational goals but which can create unsatisfied expectations about product or service performance which motivate stakeholders to demand their expectations be fulfilled." (p. 144)

It is apparent that public relations practitioners must monitor the CL of their publics if their relationship building and relationship management is to be maximally effective.

The social exchange model also alerts public relations practitioners to the vital role of relational adaptation to changing needs, expectations, and environmental demands in its relationships with various stakeholders such as vendors, employees, political bodies, and suppliers, as well as individual customers. For example, a study of 237 customer–supplier relationships between European manufacturing firms confirmed that interfirm adaptations are essential elements in the social exchange process (Hallen, Johanson, & Seyed-Mohamed, 1991). Hallen and his colleagues also proposed a structural model of "interfirm adaptation" based on social exchange and resource-dependency perspectives.

There are several other relational theories closely aligned with social exchange theory that cannot be extensively covered here due to space limitations, yet they hold great promise for application to public relations. For example, several theories examine the methods used by people to lower the amount of ambiguity in their relationships. *Uncertainty reduction theory* (Berger, 1982) explains in detail a variety of strategies used by communicators to gather information about the people with whom they interact. The theory shows the importance of uncertainty reduction, especially in the early stages of relationships.

Gudykunst (1988) applied the theory to intercultural situations and Sunnafrank (1986) evolved the theory into what he termed the *predicted outcome value theory*. Sunnafrank contended that most people do not seek information just to reduce uncertainty for its own sake, but rather to use that information to determine potential negative or positive communication outcomes and partner selection. The theory suggests that people tend to pursue those relationships that they predict will produce the most positive outcomes and, in initial relationships, those topics that they believe will be most rewarding. In addition to Sunnafrank's theory, there are several other decision theories such as Ajzen and Fishbein's (1980) *theory of reasoned action*. As with social exchange theory, these *subjective expected utility theories* were originally developed to analyze and explain decisions in economics (Liska & Cronkhite, 1995), but potential applications to relationship communication and public relations are many.

Stages of a Relationship

Researchers, theorists, and scientists are constantly attempting to find order and systemization in our rather chaotic and unstable world. Child development experts note general patterns in the stages of growth from infancy through childhood and adolescence and into maturity. Biologists divide plants and animals into various categorical families or phyla based on similarities and life cycles. Interpersonal communication theorists likewise seek to find patterns to systematize the blended stages of relational development. Relationship development models generally view relationships as developing systematically and incrementally. However, it should be remembered that the process is seldom as simple or the transitions to other stages as quick as represented in these relational development models.

Numerous theories and models on the stages in the development, maintenance and dissolution of relationships have been devised since the 1960s. For example, the concept of *selective filtering* (Kerckhoff & Davis, 1962) hypothesized that we use different criteria in deciding whether to continue a relationship at different stages in that relationship. This view says our filters serve as gates for determining entrance into the next progressive stage of relational development (Duck, 1976). Such models of relationship filters suggest that each of us has our own somewhat unique set of relationship categories such as strangers, acquaintances, friends, close friends, and best friend. Each category has its own set of criteria for filtering out those who will move on to the next stage, which is more intimate or has a stronger bond. Each progressive stage has fewer people in it because the criteria for exclusion are more stringent with each stage, making it increasingly difficult to "qualify" for the next stage.

Many advocates of exchange theory believe that participants go through a series of four stages in their relational development. *sampling*, in which we seek those who fit our needs and reward us; *bargaining*, in which both partners work at developing a mutually satisfying relationship; *commitment*, the stage in which bonds are formed; and *institutionalization*, in which there is a public declaration or affirmation of their continued relationship (Thibaut & Kelley, 1959). Institutionalization can take many forms ranging from marriage to business partnerships.

One of the most interesting and comprehensive incremental relational development and deterioration models is an *interaction stages* paradigm originally proposed by Knapp (1978, 1984) and later refined with Vangelisti (Knapp & Vangelisti, 1992). The "creeping incrementalism" or movement from one stage to the next is generally systematic and sequential, but there can also be movement within stages and forward or backward movement between stages. The interaction stages of Knapp and Vangelisti's model (Fig. 10.6) are as follows:

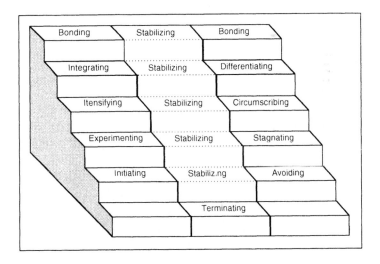

FIG. 10.6. The staircase model of interaction stages.
Note. From *Social Intercourse: From Greeting to Good-bye*, by Mark L. Knapp, Boston: Allyn and Bacon, 1978, p. 33. Reprinted by permission of the publisher.

1. *Initiating:* The first contact with another and initial reactions.
2. *Experimenting:* Exchange of basic information and attempting to discover the unknown about each other; smalltalk or phatic communion is common. Most relationships do not progress past this point.
3. *Intensifying:* Disclosure of more personal and specific information; forms of address become more informal; more use of inclusive terms such as "we" and "our."
4. *Integrating:* When two become a pair or act as a unit, develop a shared history, merge their social circles or do all three. The relationship can be between family members, romantic partners, friends, or business colleagues.
5. *Bonding:* A public ritual or formal contract binds the relationship such as marriage, christenings, adoptions, business partnerships, and ceremonies of unity. There is a public commitment to the relationship and communication can now be based on the interpretation and execution of the commitments contained in the contract. Bonding is a method of gaining social or institutional support for the relationship.
6. *Differentiating:* The start of uncoupling and the establishment of more separate identities with fewer joint endeavors. Differentiating can be the result of bonding too quickly without sufficient breadth and depth to the relationship.
7. *Circumscribing:* The communication concentrates more on superficial and public topics with less breadth or depth. Communication decreases in amount and becomes more restricted to certain "safe" topics.
8. *Stagnation:* Communication about the relationship ceases; participants may sit in each other's presence for long periods without communicating. There is a great amount of tension in the relationship and it is evident the relationship is in jeopardy.
9. *Avoiding:* Efforts are made to avoid contact with the other party. This includes avoidance of physical contact as well as ignoring the other nonverbally and verbally when they are in the same physical space.
10. *Terminating:* The stage in which one or more participants end the relationship. Open access ceases and it is clear the relationship, in its current form, no longer exists.

This model indicates that movement is always to a new place and that relational experiences are always unique to some degree and therefore cannot totally be repeated or erased from one's relational history. Knapp (1984) stated that although the communication cannot be precisely predicted, certain patterns are likely. He explained:

> We would expect the Initiating and Terminating Stages to be characterized by communication that is more narrow, stylized, difficult, rigid, awkward, public, hesitant, and with overt judgments suspended; the stages of Integrating, Bonding, and Differentiating should show more breadth, uniqueness, efficiency, flexibility, smoothness, personalness, spontaneity, and overt judgments given. (pp. 34–35)

It would logically follow that an examination of the language and of other communication behaviors manifested in a relationship could be utilized to determine the probable relational stage. This model highlights the overall development of relationships across time and the connection between the stages of a relationship. Knapp and Vangelisti (1992) pointed out that the process is not fixed and linear, but rather a matter of trends or tendencies. Wilmot (1995) observed that the model is biased toward romantic relationships and may not easily apply to other types of relationships. However, the general concept of progressivism in relationship building clearly has multiple applications in a variety of contexts and types of relationships, including those between organizations and their significant publics.

An alternative perspective is offered by the *plateau/change model* . It argues that the creeping incrementalism or progressive development of relationships through a series of stages is not an accurate depiction of the dynamic, subjective, nonlinear nature of human relationships. Duck (1988) characterized this model by stating: "We rise from plateau to plateau rather than up a continuously rising gradient of intimacy" (p. 49). The patterns of relational change presented by this model can be summarized as follows:

1. *Alternating times of stability followed by "turning points"* that are relatively rapid rather than the slow incrementalism depicted by the Interaction Stages paradigm of Knapp and Vangelisti (1992).
2. *Oscillation between closeness and more distance*, leading to increased pressure for change in the relationship.
3. *Continuous change* even when the relationship is relatively stable.
4. *Quality of interaction influences relational change* more than the mere quantity of communication.

5. *Changes in role relationships require a change in the relationship definition*, such as from stranger to friend or from prospect to customer.
6. *A predominant pattern of behavior* surrounds most relationships and most do not have intimacy as their central purpose (Wilmot, 1995).

It is not necessarily the frequency of interaction that pushes the relationship to the next plateau; it is mainly driven by how each relational participant perceives the relationship and their self. A relationship can be maintained at a particular level and endure numerous changes until some significant occurrence moves the relationship to a new level. This applies to movement toward a closer, deeper relationship, as well as to movement toward a more distant or dissolving relationship. Friendship, work, business, and family relationship contexts all experience these oscillations both between and within plateaus.

The Coorientation Model

Theodore Newcomb (1953) developed a *coorientation model* as a helpful tool in relational analysis of dyadic pairs. This simple yet insightful model consists of two communicators, A and B, and their "orientation" toward some "object of communication," X. The object of communication could be an actual physical object (i.e., a house that the couple is considering purchasing or a painting in a museum), an event (i.e., a baseball game, a rock concert, or a christening), an activity (i.e., playing cards or watching football on television every Sunday), an attitude (i.e., loving action movies or being opposed to abortion), or a behavior (i.e., selling Aunt Molly's antique quilt without conferring about it first or donating uniforms to the local little league baseball team). Any subject, behavior, attitude, belief, event, or object that is the focus of communication for the two participants has the potential to be the object of communication. Each communicator, A and B, has a simultaneous coorientation toward his or her communication partner (usually the level of attraction and feelings toward the partner) and toward the object of communication (the degree of positive or negative attitude about X). Figure 10.7 illustrates the model.

Newcomb (1953) saw four basic components of this relational system: A's attitude toward X, A's attraction to B, B's attitude toward X, and B's attraction to A. According to the model, both A and B have a natural propensity toward balance in their coorientation toward X and their

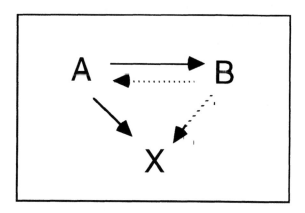

FIG. 10.7. Newcomb's A-B-X or coorientation model.
Note. From "An Approach to the Study of Communicative Acts," 1953, in *Psychological Review*, 60: 393-404, 1953, as presented in *Dyadic Communication* , 3rd ed., p. 104, by W. W. Wilmot, 1987, New York: Random House.

partner. If A has a negative attitude toward smoking (X) and a very positive attraction toward B, but B has a positive attitude toward smoking (X) and toward A, then A will experience an imbalance resulting in a push toward revision of attitudes to regain balance. This "strain toward balance" can be resolved by one or a combination of A decreasing the amount of liking for B, A changing his or her attitude toward X, and A changing B's attitude about X to align with A's. A's actions are dependent on A's own orientations as well as on A's perceptions of B's orientations, and vice versa for B. Thus, both communicators are continually making predictions or estimates of their partner's orientations. A has perceptions of what B is thinking and feeling, just as B has perceptions of what A is thinking and feeling. Based on this model, Wilmot (1987) concluded that at the very minimum, any thorough index of a dyadic relationship should include the following two items of information: each person's orientation (that is, their attitude toward the object of communication and their attraction toward their communication partner) and what each person perceives their partner's orientations to be.

This is sound advice for anyone interested in examining the intricacies of relationships, whether they be personal ones or public–organizational ones. Because of the strain toward balance or symmetry, actions and stands taken by organizations have direct impact on the amount of positive or negative perception of the organization by its significant publics. This model also lays the foundation for several other relational models of "interpersonal perception" (Drewery, 1969; Ichheiser, 1970; Laing, Phillipson, & Lee, 1966). Further, there are also numerous balance or cognitive consistency models, such as Festinger's (1957) *cognitive dissonance theory*, which offer insights about perception based on the desire for balance between behaviors and beliefs. Such constructs could make important contributions to public relations theory and model building.

Metaperspectives

As the coorientation model illustrates, communication behavior is directly influenced by a person's experience of his or her partner. Behavior (such as a touch on the arm, a handshake, or a wink) is observable, whereas an individual's experience of that behavior is a personal, internal process based on a wealth of factors ranging from context, culture, past experiences, perceived nature of the relationship, roles operating, and so forth. A person can only infer another's experience. A relationship is defined by one's perceptions of the other's behaviors and feelings. Laing's (1969) relational perception theory holds that our communication is affected by our perception of the relationship and that communication partners are mutually affecting each other continuously during a transaction. He believed that an aware communicator understands that the behavior of one's partner is a function of one's own behaviors and perceptions.

The *Interpersonal Perception Method* (Laing et al., 1966) can be useful in unwrapping the perceptual layers in any type of relationship, ranging from personal to business settings. Each person in a relationship has three major levels of experience or perception named "perspectives": direct perspective, metaperspective, and meta-metaperspective. Although these layers of perspectives can theoretically go even deeper (meta-meta-metaperspective, etc.), the first three levels are sufficient for the analysis of most interpersonal interactions.

A *direct perspective* is a person's view of a behavior, object, person, event, activity, or anything else one observes and interprets in his or her daily world. There is often an evaluation attached to the direct perspective: "I like this fruit," "I love her," "I hate broccoli," "I like that commercial," "I trust that company," "She genuinely cares about my needs." A *metaperspective* is what a person imagines that another is thinking or feeling. For example, "He likes my hair style," "She is in love with me," "She is afraid of commitment," "That business doesn't care about their customers." A *meta-metaperspective* is what a person thinks another's metaperspective is: "She thinks I like her poetry," "He believes that I love to ride horses," "She thinks I am in love with her," "Our customers think we are committed to environmental safety." In other words, it is what A thinks B sees as A's direct perspective. Whenever a person attempts to determine another's experience of him or her, meta-metaperspectives are present. Or, put another way, whenever one person presumes to know another person's metaperspective, meta-metaperspectives are present.

Perhaps an illustration will clarify this model (see Fig. 10.8). Tom loves to go to see movies (his direct perspective) and he thinks Barb also likes to go to see movies (his metaperspective). Furthermore, Tom believes that Barb thinks he loves going to movies (his meta-metaperspective). Now, from Barb's point-of-view things look a little different. Barb feels that going to the movies is boring (her direct perspective), but she also believes that Tom loves to go to movies (her metaperspective). In addition, she believes that Tom thinks she likes going to movies (her meta-metaperspective).

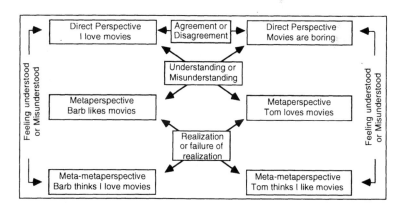

FIG. 10.8. The Interpersonal Perspectives Model.
Note. From *Relational Communication* by William W. Wilmot, New York: McGraw-Hill, Inc., 1995, pp. 13–14. Composite graphic of two models. Adapted and printed with permission of McGraw-Hill Companies.

The degree of matching perspectives is of crucial importance in relationships. The greater the perceptual accuracy, the healthier and more fulfilling a relationship will be. However, as this simple example with Tom and Barb shows, our perspectives are not always accurate and they are not always congruent with our partner's actual experience. On any particular issue, there are four key areas of comparison of perspectives in any dyadic transaction:

1. Comparison between direct perspectives on the same issue results in *agreement or disagreement.*
2. Comparison between one's own metaperspective and the other's direct perspective results in *understanding* or *misunderstanding.*
3. Comparison of one's meta-metaperspective and one's own direct perspective results in feeling *understood* or *feeling misunderstood.*
4. Comparison of one's meta-metaperspective and the other's metaperspective results in *realization* or *failure of realization* (Littlejohn, 1996).

Tom and Barb can again be used to illustrate how these comparison areas help pinpoint the specific causes of conflict or confusion in relationships. Because the direct perspectives of the two do not match, this incongruity yields disagreement regarding movie attendance. Tom thinks it is a very enjoyable activity, whereas Barb thinks it is boring. However, for some reason Tom is not aware of Barb's feelings about attending films. He thinks that she likes going to the movies. This incongruity between his metaperspective (she likes going to movies) and her direct perspective (going to movies is boring) results in a misunderstanding. Interestingly, Tom feels understood because he is experiencing congruence between his direct perspective (I love going to movies) and his own meta-metaperspective (Barb thinks I love going to movies). It should be noted that *feeling understood* is not the same as *being understood.* Furthermore, Tom's meta-metaperspective (Barb thinks I love going to movies) is congruent with Barb's metaperspective (He loves going to movies), resulting in the realization that Barb knows he loves movies. To summarize, Tom and Barb have a disagreement but he is not aware of it because he has a misunderstanding regarding how she feels about movies. On the other hand, Barb understands that they disagree on movie going (direct to direct). As a result, she feels misunderstood because she realizes that Tom misunderstands how she feels about movies.

As this simple example illustrates, disagreements generate far fewer problems in relationships than do misunderstandings and lack of realization of disagreements. Barb's and Tom's problem was not caused by the disagreement; it was caused by misunderstanding their level of agreement on this issue and a lack of realization of that disagreement. If two communicators understand that they disagree, the issue can be discussed and negotiated. For example, Tom agrees to attend philharmonic concerts that are enjoyed by Barb, and Barb agrees to attend the next film that Tom wants to see. We know that experience affects behavior, so we often behave according to our metaperspectives. Unfortunately, communicators often assume that their metaperspective is the same as their partner's direct perspective. Likewise, members of organizations often assume that they know what their employees, customers, vendors, suppliers, and other significant publics want. In traditional approaches to public relations, the focus was on manipulation and control of the metaperspectives of significant publics. If a business organization has a lack of realization or a misunderstanding of its publics' perception of the business' community commitment, then the business may suffer financially.

Dimensions of Communication Behavior Model

Most communication models have taken an either–or stance with respect to mediated interaction. That is, traditionally scholars have assumed that communication is either mediated, such as newspapers and television , or not mediated, such as face-to-face interpersonal communication. The *dimensions of communication behavior model*, which offers an alternative perspective, was developed by Lievrouw and Finn (Ruben & Lievrouw, 1990). They contend that all communication is mediated at some level. Although face-to-face interaction does not utilize the hardware and technology of mass media, this communication is still mediated through the five senses by natural communication channels such as air and light. There is no way to directly experience the messages of others without some form of intermediary means. Thus, according to Lievrouw and Finn, the focus should be on how communication is mediated rather than taking the bipolar perspective of whether it is mediated.

Their model centers on what they call the fundamental dimensions of all communication behavior: involvement, temporality, and control. *Involvement* refers to the transcending of both physical and psychological distance, ranging from high involvement to low involvement. *Temporality* focuses on how communicators experience time in their relationships, ranging from simultaneous interaction (participants are sending and receiving messages at the same moment in time) to nonsimultaneous events (there is a time delay between sending and receiving messages). *Control* involves how much influence is present in the context and how much is exerted by each participant, ranging from equal sharing to dominance by one party.

Lievrouw and Finn's model offers a means of locating in physical space the relationship between a particular type of communication and their three basic dimensions of communication. The model also provides a way to visually demonstrate the impact of each dimension and its relationship to the other dimensions. For example, it is clear from Fig. 10.9 that live non-interactive television, such as a local newscast,

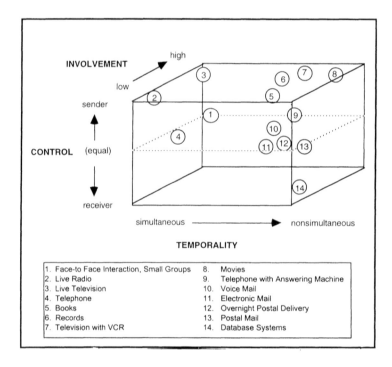

FIG. 10.9. Lievrouw and Finn's dimensions of communication behavior model.
Note. From *Mediation, Information, and Behavior* by B. D. Ruben and L. A. Lievrouw (eds.), New Brunswick, NJ: Transaction Publishers, copyright © 1990; all rights reserved. Reprinted by permission of Transaction Publishers. As presented in *Questions of Communication: A Practical Introduction to Theory* by R. Anderson and V. Ross, New York, NY:

possesses high sender control, along with high involvement and high simultaneous usage. Likewise, face-to-face interaction has high involvement and high simultaneous usage, but it is generally more equal on control.

Although one may disagree with the particular placement of some of the means of communication, the model has strong heuristic value. This model provides an excellent method of comprehending the nature of different mediated social contexts, the characteristics that each type of communication shares or does not share with other means of communication, and the spatial relationship between each. Additionally, the model removes the artificial chasm in thinking and research that has traditionally existed between those engaged in the study and practice of mass communication and those who study and practice interpersonal communication. It is a method of viewing the commonality of the various multiple means of communication rather than concentrating on their differences. Its creators also emphasized that the specific cultural context of that communication is a key factor in placement on the model. As technology continues its ever-growing number and combinations of ways for human beings to interact, the model provides a convenient and adaptable way to continually update the location and relationship between these methods of mediated communication.

Developing strong relationships with an organization's individual publics requires that public relations practitioners do more than just utilize a mix of mediated communication. The overriding perspective advocated throughout this text is that these are only tools that provide ways for communicators to interact and grow relationships. Rather than being the goal, they are simply a means to an end: building a relationship that can endure the tests of time, adversity, and competing interests. Communication designed to use these tools in order to manipulate and control is monologic, whereas the goal of public relations should be to establish dialogic communication.

SOME OVERALL IMPLICATIONS FOR PUBLIC RELATIONS

1. Traditional mass media models lack the level of sophistication needed to understand, develop, maintain, grow, and nurture relationships between organizations and their significant publics.

2. The range of interpersonal communication theories and models offers a wealth of opportunities for researchers, theorists, and practitioners of relational management.

3. Public relations practitioners may be able to improve the quality and longevity of their relationships with significant publics by including Wood's (1995) four essential dimensions of satisfying interpersonal relationships: investment, commitment, trust, and comfort with relational dialectics.

4. The Transactional Model of communication that demonstrates the interdependence of actors in the relationship and the simultaneity of roles can serve as a basis for modeling the potential interaction between organizations and their key publics.

5. The basic axiom that one cannot avoid communicating can likewise be a useful axiom to public relations practitioners, reminding them that lack of communication still sends a message to their publics.

6. Models that identify the progressive stages of relationship development can provide a basis for similar categorization of organization–public relationships.

7. Balance or equilibrium models developed around the notion of relational expectancies could serve as the framework for identifying and monitoring mutual expectations among key members of organizations and their publics.

8. The Interpersonal Perception Method or Metaperspectives Model can provide a perspective for bringing greater agreement, understanding, realization, and feelings of being understood to relationships within a public relations context.

9. The Dimensions of Communication Behavior Model can be utilized by public relations practitioners to visualize the relationship between the various means of communication used with an organization's significant publics, as well as the interrelationship between involvement, control, and temporality so adjustments can be made as necessary for relational management.

CONCLUSION

As indicated at the outset, the primary objective for this chapter is to provide a praxis—a blending of theory and practice. The goal of this chapter and the entire text is to develop theoretically informed practitioners who can *relationalize* public relations by applying these concepts and principles. Relational management will only evolve through an awareness and understanding of this relatively new public relations paradigm and its diverse theoretical foundations. Traditional models of mass communication, grounded in persuasion and manipulation, are far from sufficient to explain and predict the intricacies of public relations as it increasingly moves toward a central focus on relationships within the organization-public context. Hopefully, the few areas for exploration offered in this primer on interpersonal communication theories and models will serve to illustrate the breadth and depth of possible uses for public relations. When publics are treated as ends rather than as means, remarkably exciting things happen in organizations. The implications and applications to the relational management perspective are limited only by the imagination of public relations practitioners, researchers, educators, and theorists.

REFERENCES

Ajzen, I. & Fishbein, M. (1980). *Understanding Attitudes and Predicting Social Behavior.* Englewood Cliffs, NJ: Prentice-Hall.

Anderson, R., & Ross, V. (1994). *Questions of Communication: A Practical Introduction to Theory.* New York: St. Martin's Press.

Barnlund, D. C. (1970). A Transactional Model of Communication. In K.K. Sereno & C. D. Mortensen (eds.), *Foundations of Communication Theory.* New York: Harper and Row.

Berger, C. R. (1982). *Language and Social Knowledge: Uncertainty in Interpersonal Relations.* London: Arnold.

Berko, R. M, Rosenfeld, L. B., & Samovar, L. A. (1997). *Connecting* (2nd ed.). New York: Harcourt Brace College Pub.

Berlo, D. K. (1960). *The Process of Communication: An Introduction to Theory and Practice.* New York: Holt, Rinehart, & Winston.

Botan, C. (1997). Ethics in Strategic Communication Campaigns: The Case for a New Approach to Public Relations. *The Journal of Business Communication, 34* (2), 188–202.

Botan, C. (1993). Introduction to the Paradigm Struggle in Public Relations. *Public Relations Review, 19* (2), 107–110.

Brehm, S. (1992) *Intimate Relations (2nd ed.).* New York: McGraw-Hill.

Cutlip, S. M., Center, A. H., & Broom, G. M. (1994). *Effective Public Relations* (7th ed.). Englewood Cliffs, NJ: Prentice Hall.

DeVito, J. A. (1996). *Messages: Building Interpersonal Communication Skills* (3rd. ed.). New York: Harper Collins.

Drewery, J. (1969). An Interpersonal Perception Technique. *British Journal of Medical Psychology, 42,* 171–181.

Duck, S. (1976). Interpersonal "Communication in Developing Acquaintance. In G. R. Miller (Ed.), *Explorations in Interpersonal Communication.* Beverly Hills, CA: Sage.

Duck, S. (1988). *Relating to Others.* Chicago: The Dorsey Press.

Emerson, R. M. (1987). Toward a Theory of Value in Social Exchange. In *Social Exchange Theory,* K. S. Cook (Ed.). Newbury Park, CA: Sage.

Ferguson, M. A. (1984, August). *Building Theory in Public Relations: Interorganizational Relationships*. Paper presented to the Association for Education in Journalism and Mass Communication, Gainesville, FL.

Festinger, L. (1957). *A Theory of Cognitive Dissonance*. Palo Alto, CA: Stanford University Press.

Fletcher, G. J., Fincham, F. D., Cramer, L., & Heron, N. (1987). The Role of Attributions in the Development of Dating Relationships. *Journal of Personality and Social Psychology, 53*(3), 481–489.

Grunig, J. E. (Ed.). (1992). *Excellence in Public Relations and Communication Management*. Hillsdale, NJ: Lawrence Erlbaum Associates.

Grunig, J. E. (1993). Image and Substance: From Symbolic to Behavioral Relationship. *Public Relations Review, 19* (2), 221–239.

Grunig, J. E., & Hunt, T. (1984). *Managing Public Relations*. New York: Holt, Rinehart, & Winston.

Gudykunst, W. B. (1988). Uncertainty and Anxiety. In Y. Y. Kim & W. B. Gudykunst (Eds.), *Theories in Intercultural Communication*. Newbury Park, CA: Sage.

Hallen, L., Johanson, J., & Seyed-Mohamed, N. (1991). Interfirm Adaptation in Business Relationships. *Journal of Marketing,55* (2), 29–37.

Heath, R. L. (1993). A Rhetorical Approach to Zones of Meaning and Organizational Prerogatives. *Public Relations Review, 19* (2), 141–155.

Hecht, M. L., Marston, P. J., & Larkey, L. K. (1994). Love Ways and Relationship Quality in Heterosexual Relationships. *Journal of Social and Personal Relationships, 11*, 25–44.

Ichheiser, G. (1970). *Appearances and Realities: Misunderstanding in Human Relations*. San Francisco: Jossey-Bass.

Kerckhoff, A. C., & Davis, K. E. (1962). Value Consensus and Need Complementarity in Mate Selection. *American Sociological Review, 27*, 295–303.

Knapp, M. L. (1978). *Social Intercourse: From Greeting to Goodbye*. Boston: Allyn & Bacon.

Knapp, M. L. (1984). *Interpersonal Communication and Human Relationships*. Boston: Allyn & Bacon.

Knapp, M. L., & Vangelisti, A. (1992). *Interpersonal Communication and Human Relationships*. Boston: Allyn & Bacon.

Laing, R. D. (1969). *Self and Others*. London: Tavistock.

Laing, R. D., Phillipson, H., & Lee, A. R. (1966). *Interpersonal Perception*. Baltimore: Perennial Library.

Ledingham, J. A., Bruning, S., & Thomlison, T. D. (1996, October). The Applicability of Interpersonal Relationship Dimensions to an Organizational Context: Toward a Theory of Relational Loyalty, A Qualitative Approach. Paper presented at The Allied Academies International Conference, Maui, HI.

Ledingham, J. A., Bruning, S., Thomlison, T. D., & Lesko, C. (1997). Transferability of Interpersonal Relationship Dimensions in Differing Organizational Contexts. *Academy of Managerial Communications Journal, 1* (1), 36–39.

Liska, J., & Cronkhite, G. (1995). *An Ecological Perspective on Human Communication Theory*. New York: Harcourt Brace.

Littlejohn, S. W. (1996). *Theories of Human Communication* (5th ed.). Belmont, CA: Wadsworth.

Montgomery, B. M. (1992). Communication as the Interface Between Couples and Culture. In S. Deetz (Ed.), *Communication Yearbook 15*. Newbury Park, CA: Sage.

Newcomb, T. M. (1953). An approach to the Study of Communicative Acts. *Psychological Review, 60*, 393–404.

Roloff, M. E. (1981). *Interpersonal Communication: A Social Exchange Approach*. Beverly Hills, CA: Sage.

Ruben, B. D., & Lievrouw, L. A. (Eds.). (1990). *Mediation, Information, and Behavior*. New Brunswick, NJ: Transaction Publishers.

Sunnafrank, M. (1986). Predicted Outcome Value During Initial Interactions: A Reformulation of Uncertainty Reduction Theory. *Human Communication Research, 13*, 3–33.

Taylor, D. A., & Altman, I. (1973). *Social Penetration: The Development of Interpersonal Relationships*. New York: Holt, Rinehart & Winston.

Thibaut, J. W., & Kelley, H. H. (1959). *The Social Psychology of Groups*. New York: John Wiley & Sons.

Thomlison, T. D. (1982). *Toward Interpersonal Dialogue*. New York: Longman Publisher.

Thomlison, T. D. (1990, April). Public Relations and Listening. Paper presented at the annual conference of the Central States Communication Association, Detroit, MI.

Thomlison, T. D., & Ledingham, J. A. (1989). The Challenge of Communication Curriculum Integration. *Resources in Education*, ERIC Clearinghouse for Reading and Communication Skills (ED 332 236).

Wilmot, W. W. (1987). *Dyadic Communication* (3rd ed.). New York: Random House.

Wilmot, W. W. (1995). *Relational Communication*. St. Louis, MO: McGraw-Hill.

Wood, J. T. (1996). *Everyday Encounters*. Belmont, CA: Wadsworth.

Wood, J. T. (1995). *Relational Communication*. Belmont, CA: Wadsworth.

11

From Personal Influence to Interpersonal Influence: A Model for Relationship Management

ಬ✧ಜ

Elizabeth L. Toth
Syracuse University

This chapter introduces a model depicting how interpersonal communication processes can build public relationships. Whereas other models, such as the new model of symmetry as two-way practices (Dozier, L. A. Grunig, & Grunig, 1995, p. 48) and the antecedents and consequences model of organization–public relations (Broom, Casey, and Ritchey, 1997), have done a great deal to explicate the function of public relations in organizations, there has been little published relating interpersonal communication processes to public relations. Welcomed exceptions have been the works of Botan and Hazleton (1989), Heath (1994), and Spicer (1997).

This interpersonal communication model follows an earlier call by Ferguson (1984) to refocus public relations researchers on the "public relationship." Ferguson called for a paradigm that focused on the relationship as the unit of analysis as opposed to studying the organization and its publics: "I am not talking about research that sees either the organization or the social grouping as the unit of analysis—rather, I'm concerned with the relationship as the major focus of the research efforts" (p. 18). Her position initiated new thinking about the relationship as the goal of public relations and the communication processes that made successful relationships possible.

Ferguson (1984) did not mean merely to concern herself with communication; however, she recognized communication processes as an important focus for the study of public relationships—yet influenced by organizational structure, the publics, and the larger social environment in which publics and organizations relate to one another.

> There will be some who at this point want to ask why not simply define the field as the study of public communication, and wouldn't this include relationships? My response to this is that in this field we usually want to believe that we are concerned with more than communication. The study of public communication implies that the focus of the paradigm community should be on the process of communication itself. While I would argue that this is an extremely important focus for the study of public relationships, understanding public relationships requires more than understanding communication processes and effects. It may require understanding organizations, understanding publics, and understanding the larger social environment within which these two social units exist. (p. 26)

This is a systems theory view of public relations.

I was among those who wanted to call public relations the study of public communication, proposing that public relations was relational communication—communication concerned with exchanging information on an ongoing basis that became as distinguishable as the two individuals engaged in interpersonal communication (Lance, aka Toth, 1983, 1988, 1989). An example of how public relations was performed because of interpersonal communication comes from Simon (1980), who cast public relations work with the media as the "buffer zone, the no man's land in which public relations practitioners so often find themselves in trying to establish and maintain credibility" (p. 273).

Simon (1980) argued that public relations people could not accomplish their objectives without credibility and trust, individual elements that could not be attributed to organizational actions or decisions but rather to what the individual did interpersonally to reach specific goals. As an example, Toth (1988) found in a survey of large Southwest corporations, that corporate decisions to hire external agency help were based, not on such organizational predictors as cost, local office, and geographical area, but on the "chemistry" between the hiring communication officer and the agency's personnel, sometimes at greater financial cost and inconvenience. This chemistry was not driven by the bottom line, but reflected how the people representing the client and the agency thought they could related to each other interpersonally. Others have called the client–agency relationship a marriage (Richie & Spector, 1990). This analogy continued the emphasis on how the two individuals will build a unique set of expectations and communication processes together.

Generally, though, definitions of public relations have focused our efforts, not on relational communication or communication, but on the management of relationships through communication. Scholars and public relations experts have made management the prominent paradigm in public relations literature. For example, Grunig and Hunt (1984) defined public relations as "the management of communication between an organization and its publics" (p. 6). Cutlip, Center, and Broom (1994) defined public relations as "the management function that establishes and maintains mutually beneficial relationships between an organization and its publics on whom its success or failure depends" (p. 6). Harlow (1976) began his definition of public relations with the statement: "the distinctive management function which helps establish and maintain mutual lines of communication, acceptance, and cooperation between an organization and its publics ..." (p. 36).

There have been very few who have argued for a different paradigm view of public relations, such as Botan (1992), who argued for a focus on the communication process rather than on the management of public relations, using communication to adapt relationships between organizations and publics: "We need a view that focuses on the process at the center of public relations—using communication to adapt relationships between organizations and their publics" (p. 153).

Our developing body of public relations research has concerned itself with answering the questions of how public relations is practiced in organizations because understanding "the hows" should help public relations practitioners become more effective in what they do. Some of the key lines of theory building have looked at organizational roles (Dozier & Broom, 1995), models (J. E. Grunig & Grunig, 1992), organizational structures and environment (L. A. Grunig, 1992) and, most recently, the dominant coalition (Dozier et al., 1995, p. 15). These concepts have formed the independent variables thought to shape the communication that public relations practitioners create and practice.

This chapter seeks to return to relational communication through the lens of interpersonal communication theory, by presenting one model among others for relationship management. It does so, recognizing the importance of organizational, management, and roles theories. These are the global perspectives through which communication processes should be viewed. The chapter advances interpersonal communication theory as one type of communication practice in managing relationships, advances a practice model of personal to interpersonal influence, and makes recommendations for testing this model further.

INTERPERSONAL COMMUNICATION

There are many definitions of interpersonal communication. Weick (1987) called interpersonal communication "the essence of organization because it creates structures that then affect what else gets said and done by whom" (p. 97). Roloff (1981) defined interpersonal communication as a "symbolic process by which two people bound together in a relationship, provide each other with resources or negotiate the exchange of resources" (p. 30). J. E. Grunig and Grunig (1992) in their review of literature on the symmetrical model of public relations confined interpersonal communication to "face-to-face":

> Much of the literature review in this section describes public relations activities that rely more on interpersonal communication than is common in public relations, where communication through the mass media or small-scale media such as brochures or newsletter's prevail. (p. 319)

They spoke of interpersonal communication again from the perspective of collaboration, after discussing theories of dispute resolution, negotiation, mediation, and conflict resolution. They wrote:

> Practitioners of the two-way symmetrical model are not completely altruistic; they also want to defend the interests of their employers—they have mixed motives. A substantial body of knowledge exists that provides practitioners with advice both on how to collaborate interpersonally with publics and on how to use media symmetrically to communication with them. (p. 320)

Ehling et al. (1992) recognized interpersonal communication as a context in "various configurations of one-way and two-way symbolic transactions" (p. 384).

However, Knapp, Miller, and Fudge (1992) in the *Handbook of Interpersonal Communication* proposed two definitions of interpersonal communication as the most representative. The first definition, given by Bochner (1989), focused on "at least two communicators; intentionally orienting toward each other, as both subject and object; whose actions embody each other's perspectives both toward self and toward other" (p. 336).

The second definition, preferred by Knapp et al. (1992), was given by Cappella (1987): "If interpersonal communication has any essential feature, it is that persons influence one another's behavior over and above that attributed to normal baselines of action" (p. 228). Capella's definition emphasized communication behavior between people that belongs to them alone

> over and above that attributed to normal baselines of action, such as social or organizational roles. It is the different or distinguishing forms of interaction that develop because of the uniqueness of the individuals involved: That (1) the probability of A enacting a certain behavior at a certain time given that B enacted the same pattern or a different behavior at some earlier time is not zero, however, this probability must be significantly greater of less than A's own baseline probability of acting or ignoring B's prior action, and interaction requires that the same conditions hold for B. (pp.188–189)

Capella (1987) further limited interpersonal communication to observable behaviors enacted by persons A and B; thereby excluding such psychological variables as "personality, affective reactions, perceived intensity, and satisfaction; and, such situational factors as role and social normative constraints" (p. 189). Included by Capella are such processes as "mutual influence, turn-taking, conversational pragmatics, and negotiation" (p. 189).

Capella's (1987) interpersonal communication emphasis on observable behaviors in mutual influence and negotiation meshed with the work of J. E. Grunig and Grunig (1992), who discussed the concept of communication as represented in the concepts of negotiation, collaboration, and mediation (p. 316). Negotiation is defined as a "process whereby two or more parties who hold or believe they hold incompatible goals engage in a give-and-take interaction to reach a mutual acceptable solution" (Wilson & Putnam, 1990, p. 375). Collaboration is defined as "All parties believing that they should actively and assertively seek a mutually acceptable solution and being willing to spend large amounts of time and energy to reach such an outcome" (Conrad, 1985, p. 243). According to J. E. Grunig and Grunig, mediation occurs when a neutral theory party enters the process of negotiation (p. 316).

Capella's (1987) definition of interpersonal communication suggests two important dimensions: that of the uniqueness of the individuals as they relate to one another; and that their behaviors are observable, such as in such efforts as mutual influence, turn taking, conversational pragmatics, and negotiation. These dimensions permit us to look at interpersonal communication in organizational settings, but outside of the organizationally related behavior, such as public relations roles.

PREVIOUS INTERPERSONAL COMMUNICATION LINKAGE TO PUBLIC RELATIONS

In the public relations literature, there have been two linkages suggested between interpersonal communication and public relations. The first linkage by Broom et al. (1997) examined the use of interpersonal communication to define organization–public relationships. Broom et al. (1987) concluded that interpersonal communication scholars operationally defined relationships as "measures of participants' perceptions or as a function of those perceptions" (p. 89). This to Broom et al. (1997) suggested a domain of research on interpersonal relationships of individualistic or psychological perspectives that would not be applicable to their efforts to understand organizational–public relationships, again demonstrating a preference for the systems view of public relations.

However, Broom et al. (1997) concluded that at least some interpersonal communication scholars believe that the psychological or mentalist approach isn't the only one, quoting I. G. Sarason, Sarason, and Pierce (1995): "At the same time, however, there is a growing recognition that the 'mentalist' approach is not the only approach and that the relationship itself has distinctive emergent properties" (p. 613).

Broom et al. (1997) chose to build a model of organizational–public relationships that identified several antecedents and consequences that maintained a global perspective of relationships along the lines mentioned earlier by Ferguson (1984). They did not eliminate communication processes from their model. Communications is a concept of their definition of organization–public relationships. They identified communication as a property of relationships, along with " exchanges, transactions, and other interconnected activities" (Broom at al. 1997, p. 94).

The other linkage between public relations and interpersonal communication theory came with the introduction of the personal influence model, a fifth model describing how public relations is practiced, introduced by J. E. Grunig, Grunig, Sriramesh, Lyra, and Huang (1995), in a broader study of the applicability of the four original models of public relations in international settings.

Previously, the four original models of public relations, introduced by Grunig and Hunt (1984), the press agentry–publicity, public information, two-way asymmetric, and the two-way symmetric models, proposed goals of establishing either a one-way or a two-way flow of communication. One- way communication, represented in the press agentry–publicity and the public information models, concerned the sending of messages from the source to the receiver. Two-way communication, represented in the two-way asymmetric and two-way symmetrical models, added the concept of feedback, either to assist in the source's attempts to control the receiver or to assist both parties in attempting to reach mutual understanding. Although Grunig and Hunt noted that the communication attempts may be between sources and receivers, people, groups, or organizations, their initial discussion featured publics or group-to-group communication (p. 24). However, the introduction of a fifth personal influence model brought to center stage the "personal" and the focus on a third communication objective—to establish personal relationships.

The personal influence model, as described by Grunig et al. (1995), depicted public relations practices used to establish personal relationships: "friendships—if possible—with key individuals in the media, government, or political and activist groups" (p. 181). The intent of establishing these relationships was asymmetrical, as illustrated in these examples: " ...of public relations practitioners in India using contacts to get journalists to write stories about the organization represented by the public relations professionals" (Grunig et al., 1995, p. 180). " ...expectations from the public relations department to develop contacts with important people in Greek society and political arena and to be good at socializing with them 'at their level'" (Lyra, 1991, pp. 128–129, in Grunig, et al, 1995, p. 181).

In the area of media relations, Grunig et al. (1995) compared this model with the earlier press agentry–publicity model; however, the press agentry model differed in the choice of techniques, such as staged events, puffery, or photo opportunities, "whereas the personal influence model concentrates on personal relationships with journalists" (p. 180)

However, Grunig et al. (1995) concluded that the personal influence model also could be symmetrical, that is sought-after personal relationships that benefited both the organization and its publics, such as "trusting relationships with reporters or leaders of activist groups such as environmental or consumer organizations" (p. 184).

Grunig et al. (1995) suggested three determinants that described whether the personal influence model would be chosen by a public relations practitioner. The first determinant was the definition of public relations held by the management of an organization. The second determinant of what model would be chosen was the education and knowledge of public relations practitioners. The third determinant was the culture and political system in which the organization existed (p. 184).

Grunig et al. (1995) concluded that the asymmetrical personal influence model seemed to work better in authoritarian political systems and rigid cultures, conditions that would permit "lasting personal relationships" to be more highly trusted than if political and social conditions were more participatory and in flux, such as those in the United States. It follows that the symmetrical personal influence model would work better in social and political conditions that were participatory and in flux. In the democratic marketplace, such as that of the United States, the ever-changing reporters, politicians, and employees should mean that those one "could count on" would be valued indeed.

FROM PERSONAL TO INTERPERSONAL INFLUENCE

The importance of the personal influence model in advancing our understanding of how public relations is practiced is three fold. First, it permitted us to apply an additional paradigm to the analysis of public relations, the worldview at the individual level. According to Grunig et al. (1995), the practice of personal relations may be more a matter of individual actions in rigid cultures that rely on social class as a means of evaluating information needed to make organizational decisions. However, there are aspects of the U.S. culture that rely on social class as well, especially in the work of race relations, community relations, or employee relations.

Second, the personal influence model proposed a separate outcome in public relations, neither asymmetrical communication focused on controlling the environment nor symmetrical communication focused on mutual understanding. The personal influence model focused on establishing and maintaining a personal relationship, sometimes aside from organizational boundaries, and perhaps extending beyond the immediate employment of the public relations professional by a specific organization. Although public relations people work for specific organizations, they seek to be recognized as professionals, adhering to a code of ethics outside their employers' influences. They seek supportive relationships from other public relations people, sometimes in competing organizations and from leaders of activist groups, who can explain, for example, why their groups are angry with and at odds with their employers. Third, the personal influence model suggested an extension from personal influence to interpersonal influence. Grunig et al. (1991) suggested this linkage in alluding to "symmetrical personal influence" as one model that may be effective over the long run (p. 26).

It is from the work of J. E. Grunig and Grunig (1992) that the extension from personal or asymmetrical influence to interpersonal or symmetrical influence can be illustrated. Citing such theorists as Hellweg (1989) and Murphy (1991), J. E. Grunig and Grunig proposed that the original four models of public relations could be reconceptualized in terms of two continua: one of craft and one of professional public relations. On one continuum, J. E. Grunig and Grunig stated that practitioners of craft public relations believed that their jobs were simply to get publicity or information into the media, making use of press agentry–publicity at certain times and a public information model at other times. On another continuum, practitioners of professional public relations used both asymmetrical (compliance-gaining) tactics and symmetrical (problem-solving) tactics, depending on the specific situation (p. 312).

This continuum model was reconceptualized by Dozier et al. (1995) in a new model of symmetry as two-way practices (p. 49). Rather than a continuum of two-way practices that recognized a mix–motive perspective on how public relations was practiced, Dozier et al. (1995) illustrated how the organization (dominant coalition) and the public would choose asymmetrical or symmetrical models of public relations. Both the organization and its publics represented the ends of a continuum (p. 48). As both sides moved toward each other in establishing common ground or understandings, they reach a symmetrical or "win–win zone" in their communication with one another. As they moved away from this midpoint, each chose asymmetrical public relations. A pure asymmetrical model meant that the organization sought to dominate the public. A pure cooperation model meant the public's communication convinced the organization to cave in to the public's position.

In a similar approach, it could be hypothesized that public relations people who practice individual influence must do so on a continuum with their publics (see Fig. 11.1), at times gaining personal favors through contacts and at other times providing assistance to individuals who are in some way bound up with the organization on whose behalf the public relations practitioner is employed.

Whereas Grunig et al. (1995) described their public relations model as "personal" in influence, I would substituted the word "individual," because the unit of analysis is the individual's actions as agent for the organization. In negotiation literature, the individual is assumed to drive the negotiation process (Putnam, 1994). Embedded in this assumption was that this individual acts independently and was accountable for his or her choices. Putnam added to this assumption by theorizing that there was a relational as well as instrumental outcome. She stated:

> A view of bargaining as relational development houses choice, action, and outcome within the dyad rather than the individual. In the relational model, the major goal or object of negotiation is to form, build, transform, or redefine the relationship. It centers on the way that the task of negotiating can serve the relationship rather than the reverse. This perspective values relationship in its own right, not for instrumental gain. (p. 341)

These individual and dyadic actions could be illustrated along a continuum, moving between organizational and public personal and asymmetrical to interpersonal and symmetrical influence.

For example, a public relations person, working for the city council in community relations, may seek out information regarding what neighborhood leaders think of council efforts to provide low-cost hous-

Organization		Public
Personal (Asymmetrical)	Interpersonal (Symmetrical)	Personal (Asymmetrical)

Type of Practice	Explanation
1. Pure personal influence	Interpersonal communication used to dominate individuals, to accept either the organization's or public's position; closed and static in attributes
2. Pure interpersonal influence	Interpersonal communication used influence to find mutual definitions, mutuality of understanding, agreement, consensus; open and dynamic in attributes

FIG. 11.1 The individual influence model.

ing that will in effect integrate neighborhoods and, at the same time, provide information to the neighborhood leaders regarding the issues that might prevent their positions from gaining city council recognition.

In this example, the public relations person sought to learn how neighborhood leaders were understanding or not understanding the actions of the city council. Why would the neighborhood leaders share their time and thoughts with a city employee? Why would the employee "tip a hand" on strategies that might be more successful with the city council's position? The hypothesis to test is whether there was something in the interpersonal interaction that led to a relationship different than the norm (employee and activist group roles) and was an acceptable risk to the community relations person to introduce. Were the elements of credibility and trust on an individual level present? Were these elements more important than organizational reputation? Was there an observable interpersonal relationship? Was it personal or interpersonal influence?

The individual influence model posits that interpersonal communication is at its core. Rather than interpersonal communication as merely a context, such as between people, typically face-to-face in a private setting, the focus is on interpersonal communication that develops a relationship between individuals. Capella (1987) outlined "second-order questions" concerning the relational pattern between people: "If interpersonal communication is anything, it is directly and deeply related to the way that one person's messages cause those of another to be different from what they would be otherwise" (p. 211).

Littlejohn (1992) summarized the work on interpersonal relationships in this way: "Relationships are based not only on the exchange of information but also on interpersonal perceptions. A relationship is defined not so much by what is said as by the partner's expectations for behavior" (1992, p. 262).

It follows that, over time, the relationship is as distinguishable as the individuals who have built it. Burgoon and Hale (1984) proposed four independent dimensions of relational communication: emotional arousal, composure, and formality; intimacy and similarity; immediacy (liking); and dominance–submission.

This last dimension dealt with symmetrical and complementary interaction. When two individuals in a relationship behave similarly, they are said to behave symmetrically, with differences minimized. When individual differences are maximized, there is a complementary relationship, a degree to which one individual is dominant and the other individual is submissive. In a symmetrical relationship, individuals seek to work together or negotiate some goal between them. For example, a public relations person and a reporter may work together to build a story based on information provided by the public relations person but also on information supplied or gathered from other sources by the reporter. In a complementary public relations situation, such as that found by Grunig et al. (1995), the practitioner asked for a favor of a story being placed in a newspaper and the reporter was happy to comply.

Littlejohn (1992) proposed other concepts of interpersonal relationships, such as conflict, control, power, mutual definition, and social meaning (p. 290) that might be useful in describing the personal to interpersonal influences of public relations practitioners. Others, including Capella and White, gave us other concepts. Capella's (1987) "third order questions" provided a category to link behavioral patterns that defined interpersonal communication to intraindividual perceptions and cognitions and the socially defined relationships that exist above or below the interpersonal level (p. 221). White (1987) sought to determine how information research was developed between public relations practitioners and members of organizational publics. He examined how public relations practitioners established trust and credibility with hostile public members while still acting in behalf of their employers.

Previous research on the four models of public relations has depended for the most part on quantitative research methods. For the findings of Grunig and associates (1995), the use of qualitative methods took on increased importance. These methods used in three international settings yielded the personal influence model when, to this point in U.S. research, quantitative research had not. One means of testing the efficacy of the individual influence method may be to look first at situations with qualitative methods.

INTERPERSONAL INFLUENCE
AND THE MANAGEMENT OF RELATIONSHIPS

Although I have proposed the existence of personal to interpersonal influence in public relations practices between organizations and their publics, there needs to be further research to make this model of use in managing public relationships. There were several dimensions that should seem critical to assess, such as the agency of the individual within organizational–public relationships; the individual attributes of credibility and trust; and the dimensions of interpersonal communication introduced by Burgoon and Hale (1984), especially intimacy, immediacy, and dominance–submission. One starting point would be to study qualitatively how much individuals in negotiation situations attribute their success to their own choices and motivations and how much their agency is influenced and distinctively built in the negotiation relationship.

Other research should look at the determinants suggested by Grunig et al. (1995). Would the choice of personal or interpersonal influence be more likely given the definition of public relations held by the management of the organization? Is the choice of where on the continuum of individual influence determined by education or by social class? Would interpersonal influence be more likely if the political system were participatory and the culture more open than rigid?

However, if there is validity to the use of individual influence, then there should be additional concerns for those who seek to manage relationships. Public relations practitioners and employers will need to examine their own reservoirs of credibility and trust and make choices that build and maintain credibility. This may mean different choices than those that could bring short-term gain to the organization.

Public relations employers would look at individual traits along with resumés of experience, education, and skills, because they could anticipate the individual influence dimension to their public relations strategies and actions. The individual influence model could help public relations people manage relationships better because there would be an understanding of this important latitude to their organizational roles and communication processes.

PROPOSITIONS

This chapter discussed the use of a new model of how interpersonal communication processes could build public relationships. From this discussion, I offer four propositions:

1. The end goal of interpersonal communication is to establish and maintain successful relationships. This is not the only communication process to do so, but it should be acknowledged for the role in plays within the more global paradigm of public relations that features organizational structures, environment, role, and dominant coalition.

2. Public relations involves communication processes within organizational and social contexts that are distinguishable by the people who communication with one another.

3. These distinguishable processes may be more or less personal or interpersonal based on the motives of the individuals.

4. Some conceptual elements to examine along an individual continuum are mutuality of understanding, trust, credibility, emotion, intimacy and similarity, immediacy, and dominance–submission.

REFERENCES

Bochner , A. P. (1989). Interpersonal communication. In E. Barnouw, G. Gerbner, W. Schramm, T. L. Worth, & T. L. Gross (Eds.), *International encyclopedia of communication*. (pp. 336–340). New York: Oxford University Press.

Botan, C. H. (1992). International public relations: Critique and reformulation. *Public Relations Review, 18*(2), 149–159.

Botan, C. H., & Hazelton, V., Jr. (1989). *Public relations theory.* Hillsdale, NJ: Lawrence Erlbaum Associates.

Broom, G. M., Casey, S., & Ritchey, J. (1997). Toward a concept and theory of organization–public relationships. *Journal of Public Relations Research, 9*(2), 83–98.

Burgoon, J. K., & Hale, J. L. (1984). The fundamental topoi of relational communication. *Communication Monographs, 51*, 193–214.

Cappella, J. N. (1987). Interpersonal communication: Definitions and fundamental questions. In C. R. Berger & S. H. Chaffee (Eds.), *Handbook of communication science.* Newbury Park, CA: Sage.

Conrad, C. (1985). *Strategic organizational communication: Cultures, situations, and adaptations.* New York: Holt, Rinehart, & Winston.

Cutlip, S. M., Center, A. H., & Broom, G. M. (1994). *Effective public relations.* Englewood Cliffs, NJ: Prentice-Hall.

Dozier, D. M., & Broom, G. M. (1995). Evolution of the manager role in public relations practice. *Journal of Public Relations Research, 7*(2), 3–26.

Dozier, D. M., Grunig, L. A., & Grunig, J. E. (1995). *Manager's guide to excellence in public relations and communication management.* Mahwah, NJ: Lawrence Erlbaum Associates.

Ehling, W. P., White, J., & Grunig, J. E. (1992). Public relations and marketing practices. In J. E. Grunig (Ed.), Excellence in Public Relations and Communication Management (pp. 357–393). Hillsdale, NJ: Lawrence Erlbaum Associates.

Ferguson, M. A. (1984, August). *Building theory in public relations: Interorganizational relationships.* Paper presented at the convention of the Association for Education in Journalism and Mass Communication, Gainesville, FL.

Harlow, R. F. (1976). Building a public relations definition. *Public Relations Review, 2*(4), 36.

Heath, R. L. (1994). *Management of corporate communication: From interpersonal contacts to external affairs.* Hillsdale, NJ: Lawrence Erlbaum Associates.

Hellweg, S. A. (1989, May). *The application of Grunig's symmetry–asymmetry public relations models to internal communication systems.* Paper presented to the International Communication Association, San Francisco, CA.

Grunig, J. E., & Grunig, L. A. (1992). Models of public relations and communication. In J. E. Grunig (Ed.), *Excellence in public relations and communication management* (pp. 285–325). Hillsdale, NJ: Lawrence Erlbaum Associates.

Grunig, J. E., Grunig, L. A., Sriramesh, K., Lyra, A., & Huang, Y. H. (1995). Models of public relations in an international setting. *Journal of Public Relations Research, 7*(30), 163–186.

Grunig, J. E., & Hunt, T. (1984). *Managing public relations*. New York: Holt, Rinehart, and Winston.

Grunig, L. A. (1992). How public relations/communication departments should adapt to the structure and environment of an organization. . .and what they actually do. In J. E. Grunig (Ed), *Excellence in public relations and communication management.* (pp. 467–481). Mahwah, NJ: Lawrence Erlbaum Associates.

Grunig, L. A , Grunig, J. E., and Ehling, W. P. (1992). What is an effective organization? In J. E. Grunig (Ed.), *Excellence in public relations and communication management* (pp. 65–90). Hillsdale, NJ: Lawrence Erlbaum Associates.

Knapp, M. L., Miller, G. R., & Fudge, K. (1994). Background and current trends in the study of interpersonal communication. In M. L. Knapp, & G. R. Miller (Eds.) *Handbook of Interpersonal communication* (pp. 3–20). Thousand Oaks, CA: Sage Publications.

Lance, (aka Toth) E. P. (1983, April). *Public relations and interpersonal communication*. Paper presented to the Central States Speech Association, Lincoln, NE.

Littlejohn, S. W. (1992). *Theories of human communication* (4th ed.). Belmont, CA: Wadsworth.

Lyra, A. (1991). *Public relations in Greece: Models, roles and gender*. Unpublished master's thesis, University of Maryland, College Park, MD. In Grunig, J. E., Grunig, L. A., Sriramesh, K., Huang, Y. H. & Lyra, A. (1995). Models of public relations in an international setting. *Journal of Public Relations Research, 7*(3), 163–186.

Murphy, P. (1991). The limits of symmetry: A game theory approach to symmetric and asymmetric public relations. In L. A. Grunig, & J. E. Grunig (Eds.), *Public relations research annual* (Vol. 3). (pp. 115–132). Hillsdale, NJ: Lawrence Erlbaum Associates.

Putnam, L. L. (1994). Challenging the assumptions of traditional approaches to negotiation. *Negotiation Journal, 10*, 337–346.

Ritchie, E. P., & Spector, S. J. (1990, October). Making a marriage last: What qualities strengthen client-firm bonds? *Public Relations Journal, 46*, 16–21.

Roloff, M. E. (1981). *Interpersonal communication: The social exchange approach*. Newbury Park, CA: Sage.

Sarason, I. G., Sarason, B. R., & Pierce, G. R. (1995). Social and personal relationships: Current issues, future directions. *Journal of Social and Personal Relationships, 12*, 613–619.

Simon, R. (1980). *Public relations: Concepts and practices*. 2nd ed. Columbus, OH: Grid Publishing, Inc.

Spicer, C. (1997). *Organizational public relations: A political perspective*. Mahwah, NJ: Lawrence Erlbaum Associates.

Toth, E. L. (1988, November). *How corporations choose external public relations–An interpretative perspective*. Paper presented to the Speech Communication Association, New Orleans, LA.

Toth, E. L. (1989, November). *The crisis: When interpersonal communication theory explains public relations behavior*. Paper presented to the Speech Communication Association, San Francisco, CA.

Weick, K. E. (1987). Theorizing about organizational communication. In F. M. Jablin, L. L. Putnam, K. H. Roberts, & L. W. Porter (Eds.), *Handbook of organizational communication: An interdisciplinary perspective* (pp. 97–122). Newbury Park, CA: Sage.

White, J. (1987, August). Public relations in the social construction of reality: Theoretical and practical implications of Berger and Luckmann's view of the social construction of reality. Paper presented to the Association for Education in Journalism and Mass Communication, San Antonio, TX.

Wilson, S. R., & Putnam, L. L. (1990). Interaction goals in negotiation. In J.A. Anderson (Ed.), *Communication yearbook 13* (pp. 374–406). Newbury Park, CA: Sage.

12

"Relationship" and the Evolution of Network News

ଊ ✧ ଌ

Steven A. Esposito and Stephen C. Koch
Capital University

Can mass-mediated messages transcend the traditional interpretational frame of "image" in order to establish an apparently more credible frame of co-orientational behavioral relationships? We believe we can show that through selection of issues, sources, and elements of rhetorical style the beginnings of an attempt to establish a relationship orientation with viewers appears to be gaining momentum within traditional mass media structures.

RELATIONSHIP RHETORICALLY DEFINED

Relationship is a very broad term in general usage. We suggest that in its broadest construction, ordinary language users are implying some level of transcendence of the merely occasional or accidental. Thus, whatever the character of that transcendence, by definition any relationship involves some kind of interpretable governing rationale. Interpersonal relationships are seen to imply very complex interlocking sets of rationales based on opportunities for extended and intimate observation of behavior. Business relationships, casual friendships, and so forth, may be seen to vary by type and by intensity according to the amount and importance of behavioral contact. When moving to consider relationships in distinctly public settings where the opportunities for observation and interaction are more highly structured, the most salient variables and the most defining rhetorical characteristics of a relationship concept may be the possession of a narrative history and a set of expectations for its future.

IMAGE OR BEHAVIOR?

Relationship may be signified by certain communication practices and established cultural or rhetorical forms, but is likely to be sustained and intensified (stabilized?) when those practices contain opportunities for interactive contact in which both parties are able to assert control over elements of their articulated identities (not only do I get to tell you who I am, but I listen to you tell me who you are as well). The rhetorical form of this act was described by the late Kenneth Burke (1969) as "consubstantiality" in which a rhetor demonstrates continuity with the audience by showing in various ways that one's own perspective encompasses key elements of the audience's point of view. We would suggest that a sense of relationship is a step beyond this rhetorical act extending into creation of both retrospect and prospect for future coarticulation of the parties.

TROUBLE AT THE NETWORKS

Journalism in all of its forms, by almost any measure of credibility, authority, and economics, is in deep trouble with the public it seeks to serve. Consider the following:

> *1994 Times-Mirror survey*: 71% agree with the statement that "The news media get in the way of societies solving its problems."
> *1996 study by the Pew Center for the People and the Press*: The percentage of people who say they "regularly" watch the networks news programs has fallen by almost a third in 3 years (42% in 1994 compared to 60% in 1994).
> *1996 Harris Poll*: Only 47% of those surveyed believe journalists "care about the people they report on." Asked to compare the traits of journalists to "most people," 42% said journalists are more arrogant, 31% said they are more cynical, and 33% said they are less compassionate.
> *1996 Time/CNN Poll*: The audience for network news is dropping. In 1980, 41.2% of all American TV homes were tuned to the evening newscasts on ABC, CBS, and NBC. By 1995, that number sank to an all-time low of 26.1%.

This public relations problem, however, appears to be more than just one of image. By way of their declining attentiveness and appreciation, viewers and readers are telling journalists that providing information—telling the news "the way it is"—is simply not sufficient.

Scholars such as Wiebe (1963) and Grunig (1993) would likely suggest that journalism managers look beyond mere images to deeper relationships among their organizations and their publics. Wiebe would suggest that for journalism organizations to improve their relations with their publics, they need to nurture the larger society from which they receive their sustenance and to participate in the solution of what members of these publics perceive to be their own problems. Grunig's work suggests that the journalism industry build long-term behavior relationships with their publics in which reciprocity, trust, credibility, mutual legitimacy, openness, mutual satisfaction, and mutual understanding are at the heart of the relationship.

Facing declining viewership in the face of changed lifestyle habits and of a proliferation of alternative news choices, network television news appears to have little choice but to change. In fact, one can argue that a large part of network news' ongoing metamorphosis is an attempt at redefining this relationship between the news organizations and their viewer–publics. For network news this redefinition is doubly complex because its public relations is in a sense its product. That is to say that because communication is its product (as opposed to refrigerators for example), its image and its product are indistinguishable to all except expert or professional viewers. Considering this perspective, we might suspect that network news operations would be at the forefront of sensitivity and responsiveness to some form of a relationship paradigm.

RELATIONSHIP IN CONTEMPORARY NETWORK NEWS COMPETITION

The *NBC Nightly News*, which, in early 1997, ended *ABC's World News Tonight's* 8-year reign as the network news ratings king, is leading the change to more user-friendly relationship news. From a content perspective, there is a shift from the traditional news fare of government institutions and public officials to news that is more relevant to viewers' lives.

Andrew Tyndall, who tracks network news trends through a widely distributed weekly flier called the *Tyndall Report*, said that NBC has implemented a dramatic cutback in overseas coverage, offering only 1/3 as much foreign news as it did at the start of the 1990s decade (Carman, 1997). Domestic coverage has risen sharply to fill the void, but not domestic coverage from Washington, D.C. The new wave of domestic coverage centers on the common man and woman—with which individuals viewers can identify. According to Tyndall, in 1996 NBC devoted only half as much air time as ABC and CBS to the former Yugoslavia and the introduction of U.S. forces in Bosnia. Domestically, NBC devoted less time than its competitors to the national political conventions, the presidential campaign, and the Whitewater investigation (Carman, 1997).

AN APPROACH TO
OPERATIONALIZING RELATIONSHIP

Notwithstanding the obvious pressure exerted through new electronic media to create a symbolic analogy to interactive linkages with "users," major national media outlets have always struggled vis-à-vis their local counterparts to establish close ties with audiences. The recently noticed, but what we believe to be historically gradual, changes in broadcast network news seem to exhibit evidence of an ongoing attempt to substitute co-orientational behavioral relations for the more traditional audience image-based concept.

Working from this premise, we have attempted to identify some key characteristics of "relationship news" in network news programming. We have begun by asking: What sorts of content would constitute relationship news? What differences in news sources would be employed in relationship news? Finally, what stylistic differences might account for the perception of a relationship orientation in news coverage?

COMMUNITY AND RELATIONSHIP

Ledingham, Bruning, Thomlison, and Lesko (1997) suggested that "if an organization is seen as involved in and committed to the interests of a community, the aware members of that community will be positively predisposed toward loyalty to that organization (in the face of competition)"(p. 41). Working from the premise that network news would view creation of a relationship with diverse individuals an impossible task, and following the lead of Ledingham et al., our focus fell upon the concept of community as a viable means through which a national-level entity could signify consubstantiality with a large, heterogenous public audience. To test the idea that such a trend would evolve, we decided to look at coverage extending over a 20-year period.

A RELATIONSHIP CONTENT ANALYSIS SURVEY

Using the *Vanderbilt University Evening News Abstracts*, coders were asked to select relationship news stories—stories in which they felt the networks were demonstrating a responsibility to the community, were involved in activities that benefited the community, exhibited a commitment to the community, and invested in the community's future (i.e., proactive in providing solutions to community problems). In other words, stories that displayed network news' involvement in and commitment to the interest of the community (America and its people).

Three coders (one of whom was one of the co-authors) working independently, examined the *Abstracts* for the months of January, February, and March for the years 1977, 1987, and 1997 (weekdays only). The coders achieved an intercoder reliability of .83 (using Holsti's R, 1969).

INITIAL SUMMARY OF QUANTITATIVE FINDINGS

Table 12.1 illustrates the trend towards more relationship news on network evening newscasts since the late 1970s. The table lists the

TABLE 12.1

Evolution of Network Relationship News

	ABC Stories/Time/%	CBS Stories/Time/%	NBC Stories/Time/%	All 3 Networks Stories/Time/%
1977	45/49:30(3.7%)	50/69:00(4.9%)	86/135:30(10%)	81/254:00(6.2%)
1987	43/116:40(8.8%)	54/118:10(8.7%)	52/181:10(13.6)	149/416:00(10.3%)
1997	76/214:15(17.4%)	59/120:20(9.3%)	71/187:40(15.3%)	206/522:15(13.9%)

Note. Shrinking news-hole—In 1997, there were more teases, bumps, and promos to keep viewers tuned in. The typical news-hole (minus intros, teases, bumps, promos, closes, and commercials) was between 19 and 20 minutes. In 1987, the news-hole was closer to 21 minutes. In 1977, the news-hole was often closer to 21–22 minutes.

number of stories coded or identified as relationship news stories, the total time devoted to those stories, and the percentage of the networks' news-hole (total news time) devoted to relationship news stories.

A DISCUSSION OF THE HISTORICAL EVOLUTION OF CONTENT

1977

In 1977, limited time was devoted to these types of relationship news stories. The focus was on politics, foreign wars, and business. Many of the relationship stories were brief anchor readers, voice overs, or both, that lasted little more than 10 to 30 seconds in length. In fact, on ABC, only 11 of the 45 relationship news stories were packages. The rest all received nothing more than brief mentions.

The networks (specifically ABC and CBS) spent more time on commentaries and analysis. On ABC, Howard K. Smith had 28 commentaries totaling 52 minutes, whereas on CBS, Eric Sevareid had 38 totaling 91 minutes. Again, the commentaries reflected the networks' definition of "news" at this time: politics, foreign affairs, and business (i.e., topics including U.S. foreign policy decisions, U.S.S.R. problems, the Carter presidency, organized labor in government, the Kissinger memoirs, big business, U.S.–Mexico relations, etc.).

NBC was the lone network that aired longer (than the standard 1:30–1:45 package) feature-type stories. Referred to as "special" reports, they were similar to the mid-1990s "In Depth" reports on NBC. Of the 27 "special" reports that aired during this 3-month period, 14 were coded as being relationship news stories (5 of the 14 were part of a 5-part series that examined the U.S. energy problems).

To summarize, in 1977 the networks focused on politics, foreign affairs, and big business. There was no competition yet from cable TV, videocassette recorders, the Internet, or other alternatives. There was little or no concern for relationship news, with much more time devoted to (elitist) commentaries.

1987

In 1987, as competition for viewers increased, the number of relationship news stories increased. The time devoted to relationship news stories increased 61% from 1977. There were actually fewer of these types of stories, but they were being covered in much more depth. ABC and CBS no longer offered commentaries and analysis. Ironically, NBC did! A total of 31 John Chancellor commentaries were aired during this 3-month period, totaling 52 minutes. (In the mid-1990s, NBC created a new way to offer commentary. "In Their Own Words"is a segment in which average citizens comment on various issues. Although it lacked the obvious elitist views of past commentary or analysis, it was still selected and produced (edited) to re-create the news agency perspective!)

ABC and NBC were the only networks that labeled many of their relationship news stories. In fact, they called attention to the special nature of these segments, referring to them as "Special Assignment" on ABC and "Special Segment" on NBC. CBS's relationship news stories received no special packaging except for a 5-part series titled "Cons, Scams, and Rip-offs" in which they exposed various ways Americans were bilked out of their money.

In summary, in 1987, with increased competition (especially from CATV), networks began to focus more on viewers' (community) interests. Relationship news stories were up 61% from the previous decade. Many of the relationship news stories focused on medicine or health issues and concerns.

1997

In 1997, there was an explosion of competition from cable, Internet, direct satellite broadcast, TV tabloids, newsmagazine programs, and so forth. Relationship news continued to increase (up 20% from 1987). As mentioned earlier, the *NBC Nightly News* replaced *ABC's World News Tonight* as the network news ratings leader. Both relied heavily on relationship news, whereas CBS, a distant third in the ratings, did so to a lesser degree.

The trend of longer, featurelike relationship news stories continued from the previous decade, only with more variety. ABC offered "Solutions" to Americans' problems, examined community health concerns in "Your Health," and exposed ways in which Americans' money was spent or wasted in "It's Your Money." Note the emphasis on the word "your" as ABC attempted to involve viewers in the news stories, giving them more "ownership" of the news. Nonrelationship news "franchise" segments on ABC (as determined by the coders) included "Person of the Week," which aired every Friday.

NBC also exposed ways in which Americans' money was wasted, often by government, in "The Fleecing of America." "In Depth" segments examined various consumer-related issues, whereas "The Family" explored issues that were important to the families of the 1990s (i.e., pressure on children, missing father syndrome, working mothers and fathers, day care, etc.). Other NBC segments coded as relationship news included "Starting Over," a 4-part, user-friendly series that provided viewers with advice about drinking and driving, time management, losing weight, and getting out of debt; "Fixing America," in which "some average and some not so average Americans" offered solutions to the country's biggest problems. There were even two segments titled "Going Home," in which NBC news anchors or stars returned to their humble beginnings; the roots of their "community." These segments helped to humanize these bigger-than-life news stars, attempting to create the impression that they're just like the "average working man and woman"—they're one of us! Nonrelationship news franchise segments on NBC included "The American Dream" and "Norman Schwarzkopf's America."

"INTERESTING" NEWS CONTENT VERSUS RELATIONSHIP NEWS: QUALITATIVE COMMENTS

Coders commented on how NBC's relationship news stories, when compared to ABC and CBS, appeared to be more user-friendly; more applicable to viewers' everyday lives. CBS also had several franchise segments—most notably "Eye on America." Interestingly, only 9 of the 27 "Eye on America" segments that aired during this 3-month period were coded as being relationship news stories.

Other CBS franchise segments such as "Follow the Dollar" and "Reality Check," were not coded as being relationship news, nor was "Travels With Harry (Smith)"—a light-hearted kicker or fluff segment that concluded each Friday newscast. Two segments that perhaps weren't aired enough, "Best of Us" and "Class of 2000," did focus more on relationship news items such as children and smoking, and teenagers' fears of family deaths. Coders also indicated that many of CBS' relationship news stories were not as "enterprising" as those on ABC and NBC. Coders agreed that "they were often based on a just-released study."

To summarize, in 1997, relationship news continued to increase as viewers became less concerned with politics, politicians, and foreign matters. Stories on family matters, health and medicine, and government waste of taxpayers' dollars were much more prevalent than they were during the previous decade.

CONSUBSTANTIAL SOURCES

Viewers appear to be playing a more significant role in defining what is "news." In the late 1970s, news was determined solely by the gatekeepers. News was government, politicians, foreign affairs, and big business. In the ensuing two decades, however, the focus has shifted to viewers—not just "fluff" pieces (human interest), but stories that involve viewers and provide them with information to help them in their everyday lives.

Fallows (1996) suggested that one of the reasons for journalism's public relations problem is that the profession has lost touch with its audience by becoming too elitist, too self-involved, and too cynical. Faced with personalities they do not trust who interview people they do not recognize about stories they do not feel concern them, viewers are clicking the nightly news goodbye. Relationship news, however, seeks to remedy this problem. Relationship news segments create more communication between journalists and the people they ordinarily overlook or ignore. The news, therefore, becomes more relevant and useful to viewers when the news agency can connect with its audience. As DeWerth-Pallmeyer (1997) pointed out, the ultimate goal of the journalist

> is to connect with their audience in such a way as to make some impact on them, to get them to see the world in a new light, to get them to understand a complex problem and make connections to their own lives, to get them to appreciate someone else's difficulties, to get them to laugh, to get them to take action. The goal is to involve the audience member in the news. (p. 103)

One important way relationship news appears to involve its audience is by way of source identification. Issues that viewers can relate to, such as time management, credit card debt, teen drug usage, weight problems, and two-income families are addressed by people straining to comprehend them. These individuals—common folks much like the majority of the viewing audience—are often struggling in their (our) communities and among themselves (ourselves), usually outside any official effort, to find solutions to the problems they (we) face every day.

In relationship news, these average citizens, standing in for a larger community of middle-American viewers, are the "experts" because they live day-to-day with such issues. This is quite a difference from the experts in traditional news stories whom Alter (1985) referred to as the "usual suspects"—a privileged few that convey the impression that the world "contains only a handful of knowledgeable people"(p. 69).

RANDOMLY SELECTED VIDEOTAPE SURVEY

To examine the types of experts used in contemporary relationship news stories, 32 videotaped stories were randomly selected from the 206 relationship news segments coded from January 1 to March 31, 1997 (See Table 12.1). A televised news source was operationally defined as the videotaped sound bite of the news maker as seen and heard in the context of the network news report, either by way of interview, public speech, or studio setting. To systematically identify the sources televised in the randomly selected news segments, a list of source types was developed by reviewing the videotaped reports. Source type categories were mutually exclusive and included 5 source types ranging from *average citizen* to *elected official*. To establish intercoder reliability on the source type variable, a sample of 40 sound bites was randomly drawn and independently coded by 3 judges. Estimates were computed using Holsti's R. The reliability estimate obtained through this procedure was .98.

Table 12.2 illustrates the emphasis on average citizens as sources of information and the deemphasis of professionals and elected official types. In relationship news, network news producers have developed a

TABLE 12.2

Source Type in Network Relationship News (Jan. 1–March 31, 1997)

Source–type	ABC	CBS	NBC	Total
Average citizen	34 (59.7%)	14 (34.2%)	33 (47.1%)	81 (48.2%)
Health or medical experts	6 (10.5%)	18 (43.9%)	21 (30.0%)	45 (26.8%)
Professionals	7 (12.3%)	3 (7.3%)	6 (8.6%)	16 (9.5%)
Public employees	4 (7.0%)	6 (14.6%)	5 (7.1%)	15 (8.9%)
Elected officials	6 (10.5%)	0 (0.0%)	5 (7.1%)	11 (6.6%)
Total	57	41	70	168

way of telling news through the eyes of real people, in their own words. In so doing, they essentially eliminate (to some degree) the journalist and give the viewers a sense of identification. Although some of the usual suspects (i.e., doctors, scientists, researchers) still play a role in relationship news stories, their role is in offering advice to viewers.

Although source identification alone can not account for CBS' third-place ratings, it is worth noting that CBS, which remained the most traditional of the "Big Three" networks, not only aired fewer relationship news stories (see Table 12.1), but also relied less than its competitors on the average citizen as expert.

RHETORICAL STYLE AND SIGNIFIERS OF RELATIONSHIP

Visuals

A large percentage of the visuals in relationship news segments were of average people—ordinary people—in their environment (i.e., homes, schools, neighborhoods) working through their everyday problems. For example, on ABC (1/10/97) the viewer saw video of a man playing with his children in their backyard as we learned by way of voice over that he was a victim of panic attacks. Viewers were informed that this man was "typical" of the 21 million Americans who suffer from panic attacks.

On NBC (1/7/97), we saw video of the Britton family (husband, wife, and young twins) interacting, eating, and playing in their home as the reporter voice over informed us that they were attempting to work their way out of a $24,000 debt. The Brittons, we were told, were typical of the "average American family ... which is $19,000 in debt excluding housing." The father, Donald, could not look more "average" as he sat in his kitchen, wearing a black ballcap and plaid shirt offering this advice to other average Americans—"Ya gotta stick with it!"

KEY TERMS

Lots of address in the second person or first person plural, use of the word "average," and references to survey data tend to be associated with reportage in the relationship news category. Use of personal pronouns was a rhetorical strategy often used to implicitly tie the viewers and the TV news agency together in the creation of the problem and the search for a solution. For example, in an NBC "In Depth" segment (3/6/97) on overweight Americans, medical reporter Robert Bazell asked, "So is it choices *we* are all making as individuals or is it something else? ... Will *we* eat ourselves to death?" After discussing various solutions, Bazell once more used the personal pronoun "we" to identify with viewers as he concluded, "Perhaps this is another wake up call that *we* have to pay attention to how much *we* eat and how little *we* exercise."

On another NBC segment (1/9/97), anchor Brian Williams asked viewers, "Are *you* having problems squeezing all *you* have to do into one day? If so, *you're* not alone!" Reporter Kelly O'Donnell then introduced the audience to someone with whom many of them could identify—Kristen Fiss—"school teacher and mother of three." Fiss, the viewers were told, is "just like more than two-thirds of all Americans" who feel their life is rushed. Fiss—representing all average Americans—aurally described her hectic day, as viewers saw the corresponding visuals to which they could relate (blow drying her hair while getting ready for work, dealing with the hassle of getting young children up and ready for school, making and eating breakfast, making the daily commute to and from work, and so forth).

Stance for Problem Solving

The network news producers appeared to be making a concerted effort to become more involved in not just reporting community problems, but in becoming involved in the solution process as well. This involved a fundamental shift from the reportorial stance of indifferent observer and objective conveyor of information to a stance of ally and coworker in the struggle to maintain the well being of the community. Reporters were seen involved with "average citizens" in an attempt to develop a dialogue that would help people form arguments, grasp points, expand understanding, and decide on courses of action or solutions.

ABC, in fact, had a relatively new segment titled "Solutions" in which they attempted to help "solve" some of America's more pressing social problems. In one segment (1/9/97), reporter Michele Norris sat down with a group of high school students to discuss (and compare) parochial schools and public schools. The problem—the plight of public education in America. The suggested solution—catholic schools (in Chicago) can serve as models for the ailing public school system.

In another "Solutions" segment (1/22/97), reporter Deborah Amos sat down with a group of "deadbeat dads" to discuss the success of the "Children First" program in Racine, Wisconsin. The fathers talked to her about how the program had helped them find employment, pay their child support payments (on time), and become better, more responsible fathers. The problem—54% of single mothers had to get a court order to get their child support payments. The solution—programs like "Children First!"

In a third "Solutions" segment (3/4/97), anchor Peter Jennings asked viewers, "Why are there so many more young people using drugs today and what can *the rest of us*, young and old, do to reverse the trend?" Reporter Rebecca Chase then introduced viewers to a state-funded "mentoring" program in California. Problem teen drug abuse. Solution—state-funded mentoring programs.

Rhetorically, ABC displayed its commitment to community involvement in this program note by anchor Peter Jennings:

> Parents and children are having a difficult time communicating with one another about drugs (a subject addressed in a 3/3/97 news segment). *We think we can help*—we say modestly—*or at least we're gonna try.* On Sunday night—7:00 eastern—perhaps *you'll* join *me* as *we* share drug talk with an interesting collection of parents and kids, many of them who are, or have been, drug abusers. (*ABC*, 3/28/97)

Even if the viewer didn't watch this special program—"Straight Talk About Drugs"—they were left with the impression that the people at ABC news *do* care about America's (teen drug) problem and *are* doing something to help!

Similar community involvement segments were also found on CBS and on NBC. On CBS (2/13/97), an "Eye on America" segment focused on teen pregnancies. Reporter Russ Mitchell visited with residents from a small rural county in Oregon that went from having the second highest teen pregnancy rate in the country to having the lowest in just 2 years. Viewers saw video of young girls in the community playing basketball, families praying, and county employees and church leaders "working together ... agreeing to disagree" to solve this community problem. The problem—teen pregnancies. The solution—community leaders working together.

In another "Eye on America" segment (3/17/97), reporter David Martin tackled the problem of "pollution and danger in the workplace"—Department of Energy employees who had been diagnosed with chronic beryllium disease as the result of their time spent building "this country's nuclear arsenal." Martin, CBS's national security correspondent, visited the Rocky Flats plant in Denver where beryllium, a metallic element, was machined into parts for nuclear weapons. Martin, wearing protective gear, walked through the "shop" informing viewers that the plant was "still contaminated by toxic particles that need to be cleaned up." In essence, Martin was risking his own health to bring this problem to the viewer's attention! In the end, however, unlike many of ABC's "Solutions" segments, Martin provided no solution, only a health problem, as he closed by saying "The Department of Energy has a health crisis on its hands with no sure solution in sight."

On NBC, the network's segment titled "The Family" focused on what anchor Tom Brokaw described as "the changing realities and dilemmas confronting so many families these days" (2/26/97). In one segment (2/26/97), reporter Kelly O'Donnell discussed the problem of older workers losing their jobs to younger people. The story of Mike Kelly, "46 years old and fired after 19 years with Airborne Express," symbolized all Americans confronted with this ordeal—an ordeal, viewers were told, that "none of us can say *this* will never effect me." Among the solutions addressed was "Forty Plus"—a company that prepares older employees for job searches.

In another "The Family" segment (2/28/97), the subject was "that endless tug between working longer hours and ...spending more time at home." Anchor Brian Williams informed viewers that "there is a way to make it work." In this Mike Boettcher report, Javier Ramirez represented the "typical" American. In fact, Boettcher told viewers that Ramirez "shares the same problem with a lot of American workers." Essentially, the lead character in the narrative, Ramirez was working overtime to help buy a house for his family, but as a result was missing out on spending quality time with his family. The proposed "solution" was the newly enacted "Family-Friendly Workplace Act" in which parents can trade overtime for days off at work. This segment ended on a somewhat bittersweet note. While viewers saw video of Javier attending his young son's school awards ceremony, Boettcher closed the piece by saying that Javier's wife wasn't there—"she couldn't get off work!" The problem—balancing time between work and family. The (possible) solution—the Family-Friendly Workplace Act.

SIGNIFYING CO-ORIENTATIONAL BEHAVIOR IN USE OF NEW TECHNOLOGIES

In the final years of the 20th century, network news operations are battling viewer erosion by trying to expand their news offerings into new time periods, as well as into cable TV and the Internet. NBC, for example, has two cable channels, CNBC and MSNBC. They also have an Internet news service in conjunction with Microsoft and are often plugging the chance for viewers to "chat" with network news "stars" and news makers. (i.e., On 2/3/97, Tom Brokaw closed the program by inviting viewers to "Join me tonight *live* on *MSNBC InterNight* for a one-on-one talk with (basketball star) Charles Barkley.") ABC, a member of the Disney family, is involved in a number of cable endeavors and is also in the business of interacting with viewers by way of new technologies. (i.e., Following a 2/13/97 "Solutions" segment on parents becoming more involved in their children's education, Peter Jennings said "If *you'd* like to learn more about *our* solutions, *you* can reach *us* on America Online—use the keywords ABCNews or e-mail us. The address "Solution@ABC.com" is superimposed on the lower third of the screen). CBS, which has its own website, www.cbsnews.com, was the last to get involved in the cable business. "Eye On People," a cable channel that Dan Rather said "is not another news channel," but rather, "a new channel ... designed to tell stories" (Kiska, 1997), debuted March 31, 1997.

The use of these new technologies also allows the network news operations to perhaps reach a younger generation of viewers (ages 18–29) who have pretty much stopped watching the traditional 6:30 p.m. (EST) newscasts. According to a 1996 *Time/CNN* poll, regular viewership among this age demographic has plunged from 36% to 22% in one year alone, 1995 to 1996! (Zoglin, 1996).

CONCLUSION

Although the use of the new technologies allows the closest approximation of the concept of coarticulated or co-orientational behavior, the network news must still rely on means of signifying relationship in order to reach its mass audience. We have used Burke's (1969) concept of "identification" or "consubstantiality" to try to understand how relationship news enables the network news agency to relate to and involve its mass audience in an "intimate" manner and thus, "signify" substantive behavioral relationships with its viewers.

Identification, equated with consubstantiality, is the speaker's (news agency) recognition of common ground and is shared experientially with an audience (viewers). Consubstantiality is the term Burke (1969) used to explain that although the speaker and audience have joined interests that possibly can make them "substantially one," each remains independent. The higher goal is possible when the two are united and "partake in some way of the same substance: the same set of Actions ... A way of acting together achieves consubstantiality"(p. 22).

Relationship news stories succeed in achieving consubstantiality between network news and its viewers by selecting content that has immediacy of relevance for viewers in their own eyes, by utilizing sources with whom viewers can identify, and by adopting a rhetorical style that emphasizes visual and linguistic cues of commonality and a stance that makes the news organization a community participant rather than an objective viewer.

UPDATE

The networks' shift to more relationship news stories appears to be succeeding. After dropping precipitously, and fairly consistently since the late 1970s, network news viewership increased in 1997. According to *Nielsen Media Research*, the average weeknight viewership for 1997 was 32.6 million, up from 31.9 million in 1996.

While viewership was up, so too was an emphasis on relationship news. Coders, using the same methods and procedures mentioned earlier, examined network news coverage for the months of January, February, and June of 1998 (Many of CBS' March, April, and May newscasts were unavailable on the *Vanderbilt University Evening News Abstracts* so June was selected as a replacement month). As indicated in Table 12.3, 16.4% of the networks' combined news-hole was devoted to relationship news—up 2.5% from the previous year.

The *NBC Nightly News*, which completed its first year-long stretch on top of the evening news ratings since 1967, led the way in relationship

TABLE 12.3

Network Relationship News (January, February, and June 1998)*

	Stories	Time	Percentage
ABC	163	264:10	15.6%
CBS	153	270:00	15.7%
NBC	118	289:10	18.3%
"Big Three"	434	821:20	16.4%
CNN	77	117:20	4.4%

*Weekends included.

news coverage. More than 18% of NBC's coverage was of the relationship news variety. The most significant change, though, took place on the *CBS Evening News*, where the time devoted to relationship news stories nearly doubled from the previous year, up from 9.3% to 15.7%! It is worth noting that during this time, CBS climbed past ABC into second place in the network news wars. *ABC's World News Tonight*, although still committed to relationship news, was the lone network to cut back on its relationship news coverage, decreasing from 17.4% to 15.6%. Although many variables enter into ratings success, failure, or both, it may be more than just a coincidence that the network with the most relationship news is ranked first (NBC) whereas the network with the least relationship news is last (ABC).

Although the "Big Three" broadcast networks continue their attempt to build relationships and identify more with viewers, their largest cable competitor, CNN, does not. As indicated in Table 12.3, the amount of relationship news stories on *CNN's WorldView* (4.4%) was comparable to what we saw on the broadcast networks in the late 1970s (6.2%, see Table 12.1). Like ABC, CBS, and NBC in the mid-1970s, the focus of CNN's coverage in 1998 (and since its inception in 1980) has been on American politics and world affairs—topics to which few viewers can relate, or in which they have much interest. Although the broadcast networks' viewership increased in 1997, CNN's continued to shrink.

The updated results of this study indicate that the networks' move to more viewer-friendly newscasts is continuing. The emphasis on more "in-depth" stories that emphasize social trends over daily news developments has certainly played a role in the networks' evening news resurgence of 1997. Halfway through 1998, CNN continues to feed its audience a daily dose of "hard" news, whereas the broadcast networks keep on heapin' on more "softened" news servings. Relationship news appears to be working. Viewers are getting information that is more integral to their daily lives, while the networks have, for the time being, stopped the (ratings) bleeding.

REFERENCES

ABC World News Tonight, January 9, 1997; January 10, 1997; January 22, 1997; February 13, 1997; March 4, 1997; March 28, 1997.

Alter, J. (1985, March 25). News media: Round Up the usual suspects. *Newsweek*, 69.

Burke, K. (1969). *A rhetoric of motives*. Berkeley, CA: University of California Press.

Carman, J. (1997, January 23). NBC learns ABCs of news. *San Francisco Chronicle*, E1 & E9.

CBS Evening News, February 13, 1997; March 17, 1997.

DeWerth-Pallmeyer, D. (1997). *The audience in the news*. Mahwah, NJ: Lawrence Erlbaum Associates.

Fallows, J. (1996). *Breaking the news*. New York: Pantheon.

Grunig, J. (1993). Image and substance: From symbolic to behavioral relationships. *Public Relations Review, 19*(2), 121–39.

Holsti, O. (1969). *Content analysis for the social sciences and humanities*. Reading, MA: Addison-Wesley.

Kiska, T. (1997, January 24). CBS cable channel will aim its eye at "people" stories. *The Detroit News*, E1.

Ledingham, J., Bruning, S., Thomlison, D., & Lesko, C. (1997). The applicability of interpersonal relationship dimensions to an organizational context: Toward a theory of relational loyalty a qualitative approach. *Academy of Managerial Communications Journal, 1*(1), 23–43.

NBC Nightly News, January 7, 1997; January 9, 1997; February 3, 1997; February 26, 1997; February 28, 1997; March 6, 1997.

Nielsen Media Research, (1998). 1997 annual report.

Wiebe, G. (1963). The social dynamics of corporation-public relationships: A model and a parable. In J. W. Riley, Jr. (Ed), *The corporation and its publics: Essays on the corporate image* (pp. 12–23). New York: Wiley.

Zoglin, R. (1996, October 21). The news wars. *Time*, 58–64.

Author Index

୫✧ଓ

A

ABC World News Tonight 231, 232, 233, 235, 238
Ajzen, I., 188, 201
Aldrich, H., 12, 20
Aldrich, H. E., 42, 43, 46, 49
Allen, M. W., 75, 76, 77, 83, 84, 92, 109, 113
Allen, N., 46, 52
Allman, R. M., 133
Alter, J., 230, 238
Altman, I., 185, 186, 202
Amatayakul, M. K., 133, 135
Amirkan, J., 78, 93
Andersen, P. A., 8, 14t, 20
Anderson, R., 182, 201

B

Ballard-Reisch, D. S., 133
Ballinger, J. D., 9, 9t, 14t, 21
Barnlund, D. C., 182, 183f, 201
Barton, L., 77, 80, 85, 88, 92
Beavin, J. H., 136
Beck, C. S., 135
Bedeian, A. G., 76, 92
Beisecker, A. E., 134
Bell, D. D., 155, 156
Bell, T. E., 134
Bellah, R. N., 146, 151, 154, 156
Benoit, W. L., 83, 84, 85, 92

Berger, C. R., 187, 201
Berko, R. M., 178, 201
Berlo, D. K., 181, 181f, 201
Berry, L., 46, 49
Berscheid, E., 8, 10, 21
Besser, H., 149, 150, 156
Birch, J., 73, 92
Bitzer, L. F., 85, 92
Bivins, T. H., 37, 49
Boal, I. A., 149, 150, 153, 157
Bochner, A. P., 44, 47, 49, 209, 218
Bok, S., 37, 49
Botan, C., 55, 68, 177, 201
Botan, C. H., 205, 207, 218
Brehm, S., 179, 201
Bridges, J. A., 96, 113
Bridges, L. W., 96, 113
Bronson, D. L., 134
Brook, J., 150, 153, 157
Broom, G. M., 4, 5, 15, 16, 21, 26, 27, 28, 29, 33, 34, 35, 47, 49, 49, 55, 56, 57, 58, 68, 118, 130, 131, 134, 159, 160, 161, 172, 201, 205, 207, 210, 218
Brosius, H. B., 99, 113
Brown, S., 37, 40, 50, 118, 134
Bruning, S., 187, 202, 224, 238
Bruning, S. D., 58, 59, 60, 61, 66, 68, 69, 118, 129, 130, 134, 135, 137, 138, 143, 144, 144, 160, 162, 163, 168, 170, 172, 173
Buckley, W. H., 134
Burgoon, J., 42, 49
Burgoon, J. K., 215, 217, 218

239

Subject Index

ಬಿ ✧ ಚಿ

UNIVERSITY OF WOLVERHAMPTON
LEARNING & INFORMATION SERVICES